GREAT ANSWERS TO TOUGH INTERVIEW QUESTIONS

7TH EDITION

MARTIN JOHN YATE

KOGAN
PAGE

First published ̶ ̶ ̶ ̶ ̶ the United States ̶ ̶ ̶ ̶ ̶ ̶ ̶ ̶ ̶ 985 by Bob Adams Inc,
̶ ̶ ̶ ̶ ̶ ̶ ̶ ̶ ̶ ̶ ̶ ̶ usetts

First published as (̶ n in 1986 by Kogan Page
Limited
Second edition 1988
Third edition 1992
Reprinted 1992, 1993 (twice), 1994, 1995 (twice), 1996 (twice), 1997
Fourth edition 1998
Reprinted 1998
Fifth edition 2001
Reprinted 2001, 2002, 2003, 2004
Sixth edition 2005
Reprinted 2005, 2006, 2007
Seventh edition 2008

Kogan Page Limited
120 Pentonville Road
London
N1 9JN
United Kingdom
www.koganpage.com

British Library Cataloguing in Publication Data

A CIP record for this book is available from the British Library.

ISBN   978 0 7494 5196 7

Typeset by Saxon Graphics Ltd, Derby
Printed and bound in India by Replika Press Pvt Ltd

GREAT ANSWERS TO TOUGH INTERVIEW QUESTIONS

Contents

Acknowledgements

Great Answers to Tough Interview Questions is now in its twenty-second year of publication and has become a staple for job hunters around the world. This is due to the ongoing support of my publisher Bob Adams and the tireless encouragement of the Adams Media sales team, headed by Wayne Jackson. This, and my other books, are kept fresh and vibrant thanks to the ministrations of my editor Ed Walters, the Associate Publisher of Adams Media. Finally, I am indebted to Jennifer Lantagne for her indefatigable work on three simultaneous sets of proofs.

Introduction

You don't come to a book like this because everything is good in your professional life; you come here in times of crisis and change. So I'm not going to waste your time. You live in a global information economy, where corporate structures have flattened and workforces have been downsized and outsourced, where professional jobs get ever more complex and the competition for them ever greater. This is not an easy world in which to pursue a professional career – it requires serious attention.

You stand somewhere in the middle of a 40- to 50-year career, with the likelihood that you will change jobs every three or four years (not always by choice). You may have as many as three distinct careers over the span of this half-century work life.

Your career is a marathon, not a sprint, and stamina and tactics count for a lot. This is probably not the first job hunt of your life and it almost certainly won't be your last. Put your situation today in this context, and make a commitment that as you execute your job hunt it will also serve the purpose of getting a firm grip on the management of your career.

Great Answers to Tough Interview Questions will show you how to achieve this goal. I'll show you all the viable ways of digging up job opportunities, the most effective ways of turning them into interviews, and then how to turn not one but many of those interviews into job offers. I'll show you how to negotiate the best salary and benefit package for yourself. In these pages, you'll find a cohesive approach to job hunting that will not only help you land jobs, but will also supply you with the tools to make a success once you're on the payroll.

Yet, because other job changes will come along in your life, sometimes unexpectedly, the greatest benefit you will reap from this book is preparedness for those future strategic career moves. If you follow my advice you will already have a plan of attack in place, a comprehensive job map of employers who take on people like you, and an almost inexhaustible supply of professionals with whom to network – all assets that I'm prepared to wager you don't have today. In short, you will be in control of your professional destiny.

I wrote this book because too much of what I found on bookshop shelves lacked the practical advice on what actually to do. Much of what I read was infantile at best and seriously detrimental at worst. I knew there was room for a different approach. Twenty years and millions of copies later, this book has become a time-tested and proven commodity, here in the USA and around the world in many different languages, effectively helping people with job change and career management in completely different cultures. This is only possible because the approaches you will find in these pages reflect a clear understanding of what it is that makes business tick, and it couples that understanding with a unique, honest and practical way to package yourself as a highly desirable professional.

Perhaps you are trying to land your first job, or returning to the workforce after an absence. Maybe you are a seasoned executive taking another step up the ladder of success. Wherever you are at this point in your career, this book can help. It will guide you through the job-hunting process and the toughest interview scenarios you will ever face.

The book is written in four interconnected parts. 'The Well-Stocked Briefcase' gets you ready for the fray. Here, you will learn to build a CV with broad appeal and use a unique customizing technique guaranteed to make your job application stand out as something special.

Once you are ready for action, 'Getting to Square One' will show you every truly effective job-hunting technique that exists, and how to tap into thousands of opportunities that never reach the newspaper or your favourite website. You will learn simple and effective techniques for setting up multiple interviews, and how to steer yourself through the intimidating telephone screening process that companies increasingly use.

The job interview is a measured and ritualistic mating dance in which the best partners whirl away with the glittering prizes. Learn the steps and you too can dance the dance. The 'Great Answers to Tough

Interview Questions' section gives you a comprehensive understanding of why interviewers ask the questions they do, what is behind them, and how to answer in a way that advances your application. Your partner in the dance is naturally the interviewer, who will lead with tough questions that contain subtleties hidden from the untrained ear. You will learn how to recognize these 'questions within questions'. You'll get hundreds of sneaky, mean, trick questions that interviewers love to throw at you. With each question, I will show you what the interviewer wants to find out, and explain how you should reply. After each explanation, I'll give you a sample answer and advice on how to customize it to your individual circumstances. The examples themselves come from real life (I've been at this for 30 years) – they're all things that people like you have done to get themselves noticed. I'll show you how they packaged those responses, how they used their practical experience to turn a job interview into a job offer, and with this knowledge you will be cooler, calmer and more collected at your job interviews.

'Finishing Touches' assures that you will learn how to negotiate the best salary and benefits package for yourself once the offer is made, and even discover how to get a job offer after you have been turned down. Most important, the sum of all these techniques will give you tremendous self-confidence when you go to an interview: no more jitters, no more sweaty palms.

If you want to land a *good* new job, and get a better grip on the direction and trajectory of your career as you learn how to win over the interviewer *without lying*, then this book is for you. Now let's get to it!

Martin Yate

Part I

The Well-Stocked Briefcase

This section will show you how to discover, define, and package your skills and strong points, and to do the necessary legwork that will prepare you to sell them.

Have you heard the one about the poor man who wanted to become a famous bear-slayer? Once upon a time, in a town plagued by bears, lived a man. The man had always wanted to travel but had neither the right job nor the money to do so. If he could kill a bear, then he could travel to other places plagued with bears and make his living as a bear-slayer. Every day he sat on the porch and waited for a bear to come by. After many weeks of waiting, he thought he might go looking for bears. He didn't know much about them, except that they were out there.

Full of hope, he rose before dawn, loaded his single-shot musket and headed for the forest. On reaching the edge of the forest, he raised the musket and fired into the dense undergrowth.

Do you think he hit a bear or, for that matter, anything else? Why was he hunting for bears with a single-shot musket and why did he shoot before seeing a bear? What was his problem?

Our hero couldn't tell dreams from reality. He went hunting unprepared and earned what he deserved. The moral of the tale is this: when you look for a job, keep a grip on reality, go loaded for bears and don't go off half-cocked.

Out there in the forest of your profession hide many companies and countless opportunities. These are major organizations, small family affairs and some in between. They all have something in common – problems. To solve those problems, companies need people. Think about your present job function: what problems would occur if you weren't there? You were taken on to take care of those problems.

Being a problem solver is good, but companies prefer to employ and promote someone who also understands what business is all about. There are three lessons you should remember on this score:

- **Lesson 1** Companies are in business to make money. People have loyalty to companies; companies have loyalty only to the bottom line. They make money by being economical and saving money. They make money by being efficient and saving time. If they save time, they save money, so have more time to make more money.

- **Lesson 2** Companies and you are exactly alike. You both want to make as much money as possible in as short a time as possible. That allows you to do the things you really want with the rest of your time.

- **Lesson 3** There are buyer's markets (advantage: prospective employer) and there are seller's markets (advantage: prospective employee). Job offers put you in a seller's market and give you the whip hand.

Lesson 1 tells you the three things every company is interested in. Lesson 2 is to recognize that you really have the same goals as the company. Lesson 3 is that anyone with any sense wants to be in a seller's market.

If you look for jobs one at a time, you put yourself in a buyer's market. If you implement my advice in this book, you will have multiple job offers. These, however good or bad they are, will put you in a seller's market, regardless of the economic climate.

Operating in a seller's market requires knowing who, where and what your buyers are in the market for, then being ready with the properly packaged product.

In this section, you will find out how to identify *every* company that could be in need of your services. You will learn how to discover the names of the CEO or MD, those on the Board and in management; the company sales volume; complete lines of company services or products; and the size of the outfit. You will evaluate and package your professional skills in a way that is guaranteed to have appeal to every employer. You will discover highly desirable professional skills you never knew you had.

It will take a couple of days' preparation. You are going to need to update your CV (or create a new one), generate some covering letters, research potential employers and create a comprehensive marketing plan.

While I cover each of these areas in sequence, I recommend that, in the execution, you mix and match the activities. In other words, when the direct research begins to addle the grey matter, switch to CV enhancement and so on. An hour of one activity followed by an hour of another will keep your mind fresh and your development balanced.

7 The realities of job hunting

Why some people stay on a plateau longer, while others get more offers at better companies.

In years gone by, there used to be a stigma attached to changing jobs or looking for a new one. Today we live in a different climate. Everyone you speak to in your job hunt has been through your experience, so if you go about your job hunt in the right way you will come across many helpful hands and sympathetic ears. Strategic career moves and occasional unemployment can be an integral part of modern working lives and, as you'll soon discover, who you get to know over the years is incredibly important to your long-term success. So keep in touch with those helping hands and always be ready to return the favour.

I once met an executive who was job hunting for the first time in 20 years. He had been looking for seven months and wasn't the least bit concerned: 'I've been told that it takes a month for every £10,000 of salary, so I really have another 18 months to go.' He seemed to have this mistaken idea that after two years of unemployment, someone would magically appear with another chief executive's job for him.

His method of job hunting was networking, 'because that is what I've been told is the best way to find jobs'. It is if it works, but all too often that single-shot approach misfires.

There is no magic bullet when it comes to successful job-hunting techniques. The employment market varies from year to year. Sometimes it's a buyer's market and sometimes a seller's. But the fact remains that regardless of the state of the economy, there are good jobs out there for the job hunter who employs a systematic and comprehensive approach.

Career management for the long term

At the time you were born, there still existed a world where hard work, dedication and sacrifice resulted in long-term employment security and a steady and predictable climb up the ladder of success. The world in which you now work is entirely different. Companies still expect hard work, dedication and sacrifice, but their only loyalty is to the bottom right-hand corner of the quarterly profit and loss statement.

The job security and professional growth our parents thought of as the norm is a thing of the past. As mentioned before, you can over the course of a typical work life expect to change jobs every three or four years, and you may well have upwards of three or more distinct and different careers in that time. These realities dictate that you immediately discard any vestiges of unquestioning corporate loyalty and replace them with a little enlightened self-interest. I am not suggesting that you sacrifice your commitment to hard work, sacrifice and dedication in your professional life, just that you very quietly and privately do it with your own long-term economic success in mind.

Why is this important? It is because when you accept these realities you will recognize that this job hunt is probably far from your last. Keep this in mind as you read about unearthing job opportunities in Chapter 3. What I am going to tell you will not only help you get up to speed in your current job hunt, but it will also give you a head start on the next one. Follow this advice right now and you will find and land a good new job. Integrate this advice into a long-term career management plan, as I am going to describe, and your next job may well come to you. Even if it doesn't, I can promise that you will be able to create an almost unlimited personal network of professionals in your field and a comprehensive job map of every employer in your target location who takes on people like you... complete with contact information and a profile of the people they typically employ in your area.

This will all be possible if you understand the recruitment process from the employer's side and implement the job-hunting strategies exactly as I am going to recommend, matching your approaches to the preferences of the employer.

2 *All things to all people*

The goal of a CV is to show that you are a problem solver. Here are the five exercises that will help you identify the important aspects of your work history, the three types of CV you can use and the seven rules for making it broad and powerful.

HR and other managers today are continually asking for detailed examples of your past performance. They safely assume that you will do at least as well (or as poorly) in the new job as you did in the old one, so the examples you give will seal your fate. Therefore, you need to examine your past performance in a way that will empower you to handle these questions in a professional and competent manner that shows you think and act as a problem solver.

CVs are more important than ever: everyone needs a CV. On the other side of the desk, they function as a time management tool. Using them to screen candidates out, rather than interviewing every applicant, saves an employer time and therefore money.

From your viewpoint, creating a powerful CV helps you to understand better your professional self, crystallize your goals, and learn how to sell the professional you. A good CV also opens doors, acts as a road map for interviewers, and serves as your spokesperson long after you have left the interview.

Your CV needs to be 'specifically vague' – specific enough to put you in the ballpark and whet the interviewer's appetite to know more, while vague enough that he or she needs to get in touch with you to learn more.

It also needs to be future-oriented: most CVs are just a recitation of your professional job history and they simply aren't effective. To create a powerful CV, you must first look forward and create a clear picture in your mind of the job that you can land and in which you can succeed. You will identify the role and parameters of the job, noting the problems it is there to prevent and solve (how it helps contribute in some small way to the overall bottom line of the company). Then, and only then, will you look back over your professional life to pull out those aspects of your background that most suit you for this target job.

Your CV should be short, easy to read and understand, and it must use words that are familiar to the reader and which have universal appeal (for both human eyes and the CV database where it might well be stored). Most importantly, your CV should scream 'productivity-oriented problem solver'.

This chapter helps you to understand what it is you have to sell, and that will help you perform better at the interview. In the process you will develop some useful CV building skills. You will achieve all this as you evaluate your professional skills with a handful of simple but very effective exercises. In fact, you are likely to discover skills and achievements you didn't even know you had. A few you will use in your CV (merely a preview of coming attractions); the others you will use to knock 'em dead at the interview.

Building your CV

Your job hunt will be most successful when it starts with the parameters of your target job clearly in mind. When you clearly define your target job's parameters, you learn exactly what CV screeners and interviewers will be looking for. All the attributes that you develop in the following exercises are valuable to an employer. All will give you a better sense of your professional self; some you'll use in your CV and most you'll use in answers to questions during the interview process.

This questionnaire will give you the bones of an effective CV; it will not, however, give you a completely finished product. Creating an effective CV is a separate topic, and we simply don't have the space in these pages.

Exercise 1

A good starting point is your current or last job title. Write it down. Then, jot down all the other different titles you have heard that describe that job. When you are finished, follow it with a bulleted description of your job functions, relating them whenever possible to the target job. Don't think too hard about it, just do it. The titles and descriptions are not carved in stone – this is just the beginning.

Reread the written job description, and then write down your most important duty/function. Follow that with a list of the skills or special training necessary to perform that duty, and the professional behaviours you apply in its execution (see pages 128–32 for universally desirable professional behaviours). Next, list the achievements of which you are most proud in that area. It could look something like this:

I **Duty** Train and motivate sales staff of six.

I **Skills** Formal training skills. Knowledge of market and ability to make untrained sales staff productive. Ability to keep successful salespeople motivated and tied to the company.

I **Behaviours** Analytical, communication and people skills.

I **Achievements** Reduced turnover 7 per cent; increased sales 14 per cent.

Appeal to a company's interests by conservatively estimating what your achievements meant to your employer. If your achievements saved time, estimate how much. If you saved money, how much? If your achievements made money for the company, how much? Beware of exaggeration – if you were part of a team, identify your achievements as such. It will make your claims more believable and will demonstrate your ability to work with others.

Job titles may differ, yet all employees have the same opportunity to benefit their employers, and themselves, through being conscious problem solvers and doing their part to make money, save money and save time.

Today, companies are doing more with less: they are leaner, they have higher expectations of their employees, and they plan to keep it that way. The people who get taken on and get ahead today are those with a basic understanding of business goals. And successful job candidates

are those who have the best interests of the company and its profitability constantly in mind. Always think of your number one job as
being a problem solver.

Exercise 2

This simple exercise helps you get a clear picture of your achievements.

If you were to meet with your supervisor to discuss a pay rise, what
achievements would you want to discuss? List all you can think of,
quickly. Then come back and flesh out the details.

Exercise 3

This exercise is particularly valuable if you feel you can't see the forest
for the trees.

- **Problem** Think of a job-related problem you have had to face in the
  last couple of years. Come on, everyone can remember one.
- **Solution** Describe your solution to the problem, step by step. List
  everything you did.
- **Results** Finally, consider the results of your solution in terms that
  would have value to an employer – money earned or saved, time
  saved.

Exercise 4

Now for a valuable exercise that turns the absence of a negative into a
positive. This one helps you look at your job in a different light and
accents important but often overlooked areas that help make you
special. Begin discovering for yourself some of the key personal traits
that all companies look for.

First, consider actions that, if not done properly, would affect the goal
of your job. If that is difficult, remember an incompetent colleague.
What did he or she do wrong? What did he or she do differently from
competent employees?

Now, turn the absence of those negatives into positive attributes. For
example, think of the employee who never managed to get to work on

time. You could honestly say that someone who did come to work on time every day was punctual and reliable, believed in systems and procedures, was efficiency minded and was cost- and profit-conscious.

If you witnessed the reprimands and ultimate firing of that unpunctual employee, you will see the value of the positive traits to your employer. The absence of negative traits makes you a desirable employee, but no one will know unless you say. On completion of the exercise, you will be able to make points about your background in a positive fashion. You will set yourself apart from others, if only because others do not understand the benefit of projecting all their positive attributes.

Exercise 5

Potential employers and interviewers are always interested in people who:

∎   are efficiency minded;

∎   have an eye for economy;

∎   follow procedures;

∎   are profit-oriented.

Proceed through your work history and identify the aspects of your background that exemplify those traits. These newly discovered personal pluses will not only be woven into your CV, but will be reflected in the framing of your answers when you get to the interview and in your performance when you land the right job.

Now you need to take some of that knowledge and package it in a CV. There are three standard types of CVs:

∎   **Chronological** The most frequently used format. Use it when your work history is stable and your professional growth is consistent. The chronological format is exactly what it sounds like: it follows your work history backwards from the current job, listing companies, dates and responsibilities. Avoid it if you have experienced performance problems, not grown professionally (but want to) or made frequent job changes. All these problems will show up in a glaring fashion if you use a chronological CV.

I   Functional Use this type if you have been unemployed for long periods of time or have jumped jobs too frequently or if your career has been stagnant and you want to jump-start it. A functional CV is created without employment dates or company names and concentrates on skills and responsibilities. It can be useful if you have changed careers or when current responsibilities don't relate specifically to the job you want. It is written with the most relevant experience to the job you're seeking placed first and de-emphasizes jobs, employment dates and job titles by placing them inconspicuously at the end. It allows you to promote specific job skills without emphasizing where or when you developed those skills.

I   Combination Use this format if you have a steady work history with demonstrated growth and if you have nothing you wish to de-emphasize. A combination CV is a combination of chronological and functional formats. It starts with a brief personal summary, then lists job-specific skills relevant to the objective, followed by a chronological format that lists the how, where and when for the acquiring of these skills.

Notice that each style is designed to emphasize strengths and minimize certain undesirable traits. In today's world, all of us need a powerful CV. It is not only a door opener, it is also there long after we are gone and will almost certainly be reviewed just before the choice of the successful candidate is made by the interviewer.

If you already have a CV and just want to make sure it measures up, check it against the five basic rules of CV writing below:

I   Rule 1 Use the most general of job titles. You are, after all, a hunter of interviews, not of specific titles. Cast your net wide. Use a title that is specific enough to put you in the field, yet vague enough to elicit further questions. One way you can make a job title specifically vague is to add the term *specialist* (for example, computer specialist, administration specialist, production specialist).

I   Rule 2 If you must state a specific job objective, couch it in terms of contributions you can make in that position. Do not state what you expect of the employer.

■ **Rule 3** Do not state your current salary. If you are earning too little or too much, you could rule yourself out before getting your foot in the door. For the same reason, do not mention your desired salary. If salary information is requested for a particular job, put it in your covering letter and don't tie yourself down to a specific figure. Instead, give a range. (For details on developing a realistic salary range for yourself, see Chapter 19, 'Negotiating the offer'.)

■ **Rule 4** Remember that people get great joy from discovery. Show a little gold now, but let the interviewer discover the mother lode at the interview. You achieve this in part by keeping it short: one page for every 10 years and a maximum of two pages is the general rule. Longer and you are giving too much away. No one reads long CVs – they are boring, and every company is frightened that if it lets in a windbag, it will never get him or her out again.

■ **Rule 5** Finally, emphasize your achievements, problem-solving skills and your professional behavioural profile. Keep the CV general in tone but make sure it has a keyword or core competencies section that will help get an electronically stored CV called up from the database (more on this in the next section).

A CV only a computer could love

The majority of medium to large companies now have automated CV-tracking systems in place. If you're applying to a large company or suspect that a potential employer is using computers instead of human beings to scan CVs, then you should prepare a computer-friendly one as well as a more traditional version.

To prepare a CV especially for a computerized recruiter:

■ put your name on the first line of your CV and put nothing else before it. Desired job titles should be clearly visible;

■ use common typefaces, such as Times, Palatino, Optima and Courier;

■ keep the point size to between 10 and 14 – 12 is ideal;

■ if you want to use bold, save it for headings.

Also:

■ never use double columns or other complicated layouts;

■ never use any paper except white, off white, cream or beige A4;

■ never staple or fold your CV. If you are required to fax your CV, always follow it up with mailed and e-mail versions.

Keying into keywords and core competencies

When your CV is stored in an electronic database, the big challenge is to get it retrieved and reviewed by human eyes: you do this with the use of keywords or core competencies. Here is how it works.

A company manager needs a new accountant, so he or she sits down at the keyboard and types in a job title. The program then presents an extensive list of descriptors that might be used to identify the responsibilities of that job, and the manager clicks on the words that apply. The search engine then reviews all the CVs in the database, retrieving all those that contain any of the descriptors. It doesn't stop there, however: the search engine proceeds to weight the retrieved CVs by the number and frequency of those keyword descriptors. The more keywords, the higher up the list your CV appears for review.

Although it doesn't matter to the computer where this list of competencies appears on your CV, you might want to consider putting it near the beginning, after any introductory paragraph. The reason for this is fairly logical: that list paints a quick picture of the breadth and depth of your experience. It is also a very space-efficient way of introducing potentially relevant skills that aren't spelt out in the body of your CV. This core competency or keyword section should be less than 80 words, which should be easy to achieve.

You should also check online postings and the classifieds for positions similar to the one you're looking for, and cull from them any recurring core competencies that you also possess – add them to your list.

No plain, no gain

Remember, when you're preparing a CV to be scanned and understood by a computer, you are not necessarily writing one that would appeal to a human being. Your goal is not to catch the recruiter's eye with fancy fonts, a jazzy layout and exciting language, but simply to make it through the scanner intact, with enough information – in the appropriate order – so that when the computer is looking for somebody with your qualifications, your CV will pop up.

What follows is a selection of standard, non-computer-specific CVs for you to adapt as you see fit.

CHRONOLOGICAL CV

John Smith, 123 Anystreet, London, NW1 020 8123 4567

SUMMARY:	Ten years of increasing responsibilities in the employment services industry. Concentration in the high-technology markets.

EXPERIENCE: Howard Systems International, Inc.   2002–Present
Management Consulting Firm
Personnel Manager

Responsible for recruiting and managing consulting staff of five. Set up office and organized the recruitment, selection, and hiring of consultants. Recruited all levels of MIS staff from financial to manufacturing markets.

Additional responsibilities:

- coordinated with outside advertising agencies
- developed PR with industry periodicals – placement with over twenty magazines and newsletters
- developed effective referral programmes – referrals increased 32 per cent

EXPERIENCE: Technical Aid Corporation   1993–2002
National Consulting Firm. MICRO/TEMPS Division

Division Manager   1998–2002
Area Manager   1995–1998
Branch Manager   1993–1995

As Division Manager, opened additional offices, staffed and trained all offices with appropriate personnel. Created and implemented all divisional operational policies responsible for P & L. Sales increased to £20 million from £15 million in 1998.

- Achieved and maintained 30 per cent annual growth over seven-year period.
- Maintained sales staff turnover at 14 per cent.

As Area Manager, opened additional offices, hiring staff, setting up office policies and training sales and recruiting personnel.

Additional responsibilities:

- supervised offices in two counties
- developed business relationships with accounts – 75 per cent of clients were regular customers
- client base increased 28 per cent per year
- generated over £200,000 worth of free trade-journal publicity

As Branch Manager, hired to establish the new MICRO/TEMPS operation. Recruited and managed consultants. Hired internal staff. Sold service to clients.

EDUCATION: London University
BA (Hons) Public Relations, 1990

FUNCTIONAL CV

John Smith
123 Anystreet
London NW1
020 8123 4567

OBJECTIVE:	A position in Employment Services where my management, sales, and recruiting talents can be effectively utilized to improve operations and contribute to company profits.
SUMMARY:	Over ten years of Human Resources experience. Extensive responsibility for multiple branch offices and an internal staff of forty-plus employees and 250 consultants.
SALES:	Sold high-technology consulting services with consistently profitable margins throughout the United Kingdom. Grew sales from £15 million to over £20 million a year.
	Created training programmes and trained salespeople in six metropolitan markets.
RECRUITING:	Developed recruiting sourcing methods for multiple branch offices.
	Recruited over 25,000 internal and external consultants in the high-technology professions.
MANAGEMENT	Managed up to 40 people in sales, customer service, recruiting, and administration. Turnover maintained below 14 per cent in a 'turnover business'.
FINANCIAL:	Prepared quarterly and yearly forecasts. Presented, reviewed, and defended these forecasts to the Board of Directors. Responsible for P & L of £20 million sales operation.
PRODUCTION:	Responsible for opening multiple offices and accountable for growth and profitability. One hundred per cent success and maintained 30 per cent growth over a seven-year period in ten offices.
WORK EXPERIENCE: 1999–Present	HOWARD SYSTEMS INTERNATIONAL, London National Consulting Firm Personnel Manager
1990–1999	TECHNICAL AID CORPORATION, London National Consulting & Search Firm Division Manager
EDUCATION:	BA (Hons) 1990, London University
REFERENCES:	Available upon request

COMBINATION CV

EMPLOYMENT SERVICES MANAGEMENT

John Smith
123 Anystreet
London NW1
020 8123 4567

OBJECTIVE:
Employment Services Management

SUMMARY: Ten years of increasing responsibilities in the employment services marketplace. Concentration in the high-technology markets.

SALES: Sold high-technology consulting services with consistently profitable margins throughout the United Kingdom. Grew sales from £15 million to over £20 million a year.

PRODUCTION: Responsible for opening multiple offices and accountable for growth and profitability. One hundred per cent success and maintained 30 per cent growth over a seven-year period in ten offices.

MANAGEMENT: Managed up to forty people in sales, customer service, recruiting, and administration. Turnover maintained below 14 per cent in a 'turnover business'. Hired branch managers, sales, and recruiting staff throughout United Kingdom.

FINANCIAL: Prepared quarterly and yearly forecasts. Presented, reviewed, and defended these forecasts to the Board of Directors. Responsible for P & L of £20 million sales operation.

MARKETING: Performed numerous market studies for multiple branch openings. Resolved feasibility of combining two different sales offices. Study resulted in savings of over £5,000 per month in operating expenses.

COMBINATION CV (page 2)

EXPERIENCE: Howard Systems International, Inc.   2002–Present
Management Consulting Firm
Personnel Manager

Responsible for recruiting and managing consulting staff of five. Set up office and organized the recruitment, selection, and hiring of consultants. Recruited all levels of MIS staff from financial to manufacturing markets.

Additional responsibilities:

- developed PR with industry periodicals – placement with over twenty magazines and newsletters
- developed effective referral programmes – referrals increased 320 per cent.

Technical Aid Corporation   1993–2002
National Consulting Firm. MICRO/TEMPS Division
Division Manager   1998–2002
Area Manager   1995–1998
Branch Manager   1993–1995

As Division Manager, opened additional offices, staffed and trained all offices with appropriate personnel. Created and implemented all divisional operational policies. Responsible for P & L. Sales increased to £20 million from £15 million in 1988.

- Achieved and maintained 30 per cent annual growth over seven-year period.
- Maintained sales staff turnover at 14 per cent.

As Area Manager, opened additional offices, hiring staff, setting up office policies, training sales and recruiting personnel.

Additional responsibilities:

- supervised offices in two counties
- developed business relationships with accounts – 75 per cent of clients were regular customers
- client base increased 28 per cent per year
- generated over £200,000 worth of free trade-journal publicity.

As Branch Manager, hired to establish the new MICRO/TEMPS operation. Recruited and managed consultants. Hired internal staff. Sold service to clients.

EDUCATION: BA (Hons), 1990, London University

The executive briefing

If you know the specific requirements of a particular opening, the executive briefing will quickly – and impressively – line them up with your skills and qualities. Once you have a few years of professional experience, it is likely that you will be qualified for more than one job, so it is a good idea to create one CV for the main thrust of your job search, and then adapt it for special circumstances. Ultimately, you could have three to five CVs for different opportunities. It's a smart step to take, because there is no such thing in life as 'one size fits all', and the less specific your CV is to a target job, the less effective it will be.

Nevertheless, circumstances will arise where none of your CVs fit a particular opportunity and there is no time to adapt the closest matching CV. When this happens, you can employ the executive briefing (which is, by the way, a useful tool even when your CV does match).

An *executive briefing* enables you to customize your CV quickly to any specific job and is especially helpful on the other side of the desk, to overworked secretaries and HR personnel who may not understand all the niceties of a specific job function.

While the executive briefing is only one form of CV covering letter, I am including it here because in your research you will come across great opportunities before your new CV is finished. The executive briefing will allow you to update and customize that old CV with lightning speed without delaying the rest of your research, or missing out on the opportunity.

Like many great ideas, the executive briefing is beautiful in its simplicity. It is a covering letter on your standard letterhead or e-mail, with the company's requirements for the job opening listed on the left side, and your skills – matching point by point the company's needs – on the right. It looks like this:

From: A1coordpro@earthlink.net
Subject: Assessment Coordinator
Date: February 28th, 2005 11:18:39 PM
To: jobs@abc.com

Dear HR Staff,

Your advertisement in the Times, on February 27th, 2007, for an **Assessment Coordinator** seems to perfectly match my background and experience. As the International Brand Coordinator for Kelco, I coordinated meetings, prepared presentations and materials, organized a major off-site conference, and supervised an assistant. I believe that I am an excellent candidate for this position as I have illustrated below:

YOUR REQUIREMENTS	MY QUALIFICATIONS
Highly motivated, diplomatic	Successfully managed project teams involving different flexible, quality-driven professional business units. The defined end results were achieved on every project.
Exceptional organizational skills and attention to detail	Planned the development and launch of the Kelco Heritage Edition bottle series. My former manager enjoyed leaving the 'details' and follow-through to me. Coverdale project management training.
University degree and 6yrs exp	B.A. from Exeter University (1998). 6+ years relevant business experience in productive, professional environments.
Computer literacy	Extensive knowledge of Windows & Macintosh applications.

I'm interested in this position because it fits well with my new career focus in the human resources field. Currently, I am enrolled on an adult career planning and development certificate programme and working at Harrison Curtis Ltd.

My CV pasted below and attached in MSWord will provide more information on my strengths and career achievements. If after reviewing my material you believe that there is a match, please call me. Thank you for your consideration.

Sincere regards,
Jane Swift

This briefing ensures that each CV you send out addresses the job's specific needs and that every interviewer at that company will be interviewing you for the same job.

Send an executive briefing with every CV where you have some knowledge of the requirements; it will substantially increase your chances of obtaining an interview with the company. The use of an executive briefing is naturally restricted to jobs that you have discovered through your own efforts or seen advertised. It is obviously not appropriate for sending when the requirements of a specific job are unavailable.

An executive briefing sent with a CV provides a comprehensive picture of a thorough professional, plus a personalized, fast and easy-to-read synopsis that details exactly how you can help with current needs.

Using the executive briefing as a covering letter to your CV will greatly increase the chance that your application will be picked out of the pile in the Human Resources department and hand-carried to the appropriate manager.

3 Networking and the successful job search

Here's how you can use a wide variety of networks and associations to get the referrals that lead to the perfect position.

As you tune up your CV, simultaneously piece together a plan of attack for your job hunt. To make that plan of attack most effective, take a couple of minutes to understand how companies like to hire people, because understanding corporate recruitment preferences will help you fine-tune your job hunting approaches to make them maximally productive.

How companies recruit employees

At most companies, taking on new staff is planned up to 12 months in advance (apart from staff replacements due to employee turnover). So the interviews you go to this year were mostly planned and budgeted last year. Once recruitment budgets are approved, they can then be swung into action at any time, but most often they open up at the start of the new calendar year and are staggered throughout the year. This means that the early part of every year usually has plenty of opportunities, so if you read this in November you should be especially diligent about working on your job hunt right through the holiday season! It most certainly does not mean that you can't find jobs at other times of the year; there are always jobs available, just so long as you know how to find them.

The cost of employing and training personnel runs into thousands and sometimes tens of thousands of pounds, so the entire recruitment process is entirely cost/productivity conscious (ok, so tell me something in business that isn't). The people involved in a specific search – the manager and the assigned human resources people – all want the same thing: good recruitment, fast recruitment, and recruitment done as cheaply as possible. When you understand how and why things are done, and in what sequence they are done, it will help you focus your efforts on the most effective job-finding techniques.

Put yourself on the other side of the desk for a few moments. You would naturally start the recruitment process by asking yourself, your peers and your staff who within the company can do this job. If possible, you will want to recruit from within, because it's the cheapest way, you are dealing with known quantities, and it is motivating to everyone to see internal promotion. About 30 per cent of positions are filled this way. This should tell you that becoming connected to your profession, and getting to know and be known by your professional peers, can only give you a head start on the competition whenever you hear about internal promotions and transfers at your own, or other companies, because that promotion also speaks of another opening created by that promotion or transfer.

This is reinforced by the next step taken in the recruitment process. When a manager can't recruit internally, he or she will logically ask, 'Who do we know, and who do my people know?' This goes beyond the casual inquiry, and it includes who might be in the company's database, who has been interviewed in the past, internal posting of recruitment requirements (often tied to cash incentives for employee referrals), and who might be known in the professional community. These approaches account for 3 out of every 10 appointments that are made externally, and the questions you have to be asking yourself are, 'How do I get better connected to my local profession? How do I get to know and be known by my peers? How do I become more visible in my professional community?'

The next step – one slightly less reliable, as well as more expensive and time-consuming – is to look outside the company for people of whom the managers seeking staff have no direct knowledge; the first choice is often the internet. As cost now becomes a serious consideration, it won't surprise you to learn that the vast majority of internet appointments – 68 per cent, according to a recent study – come directly through the company's own website. The balance of internet appointments will come as a little surprise. Less than you might expect, 14.5 per cent, come from the big job boards, while significantly more of them (17.5 per cent) come from speciality sites that focus on a particular profession. After a little thought, the explanation is obvious: we don't pay fees when people come to our door on their own, so we naturally look more favourably on applicants coming to us through the company website. And it is also logical to expect a better-qualified candidate to come from an advertisement placed, let's say, on the site of a professional association.

When it comes to advertising on the internet and newspapers the picture gets a little murkier. While the internet as a recruiting tool is shown in some studies to outperform newspapers by a factor of 8 to 1, the issue isn't quite as clear-cut as it might appear. Recruitment advertising agencies encourage cross-media packages that include newspapers and advertising, and most newspapers post print advertising on their own sites.

Beyond the internet and newspaper advertising (which, by the way, has many job leads beyond the 'appointments' section) the balance of recruitment, about 30 per cent, come mainly from job fairs (both virtual and local), temporary to permanent appointments, and headhunters.

So the breakdown of effective recruitment strategies is very roughly split into thirds: one third of appointments coming from personal/professional networks and prior contacts, one third from the internet and cross-media advertising, and one third from the remaining sources. We'll now put together a job-hunting plan that reflects these realities.

The hidden job market

On a radio talk show I listened to a caller's problem. She said, 'I'm in the academic field and I've been unemployed for two years, and I don't know what to do.' I asked her how many possible employers there were, and she said about 3,000. I said, 'Next caller, please.' The world owes no one a living. You have to go out and find that next job.

About the same time I also heard from the producer of a national talk show on which I had recently appeared. She told me she used the techniques described in this part of the book to get 30 interviews in three weeks! I can't promise you those kinds of results, as that depends on your level of commitment and execution, but I can promise you that the following approaches really do work, and that you won't find a more practical or comprehensive approach anywhere. Implement these approaches with your head and your heart and you are going to generate more interviews than you have ever had in your life.

There is no magic bullet when it comes to successful job-hunting techniques. The employment market varies from year to year. Sometimes it's a buyer's market and sometimes a seller's. But the fact remains that regardless of the state of the economy, there are good jobs out there for the job hunter who employs a systematic and comprehensive approach.

Anyone struggling in a job hunt 10 years ago was probably relying exclusively on the situations vacant ads in the newspapers. That same person struggling today is probably relying on its modern equivalent: internet job boards. This is not to say that any of these approaches are invalid. On the contrary, each is a valuable resource, just so long as you know how to use it to best advantage and integrate it into a comprehensive overall plan.

Your goal is to land the best possible job for your professional needs. The problem is, you won't have the chance to pick the best opportunity unless you check them all out. It is nothing short of arrogant to imagine that the only companies with vacancies are the employers that are advertising where you happen to look.

Job hunters who go beyond scanning the job ads and posting a CV on the job sites all too often then fall back on applications to the large, well-known companies. They forget that 90 per cent of the growth in commerce is among small companies with fewer than 500 employees.

Average employee turnover from resignations, retirements, relocations and terminations in the workplace remains fairly steady at about 14 per cent. In other words, just about every company in your target area will be looking for someone during the year. What you have to do is to make sure that you are aware of the opportunities as they arise, and that the companies in turn are aware of you. This is where strategy comes into play.

You need to organize a comprehensive job-hunting strategy that will give you maximum penetration in your target area, and the ability to keep track of all the opportunities and potential employers you unearth. I'm going to help you do this in three steps.

You'll remember that about one-third of appointments come from internet resources and cross-media advertising. Here I'll help you get the most out of posting CVs on online job sites; how to find and use tools that lead you directly to employers in your profession and target location; and how to use the online and print versions of newspapers, business and trade publications to locate local opportunities.

Another one-third of appointments tend to come from employers' personal networks and prior contacts. I'll outline effective networking techniques using your personal networks, and ways for getting connected to your professional community through involvement with professional associations, college placement offices and alumni associations.

The balance of appointments – the remaining third – come from job fairs, third-party employment suppliers including temporary employment companies, employment agencies and headhunters, and what is quaintly referred to as 'smokestacking' – that is, keeping an eye out for potential employers as you go about town on your daily business.

The new networking

As you have probably grasped by now, choosing the best job hunting approach isn't as simple as choosing the Internet over your local newspaper; it is a matter of understanding how companies set about finding employees, and implementing an action plan that matches your job-hunting approaches to corporate recruitment practices.

Employers favour personal referrals above all other methods because they look easier, faster, and cheaper; and they are thought to result in an employee who is productive more quickly and who stays with the company longer. All job hunters like the idea of networking, but for fully two-thirds of us it doesn't work as effectively as it should because our networks lack depth and relevance (employers strongly prefer to hire through this channel but they only recruit about one-third of their employees this way). It is also the most time-consuming job-hunting approach to get up and running, so with these combined reasons we'll handle the ways to build broad and relevant networks first.

Effective networking practices will help you land that next job, increase your visibility and credibility within your field, increase your skills, and forever enhance your employability and promotability; through networking you will find mentors and become a mentor yourself, further enhancing your abilities and your connectivity. In the short term, getting personal referrals to job openings demands that you get connected to both your professional community and to the diverse networks that make up your local community. In some professions, as your career progresses further up the ladder of success you may eventually need to become connected to your professional communities on a national level.

When you connect with your professional community, beyond the people you work with, you get to know all the most dedicated and best-connected professionals in your area, and in turn you become known by them. You should think in terms of *networks*, rather than a single *network*. We all have a number of networks available to us, any of which may produce that all-important job offer. Here are the typical networks we can all tap into:

Professional networks

I other job hunters. Professionals seeking a position in the same profession or industry can be valuable resources; they don't have to be looking for the same type of position;

I managers, past and present, and your references. They can be useful to you throughout your job hunt;

I colleagues. This includes professional colleagues, past and present;

I other professionals in your field. Professional associations are a good place to start in order to find these contacts;

I college alumni. Educational institution networks are a valuable job search resource;

I company alumni associations. Companies increasingly see the value in maintaining contact with ex-employees.

Community networks

I family and relatives. This includes your spouse's family and relatives;

I friends. This includes neighbours and casual acquaintances, and those you know through your personal interest;

I service industry acquaintances. This includes your banker, lawyer, insurance agent, doctor, dentist, hairdresser, and the like;

I social and civic associations, including business groups, sports clubs, etc;

I hobbies. This includes everything from the golf club to chess club, and any activity you enjoy that involves a loosely knit group of similar people.

Networking approaches

You will have networks of people you can approach now and networks you will have to build today for use tomorrow. Ultimately, the effectiveness of your networking will depend largely on the scope of your networks and their relevance to your life. Whatever the network you have choices for making contact and nurturing those relationships:

▌ Electronically. By letter, over the telephone, via e-mail, online chat, or message posting.

▌ In person. Conventions, association meetings, class reunions, fundraisers, continuing-education classes, community groups, and events.

In practice, the professional who integrates intelligent networking into his or her professional life will use all of these approaches. Networking is a tremendously valuable survival tool for your entire career, but it is much more than a series of single events. It is a *process* of building relationships; your networks become more effective with the effort you put into their development.

In the following section, you'll learn how to build and nurture networks in both your professional and personal life.

Professional associations

Joining and being active in a professional association is the best long-term vehicle for increasing your professional visibility to future employers. In fact, if you have heard disgruntled job hunters mutter, 'It's not what you know, it's who you know,' it probably means they are not members of a professional association, and they don't understand networking.

Associations have monthly meetings in most major towns and cities, plus regional and national get-togethers every year. Of immediate interest are the local meetings. When you join, you get to know and be known by the most committed and best connected people at all levels of your profession. Your membership will help you stay attuned to what is going on in your profession. These associations also offer training programmes that make you a more knowledgeable and therefore a more desirable employee.

Your membership also becomes a link to colleagues, most of whom will gladly talk to you, based on your mutual connectivity through the association. The professional association is a new 'old boy/old girl' network for the modern world.

If you fit the profile of a special interest or minority group you will find professional associations that cater to another dimension of the professional you. If you can find a niche association that's a fit, join it as well, as it represents another even more finely tuned network.

If you are smart enough to join an association, you'll get the most benefit if you attend the meetings, because this is where you will meet fellow dedicated professionals. But don't just attend the meetings; volunteer to get involved. Associations always need someone to set out chairs or hand out paperwork and nametags. The task itself doesn't matter, but your visible willingness to be an active participant most certainly does and will get you on first-name terms with people you would probably never otherwise meet.

The association directory, which comes with your membership package, provides you with a superb networking resource for verbal contact and e-mail networking campaigns. You can feel comfortable calling any other member on the phone and introducing yourself: 'Hi, Brenda Massie? My name is Martin Yate. We haven't spoken before, but we are both members of the ABC Association. I need some advice; can you spare a minute?'

Your mutual membership, and the commitment to your profession it bespeaks, will guarantee you a few moments of anyone's time. Your association contacts will also feel more comfortable about referring you to others in their own networks and to employment needs at their own companies.

You can also use your association membership directory to generate personal introductions for jobs you have heard about elsewhere. Rather than apply cold, return to your membership directory and find people who work for that company. A judicious call or two will frequently get you a personal referral and some inside information on the opening. Once you have an interview scheduled, these same contacts can help you prepare for the interview with insider knowledge about the company, the department, and the hiring manager.

Professional associations all have newsletters, usually online and print. Many have a jobs section on the Web site or linked to the newsletter, where companies advertise because of the qualified response. Consequently, you will see recruitment ads that often don't appear anywhere else.

Active association membership puts you on the radar of all the best-qualified and connected professionals in your area. You can also list it at the end of your CV under a *Professional Affiliations* heading. This is guaranteed to get a second glance, as it signifies professional awareness.

Internet working

A new rage on the Internet that helps all of us to build deeper, more relevant networks is 'internetworking'. It revolves around various professionally oriented online networks created expressly to help you develop your professional expertise through connecting with others in your professional area and with whom you share common experiences or interests.

Internet working can get you useful introductions to people throughout the country and the world – people who might know of jobs at their own companies or who can introduce you to people at companies that do have openings. This new application of technology enables you to reach out to an endless horizon of relevant networking contacts.

It works quite simply: you join a social networking site, fill out a profile, and you are ready to go. For employers and recruiters, networking sites are a reliable pathway to the passive job seeker. For a job hunter or career changer, it's a reliable pathway to jobs through the people connected to them.

Some professionally oriented networking sites are general in nature, others are profession-specific. These sites may also offer an array of services useful to your networking activities:

I job postings from employers and headhunters;

I reminders of when to follow up with a call or e-mail to nurture your relationships;

I message boards and forums for common-interest groups, such as women in business;

I links to job boards;

I offline social events to meet and mingle in person.

One word of caution: online networking is a tool, a new and seemingly very attractive tool, but a single tool nevertheless. Use it in proper combination with other job search approaches.

If you are graduating, take advantage of this resource, but remember that the college placement office is not a substitute for your mother. It is not there to hold your hand or provide you with job offers. Career services and their staff are horrendously overworked and they work hard merely to keep pace with the Herculean task of providing assistance to the student body.

Take the time to make yourself known here, and stress your willingness to listen to good advice. If you are then seen to act on that advice and come back for more you will have earned your departments' respect and will garner yourself extra attention and guidance. Treat your entire interaction with career services in the same way you intend to treat the interview process. Make a real effort with your appearance and professional demeanour and, of course, you'll find that courtesy will go a long way.

Alumni associations

Almost every school, college and university, has an alumni association, and being a member of your alma mater's association can have a pivotal role in your professional life, if handled correctly. Going to the meetings, networking at the online site, and occasionally volunteering for some task are all activities that will ease you into collegial relationships with men and women on every rung of the corporate ladder – people who are in a position to boost your career.

The alumni association membership directory puts you in touch with the other graduates from your alma mater, and people hire people like themselves, people with whom they share something in common. Alumni associations all have newsletters (see how to use this tool in 'Newspapers and magazines', pages 53–55), and many include information about job openings. Some alumni associations even have semiformalized job-hunting networks where alumni are encouraged to pass on their company's employment needs. As a member of an alumni association, you can also continue an informal relationship with the school's director of career services and get some inside knowledge of corporate hiring plans. Even when your school days are in the misty past, don't forget these people and the valuable resource they represent.

Company alumni associations

Companies increasingly see the value in maintaining contact with ex-employees through online corporate alumni associations, as a source for future hires and for leads on future hires.

Your past managers and other references as a networking resource

As a rule, we are confident that our referees will speak well of us. The fact is, however, that while some of them will speak well of us, some, we might be surprised to hear, bear us no good will. It isn't wise to discover this as one potential offer after another bites the dust. Another mistake is not to speak to those referees at all or only at the end of a job hunt when a job offer is imminent. (For a discussion of how to handle your references when you are under serious consideration for a position, see Chapter 19, 'Negotiating the offer'.) If these are people you know well and whom you believe will speak well of you, why not use that goodwill throughout your job hunt?

At the very start you should identify as many potential references as possible. The more options, the better your likelihood of coming up with excellent references. With some experience under your belt you might be pursuing different job titles, and consequently different references might be appropriate for some of those jobs; of course, when employed, avoid using current managers and colleagues as references.

Yet at this point of the job search, excellent references, though important, are simply an added bonus. Your real agenda is to use these contacts as another aspect of your professional network.

The process is simplicity itself, starting with an introduction: 'Bob, this is _____. We worked together at XYZ between 1998 and 2003. How's it going?' It is appropriate here to catch up on gossip and the like. Then broach the subject of your call.

'John, I wanted to ask your advice.' (Everyone loves to be asked for an expert opinion.) 'We had some cutbacks at Fly-By-Night Finance, as you probably heard,' or 'The last five years at Bank of Crooks and Criminals International have been great, and the _____ project we are just winding down has been a fascinating job. Nevertheless, I have decided that this would be a perfect time for a strategic career move to capitalize on my experience.'

Then, 'John, I realize how important references can be and I was wondering if you would have any reservations about my using you as a reference?' It's better to find out now rather than down the line when it could blow a job offer. The response will usually be positive, so you can then move to the next step.

'Thanks, John, I hoped you would say that. Let me update you about what I have been doing recently and tell you about the type of job I'm after.' Give a capsule description of what you've done since you worked together and specifically what you are looking for. Also ask your contacts if they will keep an ear to the ground for you, and ask if they would mind giving you advice as situations arise during your job hunt. You'll also want to show courtesy by following your call with a thank-you letter.

With the scene set in this manner, you can network with each of these potential references every month or two, either for input on a particular opportunity and/or to ask who they know who might be looking to hire. With this approach you will have developed another small but very finely tuned networking resource for your job hunt.

Personal networks

Personal networking means more than annoying your friends until they stop taking your calls; it means using others within your personal sphere of influence to assist in your job search. Friends and acquaintances like to help, but as a group resource they can easily be exhausted. If you are like most people your personal networks aren't going to be wide enough or relevant enough to support a job hunt on their own. The typical personal networks we can all tap into include:

▪ family and relatives and friends. This includes your spouse's family and relatives and their networks;

▪ service industry acquaintances. Electricians, plumbers, carpenters, accountants, lawyers, hairdressers – anyone whose services you employ is a potential networking resource;

▪ hobby and special-interest networks. This includes anyone with whom you share a common interest;

▪ social community groups. This includes all the networks that become available to you when you reach out to help others.

While networking should become an integral part of your life, it will always move into a higher gear when strategic career moves are on your front burner. There are a wide variety of personal and community-based networks available to you, depending on your interests and willingness to become an active member of your local community.

Your personal networking efforts break into two categories: those people you already know personally, and those you can meet through involvement in your community. With the first you can be direct, while the second group requires a little more time and diplomacy. You might contact some of these networks by phone or e-mail, and some will combine both personal interaction and telephone or e-mail communication, but on the whole most of your personal networking will be done, well, personally.

Family and friends

The good news is that the people who know you best, your family and friends, will really try to help you. The bad news is that since most of them may have known you since you were a runny-nosed ten year old, you have been categorized, stereotyped, and pigeonholed. They might not really know what it is you do. They probably don't know what you are capable of doing or what you want to do.

When job hunting you tend to compound the overfamiliarity problem by tapping into this valuable network too soon and too often, before you have really thought out what your next job is going to be and what kind of leads will get you there. Still, you can get good mileage out of your family and friends network by retooling your approach.

Here are the steps to help your loved ones help you:

1. Think carefully about what you do for a living and put it in a one- or two-sentence description that even Aunt Aggie can grasp: 'I am a computer programmer; I write the instructions that help computers run.'

2. Think carefully about the job you want, the kind of company you will work for, and the kind of people you need to talk to; condense it into a one- or two-sentence explanation: 'I'm looking for a job with another computer company. It would be great if you or your friends know anyone I could talk to who works with computers.'

3. Give them the information you need to get in touch with these people: 'I am looking for the names and telephone numbers of anyone in these areas. I'm not looking for someone to hire me; I'm looking for people in my field with whom I can network.'

This process of breaking your networking needs into three or four simple statements gives the people you know socially something they can easily remember and something they can really work with.

Civic, social, volunteer and special-interest networking groups

It is good to be involved in your local community. Your involvement will reward you with a richer personal life, as well as a wide array of networking opportunities. You will find that effective networking in these groups is a little more time-consuming than with professional groups; after all, you have no prior professional relationship, and they don't have a familial 'obligation' to help you out.

At the same time, you can't possibly join all the groups your community has to offer, so you will have to make some decisions about what is practical and which activities are going to have a value to you in and of themselves. Most people have time for no more than three ongoing social activities. These might comprise:

▌ A community volunteer group – volunteer communities help us achieve a sense of meaning and balance in our lives, and such groups are especially helpful in the emotionally troubled times of job and career change. They get you involved with others who wish to make a difference.

▌ A hobby or special-interest group – this could be a chess club, a women's/men's group or a dance class. It doesn't matter as long as the activity is one that energizes you. The people you meet will all share a common bond based on your special interests.

▌ Business, professional, and civic groups – all communities have networks of professionals: Rotarians, Chamber of Commerce, women in business etc. These community-based associations are professionally oriented in membership, but they aren't focused on one profession; they straddle the line between your professional and community-based networking activities. Belonging to one will give you another angle of attack for your job hunt and perhaps improve your social life.

In all these groups your need for job leads must first take a back seat to becoming involved as a productive member. Soon enough you'll learn what people do for a living, as they learn about you both as a professional and as a human being. As opportunities arise you can talk about your job-hunting needs; we'll talk about how to manage these conversations shortly. You can find out about these groups in your local newspapers, at the library or by using your internet browser.

Gathering leads and referrals from networking conversations

You get a personal referral to a professional colleague or find a suitable name from a professional association directory, or maybe you get a referral from a friend. You might need to follow up with people you have met briefly on some prior occasion. You never know whom you are going to meet at the hairdresser, or gym. For your networking in any of these situations to be maximally effective, you need a 'networking mindset' that you can apply as readily in person as you can over the telephone, when you have copious notes in front of you and all the time in the world to prepare.

A 'networking mindset' means you are always prepared to show an interest in, and to speak to, others in a friendly way, so you won't let casual opportunities for expanding your networks slip by. With a networking mindset, you will be surprised at the range of useful people you will meet. Even when those people know nothing about your profession, they might know someone involved in the same field as yourself; everyone you meet has the potential to know someone who can be useful to your job hunt.

It's one thing to have an introduction and quite another to make the ensuing conversation productive. You can network with others at conventions, association meetings, class reunions, fundraisers, continuing-education classes, or at community, social and sporting events; or from a distance over the telephone, by letter, via e-mail, online chat, or message posting. While the information-gathering aspects of these conversations will remain fairly constant, regardless of the communication medium, there are one or two unique considerations about networking in person.

In-person networking

Always carry business cards. If your company doesn't supply you with cards, get some made at your own expense. When you attend social and professional events, keep those business cards handy (though, unless you are attending a job fair, leave your CV behind, as thrusting your CV at every new contact will be seen as overanxious and unprofessional).

You will need an introduction for yourself, which might vary slightly depending on the context, and while it's tough to do, you have to make the effort to reach out to others; as everyone knows what it is like to be looking for a job, you will find the majority of people friendly and responsive. 'Hello, I'd like to introduce myself. My name is Mark Germino. I'm in accounting/just started playing tennis; how about you?' Always try to end with a question that encourages your contact to introduce and talk about him- or herself; it doesn't really matter what question. Once there has been a conversational exchange, you can begin to move forward with your networking agenda. (We'll go into a whole series of networking questions shortly.)

Even though gatherings of associations, clubs, and societies provide excellent networking opportunities, they are not set up specifically for that activity. The same goes for any type of casual interaction. Try to keep your initial in-person networking conversations to under five minutes. You can end them gracefully with an offer of your business card. Similarly recognize that a request for yours is a signal for you both to move on. If someone you meet isn't carrying a card, have him or her write a name and contact information on the back of one of yours; always try to get both a telephone number and an e-mail address.

Whenever you meet someone in person, send an e-mail a few days later to thank him or her for any helpful information you may have gathered from the conversation; it also serves to keep you on that person's radar.

The secrets to all fruitful networking conversations

Your networks grow depending on the energy you put into them. That energy will express itself in the number of networking events in which you participate and how intelligently your networking conversations are structured. These events can happen in person or over the telephone. They can happen through e-mail as well, but actually talking with someone will always generate the most consistent results.

While your communication medium will vary, the agenda of your conversations will remain logical and constant. Here are some ideas for the content of those in-person conversations, telephone calls, and e-mails. Show interest in your contacts as human beings, then – and only then – move on with your agenda.

It's a good idea before leaving for an in-person event, or making a telephone call, to consider what information you want to gather and what messages you want to get across. As we spend the majority of our waking hours at the office, most people are happy to talk about their work. Discovering what someone does for a living makes a useful opener, and if the answer puts the contact in your professional field, great; you can draw the connection and go from there. If not you should still show an interest in your contact's interests, because this person may well know some of the people you need to know.

If you have spoken to the contact before, recall the last memorable interaction you had with that person or mention someone you both know. Ask what is happening in that person's personal and professional life, then listen to what is said and respond appropriately.

When it is time to move on to your information-gathering questions, prepare a statement that allows you to encapsulate your situation succinctly: 'I just got laid off with one thousand others' or 'We have a baby on the way, and XYZ is a company where there just isn't the room for me to grow professionally' or 'My job just got sent to Mumbai, India, so it's time for me to make a move.'

When common professional ground exists through an association or other social network, you can assume that your listener will be well disposed toward you; you can repay this goodwill by showing respect for that person's time and politely cutting to the chase. You could also begin, 'Brenda, I have been an accountant with Anderson for the last four years. I work in the small business area, and I'm looking to make a change.' Rather than rambling, in less than ten seconds you have courteously provided a focus, and it is here that you have to avoid the next gaffe by saying something like, 'My ideal job would be...' or 'The next step I'd like to take is...'

By describing an ideal job or your desired next step up the professional ladder, you make things more difficult for the listener, who thinks, 'This person is looking for something very specific, and any introductions I can make will probably be a waste of everyone's time.' It is more productive to talk in terms of what you do day-to-day, or even just tell the contact you are an accountant looking for a new opportunity.

(*Note:* The nature of these networking conversations assumes you are talking to professional colleagues and seeking leads on job openings, rather than talking to the managers, directors, vice presidents, and presidents who can make those hiring decisions. The conversations with anyone who has the potential to hire you are different because you are then making a marketing presentation; this will be handled later in this chapter.)

At this point, your conversation can move on to a discussion of the profession or industry, the areas of opportunity, and the direction you hope to pursue. If you handle yourself in a pleasant and professional manner, most people will try to be helpful. It helps to let your contacts know in general terms the job you intend to pursue, because while people usually want to help, they need a framework within which to target their efforts.

You can ask for general guidance about your tactics: 'If you were in my situation, Charlie, what would you do?' You can ask if he or she has heard about local companies hiring. If appropriate you can ask whether your contact would take a look at your CV – because you'd appreciate an objective opinion from someone in the profession. These are all good questions, and they typically comprise the content of 99 percent of all networking calls, but you can achieve more.

We are now going to proceed with a comprehensive sequence of interview development questions that will lead you to a substantial number of jobs in the hidden job market. These are exactly the question sequences asked by the headhunting and employment services industry when prospecting for job openings.

The questions follow a logical sequence – but that order might not suit your needs. As you look at the questions, decide what question you would ask if you had time for only one. Write it down, and repeat this with the remaining questions on this list; the result will be a comfortably prioritized set of questions. During each conversation you will only have so much time to gather information, so avoid questions like 'How's business these days?' Each question you ask should be specific. When you're satisfied with your list of interview development questions, print them out on a fresh sheet of paper and keep it by the telephone.

Questions for leads at your contact's company

You can ask if there are openings in the department or at the company and whom you should speak to about them. Don't ask, 'Can you or your company hire me?' You can ask:

■ 'Who else in the company might need someone with my qualifications?'

■ 'Is the company/department planning any expansion or new projects that might create an opening?'

■ 'When do you anticipate change in company manpower needs?'

■ 'Does your company have any other divisions or subsidiaries that might need someone with my attributes?'

Always ask about headhunters your contact might hear from and if he or she would pass on your name and contact information.

You might need to add some profession-specific questions. For instance, people in Information Technology might find questions about the operating systems, communication protocols, programs and languages a company uses to be useful. In this instance, after receiving an answer add a similarly focused follow-up question: 'Thanks, Gail. Who else do you know who uses these configurations?' Be sure any question you add to your list is geared toward identifying people and companies in your areas of interest.

Even when an offer of an introduction is made – 'Let me speak to Charlene Howarth for you,' (rather than being told to make direct contact yourself, 'call Charlene at extension 912') – don't rely on your contact to get you into that company. If the door hasn't opened in a few days, it might not. You should execute your own plan of attack, seeking other personal introductions within the company from your networking resources and making direct application by telephone or by e-mail and traditional posted CV submissions.

Questions for leads at other companies

When you are sure that no job openings exist within a particular department or company, move on to gathering leads in other companies: 'Do you know of anyone at other [banks] in town I might speak to?' or 'Whom do you know in the business community who might have a need for someone like me?'

If your contact can't think of a person, ask about other companies: 'What companies have you heard about that are hiring now?' or 'If you were going to make a move, what companies would you look at?' or 'Which are the most rapidly growing companies in the area?'

Whenever you are offered a lead, say, 'That's a great idea. I never thought of IBM,' as your encouragement is positive reinforcement. Then after a suitable pause, ask for another company name, as in, 'I really appreciate your help, Sam. I never thought of IBM... Who else comes to mind?' When people see that their advice is appreciated, they will often come up with more helpful information. When you have gathered two or three company names, you can backtrack with a request for contact names at each of the companies: 'Do you know of anyone I could speak to at _____?'

You can also ask for leads at companies you plan to call, or even ones you have already called: 'Jack, I was planning to contact _____, Inc. Would you happen to know anyone there?'

If you are changing or considering a career change, your priorities might be different. In this case you can explain that you are considering a particular profession for a new career direction and ask what it is like working in the profession; what your contact likes least and most about the work; what education, experience, and professional behaviours help people succeed in the profession; who fails and why; and how one gets into and moves ahead in the profession.

What to do when you get a referral

When you get leads on companies and specific individuals to talk to, be sure to thank your benefactor and ask to use his or her name as an introduction. 'Thank you, Bill. I didn't know XYZ was building a facility in town (duh!), and I appreciate getting Holly Barnes's name. May I use your name as an introduction, or would you prefer me to keep it confidential?'

Every time you get a referral be sure to ask whether you can use your contact's name as an introduction. The answer will invariably be yes, but asking demonstrates professionalism and will encourage your contact to come up with more names and leads. It is also quite acceptable to add afterward, 'That's very helpful, Bill. Does anyone else come to mind?'

When you get permission to use your contact's name, use it in an introduction: 'Jane, my name is Natalia Markowskiu. Our mutual friend

Bill Smith suggested I call, so before I go any further, Bill has asked me to say hello.' This is a bridge-building phrase and usually leads to a brief and complimentary exchange about your mutual contact before you go into your information-gathering agenda.

When you do get help, say thank you. If you do it verbally, it's a nice touch to follow it up with a note. The impression is indelible and might get you another lead. It never hurts to include a copy of your CV with the thank-you letter.

When your networking call comes to its natural conclusion, say your thanks, offer to return the favour, and leave the door open for future calls: 'Jack, thanks so much for your help. I do appreciate it. You know when you are job hunting you realize how important your colleagues are, so I'd like to give you my telephone number and e-mail so that one day I might return the favour. Thanks for your time. Might I call you again sometime?'

Other statements that you might use at the end of your conversation include:

▌ 'I'll let you know how it works out with Mary Chen.'

▌ 'Might I get in touch in a couple of months to see if the situation has changed?'

▌ When talking to a management contact in your profession, you might suggest, 'Would it be worth my e-mailing a copy of my CV for your personal management database?'

Keep in touch with each of your networking contacts, but don't overdo it. It is better to invest your energies in developing the breadth, depth, and relevance of your networks, rather than just calling people you already know.

Whether your contacts are able to help you or not, let them know when you get a job, and try to stay in contact at least once a year. A career is a long time, and it might be next week or a decade from now when a group of managers (including one from your personal network) are talking about filling a new position, and the first thing they'll do is ask, 'Who do we know?' That someone is more likely to be you when you are connected to your profession and your local community.

4 More effective job search tactics

In a competitive market, you need to make use of every tool that you can to win the job that's right for you.

All of the job-hunting tools and approaches that we will discuss in this chapter – the internet, newspapers and magazines, employment agencies, and more – have proved effective, but no single one is a guaranteed silver bullet. Any one of them could turn up the ideal opportunity for you and your future, so your plan of attack must embrace as many of these approaches as is practical in your situation. It should also include elements of all the techniques we discussed in the previous chapter for creating a personal networking system. A man who goes fishing and puts one hook in the water has only one chance of catching any one of the millions of fish in the sea; a man with two hooks in the water has double the chances of getting a bite. The more hooks you have in the water, the better your chances of getting bites.

Using the internet in your job hunt

The internet is now the most comprehensive job-hunting resource. You can search through thousands of job openings and send your CV to hundreds of employers and headhunters in just a few hours. You can also use salary calculators to help you compare earnings and the cost of living in different parts of the country. You can ask questions of career experts, live, and there are special-interest forums for virtually all professional areas. Job hunting on the internet can make your job hunt faster, more efficient and more comprehensive. Use this tool to stack the odds in your favour.

My advice is to spend a couple of days at the start of your job hunt kick-starting your search with internet tools. Visit the incredible job banks to look for suitable openings and sign up for the e-mail alerts that will automatically update you when jobs matching your needs appear. Post your CV on the CV banks – employers and headhunters are scanning them daily.

Do all these things and whatever else the internet offers your unique job hunting needs, focusing on it for three or four full days to get the best out of the medium and the stars out of your eyes. Then, focus on the traditional job-hunting techniques explained in the rest of this chapter. Then, take an hour at the end of the day to maintain your online momentum. If you continue ad nauseum to potter around the internet, surfing from this site to the next, you will feel busy but you won't be maximally productive.

Registering on job sites

Not all job sites and CV banks work the same way. On some, you will copy and paste your CV into dialogue boxes as directed. On others, you will be completing a profile or questionnaire that the site has developed.

Job sites are usually free for you to use, but the employers are paying to post their job openings, just as they are also paying to search the CV bank. These same paying customers want to control their search time, and the job sites work with them to develop ever more efficient screening tools. By making you, the jobseeker, fill out profiles and answer questionnaires that ask for very specific information, you are helping them screen you in – or screen you out.

Whenever you are filling out a profile or questionnaire keep two things in mind:

1.   Who will be reading this, and for what purpose?

2.   What are they really asking me?

Angle your answers accordingly and remember to include those important keywords.

Web-based CVs, e-CVs, and web portfolios

Almost all job hunting activities take time and effort on your part, so when the opportunity comes along to use passive marketing, you should seize it. Here are passive marketing approaches to increase your professional visibility and credibility:

1. Keep your CV posted and refreshed on a selection of job sites. Throughout a job hunt you need to keep your CV visible on the job banks with which you have signed up. This sometimes takes a little maintenance, as typically job sites like to purge their CV databases every 90 or 120 days so their paying corporate customers will feel they are paying for fresh candidates. When you sign up at a particular site, make a note of their policy for purging their CV databases, mark the 'kill' date in your calendar, and go in a few days before and refresh everything.

   As almost all job sites tell you when openings matching your needs are posted, you can go to the site as needed during your job hunt, maybe once a month while employed, to harvest the matching jobs.

2. Create web portfolios and web-based CVs. For some time now, artists and designers have been creating online portfolios for their work, as a cost-effective marketing device. Now that the web is becoming ubiquitous, it is practical for you to establish an online presence as a career management tool. You can build what is variously called an e-CV, a web folio, or a web portfolio for yourself, or have it built for you, where your type of work warrants it.

How to approach companies directly

Companies now overwhelmingly prefer to have you approach them directly, and you can use the job sites you visit to identify companies in your area of professional interest.

Go to any job site and do a search of their posted openings by putting in minimal keywords and restrictions. For example, if a Medical Insurance Sales Manager goes to a site and does a simple keyword search for 'insurance' he may get hundreds of results, and the vast majority will be for jobs that do not interest him. At the same time, those results will reveal recruiters and companies in his profession and target location.

With this direct research approach you can directly link to hundreds of employer websites. Visit these sites and see if they have more suitable job openings posted there. Companies all use their sites as recruitment tools and usually have most open job opportunities posted there. When they do, you'll have additional information with which to customize your covering letter and CV. Even if they do not appear to have an opening for someone like you, send them your CV anyway. You don't really know what is going on at that company, and at the very least you will be in their database and therefore on their radar when a need does arise.

Getting an inside track at target companies

This is where your networking approaches come back into play. You can use that association membership directory (and other networking resources) to get a personal introduction to the company, either a direct recommendation ('Hey, we should speak to this guy I know named Bill Hudson') or at least the name of someone to whom you can e-mail and post your CV.

Look in the membership directory for someone who works at the target company and call them. Your conversation, like those mentioned in our discussion of professional and personal networking, should run something like the following:

> EXAMPLE
> **'Hi, Carole Mixon? This is Martin Yate, We haven't spoken before, but we are both members of the _____ Association. Carole, I see that you work at Cybex Labs, and they currently have a job posted on the website for someone with my background. Do you think I could ask you a couple of questions about the company?'**

After a minute or two of conversation you can then ask for a name:

> EXAMPLE
> **'Carole, rather than just send in my CV blind, could you tell me the name of the person who this job reports to... I won't mention your name unless you want me to.'**

With a name your CV goes to a person first and not the database, again raising your visibility.

Getting the scoop on target companies

If you want to do a little research on the company to tweak your CV, or to gain information that will help personalize your covering letter, or to prepare for an interview, you can do this from your computer, too. Google News Search will search for press stories about the company, and in the process spit up names of people within the company. An employer's own website is also a major source of information.

As your job hunt picks up steam, some employers will rise to the top as particularly desirable, and you will gradually build a dossier on them. When you gather information about a company, create a company folder and paste the knowledge in; it will provide useful background information for interviews and show that you have done your homework. This is flattering to the interviewer: he or she sees it as demonstrating effort and enthusiasm, both of which can end up as being deciding factors in a tightly run job race.

Newspapers and magazines

You can't spend your whole life sitting in front of the computer screen; it's bad for your health and you'll be missing important job leads by not integrating newspapers and magazines into your campaign.

Not all companies advertise on the internet and not all companies yet have websites. For companies that rely on the local community for both customers and employees, the newspaper is still a major recruitment vehicle.

It is always a good idea to examine back issues of the newspapers. These can provide a rich source of job opportunities that remain unfilled from previous advertising efforts. I suggest working systematically through the job ads, going back 12 to 18 months. React to ads as if they were fresh: answer the ones with your job title and contact companies in your field even if they appear to be seeking people with different skills.

Sound crazy? That's what a reader said to me in a letter. He also said this technique landed him a £40,000-a-year job from a seven-month-old ad. Sometimes the position will not have been filled and the employer simply despaired of getting someone through advertising. Sometimes the person was employed but it didn't work out. Perhaps they are only now starting to look for another person like the one they had advertised for earlier, or they might even just be coming off a recruitment freeze.

Whatever the case, every old ad you follow up on won't result in an opening, but when one does, the odds can be short indeed. Smart money always goes on the short odds.

In addition to your local papers, there are regional, national and international papers that employers favour to meet their professional needs.

Your approach for mining the job ads is similar to that used on internet job sites. You will initially look for jobs relating specifically to your professional skill set, at your professional level, then above and below it. Following this you will look for other job titles that typically work in your department or whose holders perform related functions. Finally, you will look for ads from any employer in your line of work. You'll do this because you remember that employers don't always advertise exactly where you happen to be looking, and that they don't always advertise, perhaps having moved on to using employment agencies and headhunters for that particular position.

When you cruise the job ads, that is only part of your newspaper research. You should also read the business pages for both the advertisements and the articles. Advertisements can lead you to employers you might not have considered before, and the editorial copy is full of opportunities:

▌ Always check out the promotions column. It will tell you about companies, give you the name of person you can contact ('Congratulations on the promotion, Mr Byrd...') and, in most cases, if someone gets promoted or leaves one company for another, that leaves a job to be filled. Without wishing to be morbid, the obituaries column and stories of sudden death can also mean that some company somewhere now has a new set of problems to solve.

▌ The business news stories tell you about company success stories, new contracts signed, new products and services introduced, and companies coming to town.

▌ Industry overviews and market development pieces can tip you off about subtle shifts in your professional marketplace and thereby alert you to opportunities – and provide you with the chance to customize your letters, calls and CV for specific targets.

▌ Pay special attention to quotations. 'The art of press writing demands frequent quotes, and by necessity,' says Peregrine McCoy, senior partner of Connem, Covertrax and Splitt. The person quoted might just be someone in your field who you can contact. Reminding that person of the article ('I saw you quoted in the *Argus* last week...') is flattering and will get you a few minutes of that person's time to make a pitch, get an interview, and/or get some leads.

As well as the newspapers, you should also keep an eye on the trade press: professional association periodicals, trade magazines, and the general business press. You can mine them all in a similar fashion. In these publications you are likely to find articles written by industry professionals. When contacting the author of an article, you might include how much you agree with what was said, a little additional information on the subject, or words to the effect that 'it's about time someone told it like it is'. Never say anything in the vein of, 'Hey, the article is great but you missed...'.

If you have ever tried your hand at writing, trade magazines offer a ready outlet for your efforts and can get you noticed by all kinds of people. You can also use your writing ability to create what are known as *special reports*, and use these in place of a CV.

It is a good idea to cut out and keep all the pieces that give you ideas, maybe placed in a ring binder. You will have the info where you can find and use it, you can send a copy of an article where a person is mentioned with a letter and CV, and you will have a copy on file to refresh your memory before any direct communication.

There are plenty of great job leads in newspapers and magazines, if you read them with a job-hunting mindset.

Employment agencies

There are essentially four categories: state employment agencies, private employment agencies and executive recruiters, temporary help organizations, and career counsellors.

State employment agencies – Jobcentres

These will make efforts to line you up with appropriate jobs and will send CVs on your behalf to interested employers who have jobs listed with them. It is not mandatory for employers to list jobs with these agencies, but more and more are taking advantage of these free services. Once the bastion of minimum-wage jobs, the choice is getting wider, so it's a resource not to be ignored.

If you are moving to another part of the country your local Jobcentre can see what jobs might be available there. The most effective way to use the service, though, is to visit your local office and ask for an introduction to the office in your destination area.

Private employment agencies

When working with an employment agency, choose your agent, or 'headhunter' as they are sometimes called, with the same care and attention with which you would choose a spouse or an accountant. The calibre of the individual and company you choose could well affect the calibre of the company you ultimately join. Further, if you choose prudently, he or she can become a lifetime counsellor who can guide you step by step up the ladder of success.

There are different types of employment services:

▌ Permanent employment agencies where you pay the fee.

▌ Permanent agencies where the employer pays the fee.

▌ Contingency and retained search firms.

As this is the for-profit sector of the marketplace, the question arises: whose pocket is the profit coming from? To avoid misunderstanding, it is best to confirm which is which before entering into any relationships.

Only employment agencies and certain contingency search firms will actively market you to a large number of companies with whom they may or may not have an existing relationship. A true executive search firm will never market your services. It will only present your credentials on an existing assignment.

So what type of company is best for you? Well, the answer is simple: the one that will get you the right job offer. The problem is there are thousands of companies in each of these broad categories. So how do you choose between the good, the bad and the ugly?

Fortunately this is not as difficult as it sounds. Let's dispel one or two myths. A retained executive search firm is not necessarily any better or more professional than a contingency search firm, which in turn is not necessarily better or more professional than a regular employment agency. Each has its exemplary practitioners and its charlatans. Your goal is to avoid the charlatans and get representation by an exemplary outfit. Make the choice carefully, and having made the choice, stick with it and listen to the advice you are given.

Check on the date of the firm's establishment. If the company has been in town since you were in nappies, the chances are good that they are reputable.

A company's involvement in professional associations is always a good sign. It demonstrates commitment and, through extensive professional training programmes, an enhanced level of competence.

Involvement in independent or franchise networks of firms can also be a powerful plus. These networks also have extensive training programmes that help assure a high-calibre consultant. Franchise offices can be especially helpful if you are looking to change jobs and move across the country (or further) at the same time, as they tend to have powerful symbiotic relationships with other network members; in fact this is often a primary reason for their being a member of that particular franchise or network.

Experienced recruitment consultants can also be relied upon to have superior knowledge of the legalities and ethics of the recruitment process, along with the expertise and tricks of the trade that only come from years of hands-on experience. All of this can be put to work on your behalf.

It makes good sense to have a friend in the business with an ear to the ground who has your interests at heart as you continue your upward climb.

Finally, don't get intimidated. You are not obliged to sign anything, and neither are you obliged to guarantee an agency that you will remain in any employment for any specific length of time. Don't get ensnared by the occasional cowboy in an otherwise respectable profession.

Executive recruiters

These people rarely deal with salary levels under £50,000 per year. All the advice I have given you about employment agencies applies here (although you can take it for granted that the executive recruiter will not charge you a fee). They are going to be more interested in your CV for their database than in wanting to see you right then and there, unless you match a specific job they are trying to fill for a client. They are far more interested in the employed than in the unemployed, because an employed person is less of a risk (they often guarantee their finds to the employer for up to a year) and a more desirable commodity.

Executive recruiters are there to serve the client, not to find you a job. They neither want nor expect you to rely on them for employment counselling, unless they specifically request that you do – in which case you should listen closely.

Working with a headhunter

Mutually beneficial relationships can be developed with headhunters in all these categories; after all, their entire livelihood depends on who they know. But do be circumspect, as an unethical headhunter can create further competition for you when you share information about companies you are talking to. Details of a company you are in contact with are nobody's business but your own.

Ascertain network and association membership and how this might help in your job search; if you are moving across country these far-flung networks can be a real advantage. Determine who pays the fee and whether any contracts will need to be exchanged. Define titles and the employment levels they represent, along with geographical areas. Know what you want, or ask for assistance in defining your parameters. This will include title, style of company, salary expectations, benefits and location.

If the recruiter is interested in representing you, expect a detailed analysis of your background and prepare to be honest. Do not overstate your job duties, accomplishments, or education. If there are employment gaps, explain them.

Find out first what the professional expects of you in the relationship and then explain what you expect. Reach commitments you both can live with, and stick to them. If you break those commitments, expect the headhunter to cease representation and to withdraw your application from potential employers. They are far more interested in long-term relationships than passing nuisances.

Keep the recruiter informed about any and all changes in your status, such as salary increases, promotions, redundancies, or other offers of employment.

Don't consider yourself an employment expert. You get a job for yourself every three or four years. These people do it for a living every day of every week. Ask for their objective input and seek their advice in developing interviewing strategies with their clients.

Always tell the truth.

Temporary employment agencies

These provide employment services to companies in all industries and at most professional levels, from unskilled and semi-skilled labour (referred to as *light industrial* in the trade) to administration, finance, technical, sales and marketing professionals, doctors, lawyers and even interim executives.

Temporary employment services can be a useful resource if you are unemployed. You can get temporary assignments, maintain continuity of employment and skills, and perhaps enhance your marketability in the process.

If you are changing careers or returning to work after an absence, temporary assignments can help get new or rusty skills up to speed and provide you with a current work history in your field.

If you are unemployed and need the cash flow for bills, working with a temp company can supply that and get you exposure to employers in the community who, if you really shine, could ask you to join the staff full time. This 'temp-to-perm' hiring approach is becoming increasingly popular with companies, as it allows them to try before they buy. You will also develop another group of networking contacts.

Here is some advice for working successfully with a temporary employment agency:

■   Investigate the turnover of the temporary staff. If other temporaries have stayed with the company long term, chances are that company does a good job and has good clients.

■   Select a handful of firms that work in your field; this will increase the odds of suitable assignments appearing quickly.

■   Define the titles and the employment levels they represent, along with geographical areas they cover.

■   Do not overstate your job duties, accomplishments, or education.

■   Find out first what the agency expects of you in the relationship, then explain what you expect. Reach commitments you both can live with, and stick to them.

■   Judge the assignments not solely on the pay (although that can be important) but also on the long-term benefits that will accrue to your job search and career.

■ Keep the agency informed about any and all changes in your status, such as offers of employment or acquisition of new skills.

■ Resolve key issues ahead of time. Should an employer want to take you on full time, will that employer have to pay a set amount, or will you just stay on as a temporary for a specific period and then go on the employer's payroll?

Career counsellors

Career counsellors charge for their services. For this you get assistance in your career realignment or job-search skill development. What you don't get is a guarantee of employment.

If you consider this route, speak to a number of counsellors and check multiple references on all of them. As you are unlikely to be given poor references, you will want to check secondary and tertiary references. This is simple to do. Check the half-dozen references you request and then ask each of the referees to refer someone else they know who used the service. Then check that reference as well.

When it comes to headhunters and career counsellors, good people come from many backgrounds. My personal choice for someone who can give you the best possible advice is the person who has both corporate HR experience *and* employment agency or retained search experience.

Job fairs

Job fairs (sometimes called career days) are occasions where companies get together to attract large numbers of potential employees to a one-day-only event.

Job fairs aren't regular events, even in metropolitan areas, so they won't be taking much of your time, but you should become an active participant when they do occur. They are always advertised in the local newspapers and frequently on local radio, so if you stay keyed into the local news scene as part of keeping your job-hunting antenna tuned you'll hear about them. Job fairs sometimes charge a small entrance fee, in return for which you get direct access to and time with all the employers and formal presentations by company representatives and local employment experts. When you organize yourself properly, take the right attitude and make the most of what's on offer, job fairs make for a great job-hunting opportunity.

When you attend job fairs, go prepared with:

- Proper business attire. You may be meeting your new boss, and you don't want the first impression to be less than professional.

- Business cards. (If employed, remember to request the courtesy of confidentiality in calls to the workplace.)

- CVs – as many as there are exhibitors, times two. You'll need one to leave at the stand and an additional copy for anyone you have a meaningful conversation with.

- Notepad and pen, preferably in a folder.

It's easy to walk into a job fair and be drawn like a moth to just the biggest and most attractive stands, sponsored by the largest and most established companies, and ignoring the lesser one. But remember that 90 per cent of jobs are generated by small companies of fewer than 500 employees. You will want to visit every stand, not just the ones with the flashing lights and all the moths fluttering around. You should also go with specific objectives in mind:

- Talk to someone at every stand. You can walk up and ask questions about the company activities, and who they are looking for, before you talk about yourself. This allows you to present yourself in the most relevant light.

- Collect business cards from everyone you speak to so that you can follow up with a letter and a call when they are not so harried. Very few people actually get offered a post at job fairs; for most companies the exercise is one of collecting CVs so that meaningful meetings can take place in the ensuing weeks. But be 'on' at all times, because serious interviews do sometimes occur on the spot. If you have a background and CV that makes you a good match for a specific opportunity, then make a pitch, get the person's business card and fix a date for a follow-up call. If on the other hand there's a job you can do, but your CV needs some adaptation to better position your application, you'll need a different approach. By all means talk to the company representative, but don't hand over a CV that will detract from your application (you can come up with a harmless pretext, such as having run out of copies). Instead get the contact's business card and promise to follow up with a CV, which you can then custom fit to the opportunity.

▋ Collect company brochures and other materials.

▋ Arrange times and dates to follow up with as many employers as possible. 'Ms Jones, I realize you are very busy today, and I would like to speak to you further. Your company sounds very exciting. I should like to set up a time when we could meet to talk further or perhaps set a time to call you in the next few days.'

In addition to the exhibit hall, there are likely to be formal group presentations by employers. As all speakers love to get feedback, move in when the crush of presenter groupies has died down; you'll get more time and closer attention. You will also have additional knowledge of the company and the chance to spend a few minutes customizing the emphasis of your skills to meet the stated needs and interests of the employer in question.

Job fairs provide opportunities for administrative, professional and technical people, up to the middle management ranks. However, this doesn't mean that the senior executive should feel such an event is a waste of time. The opportunity still exists to have meaningful conversations with tens or hundreds of employers in a single day about company direction, from which may come further fruitful conversations. Job fairs aren't attended by employers to attract senior executives, but it doesn't mean that you can't gather information, collect cards and generate leads.

On leaving each stand, and at the end of the day, go through your notes while everything is still fresh in your mind. Review each company and what possibilities it may hold for you. Then review all the companies as a whole to see what you might glean about industry needs, marketplace shifts and long-term staffing requirements. Make notes and determine that everyone you spoke to will receive an e-mail and a follow-up call within the next week.

Part II

Getting to Square One

You have to get the word out and make contact with employers to land job interviews, and you make the most contacts in the shortest time when you do it simultaneously with e-mail, mail and by picking up the telephone.

5 *Making contact*

To land that all-important first interview, you've got to be able to recognize the 'buy signals' and make your way past the objections that can keep you from being considered for a job for which you might just be perfect.

As you identify opportunities with all the techniques we have just discussed, you need to make contact and pitch your candidacy. There are two commonsense approaches: pick up the phone and make a call; and the written approach, including a cover letter and CV, sent as an e-mail or traditional mail, and often through both mediums.

E-mail and post is likely to be more appealing because there is less likelihood of direct rejection, yet at the same time you know that interviews don't happen without telephone conversations – so you have to make calls, too.

In fact, you should be making as many phone calls as the letters and e-mails you send. As your job hunt gets up to speed you will see that both approaches are necessary steps in the same process. When you send out e-mails, letters, and CVs, you must follow up with phone calls, and when you make calls (calling employers directly to present your credentials), you will often find yourself following up with e-mailed letters and CVs. Your plan of attack needs to maintain a delicate balance between the two approaches so your calls force you to follow up in writing, and your CVs and letters force you to follow up with phone calls.

A balanced approach, using phone calls, e-mail, and post, will generate the most interviews. When you have identified names of people to talk to within companies, it's common sense to start with a conversation; yet, there will be times, especially at the very start of your job hunt, when you are still developing your contacts.

With this in mind, first we are going to address launching the e-mail and traditional mail part of your job-hunting campaign. Not because it is a more productive approach – it isn't – but because with e-mail you can get the word out without benefit of names to contact.

E-mail and letters

Must you send out hundreds or even thousands of e-mails and letters in the coming weeks? Yes and no. You should send out as much as you need and no more. Only if you approach and establish communication with every possible employer will you create the maximum opportunity for yourself. Two contacts a week is the behaviour of the long-term unemployed.

On the other hand, I am not recommending that you immediately make up a list of 700 companies and contact them today. That isn't the answer either. Your campaign needs strategy, and without follow-up calls many of your letters will get lost in the shuffle, while a quick phone conversation could well get you an interview. Every job search campaign is unique; nevertheless, you should maintain a balance between the *number* of letters you send out on a weekly basis and the *types of people to whom they are sent*. The key is to send out balanced mailings representing all the different types of leads, and to send them out regularly and in a volume that will allow you to make follow-up calls. Many headhunters manage their time so well that they average over fifty calls per day, year in and year out. While you may aim at building up your call volume to this enviable number, I recommend that you start out with more modest goals. Send five to ten contacts per day in each of the following areas:

- in response to internet job postings;
- in response to newspaper advertisements;
- to contacts in any of your professional network;
- to contacts in any of your personal networks;

■ to companies and contacts you identify from the internet, reference works, newspapers, and trade journal research;

■ to headhunters;

■ to job fair contacts.

When you apply these approaches, there are thousands of contacts waiting to be made, so this breakdown of contacts becomes a daily quota. If it seems a bit steep to begin with, scale down the numbers until they are achievable and gradually build up the volume. But remember, the lower your volume, the longer the job search.

Most people labour over each call and then agonize over its results. A very effective idea is to develop a list of 10 or 20 calls where your presentation will be the same in each instance (for example, following up on a CV you sent last week). Then write out a script for yourself, compiling a bullet list of points and questions you want to make on each call. Then screw up your courage, sit down and make those 20 calls one after the other without stopping to dwell on the rejection or dance a jig when the call goes well. When you do this, you will make more calls, get more results and get acclimatized to using the telephone effectively as a job-hunting tool. When I first became a headhunter many years ago and had to be on the phone every day talking to strangers, I was terrified at the prospect. One piece of advice really helped me, so perhaps it will help you too. I was told I would never meet these people unless they were interested in what I had to offer, in which case they'd be happy I called. Because I was on the phone, no-one would know who I was or how scared I looked.

Do you need to write more than one letter? Almost certainly. We have already made the case for having letters and CVs in more than one format. There is no need to waste precious time crafting your written communication entirely from scratch when templates exist. The key is to do each validation once and to do it right, so make sure you save copies of your letters and CVs. This way you'll be ready regardless of when opportunity comes knocking on your door.

Multiple submissions

While you might start off making single submissions to companies, you will sometimes find it valuable to make a number of contacts within a given company, especially the larger ones, to ensure all the important players know of your existence. Let's say you are a young engineer who wants to work for Last Chance Electronics. If you haven't been able to get a personal introduction through applying all the networking and direct-research approaches (unlikely but possible), it is well within the bounds of reason to post or e-mail cover letters and accompanying CVs to any, or all, of the following people (each ideally addressed to someone by name, so they have less likelihood of being lost): the Managing Director, the head of engineering, the chief engineer, the engineering manager, the head of human resources, the technical recruitment manager, and the technical recruiter. Find names on the company Web site, in membership databases of all your formal professional networks, and in professional directories.

Keep a log of your mail and e-mail contacts so you will know when to follow up with a phone call-usually between three and seven working days later; exclude Monday mornings from this count, as everyone is either in meetings or getting up to speed for the week.

Keep track of these contacts beyond the initial follow-up period. CVs do get misplaced, and employment needs change. You can comfortably resend mail to everyone on your list every couple of months if necessary. Most recipients won't register that they heard from you two months ago, and of those who do, most won't take offence. Any who do are people who have no need for your professional skill set and whom you are therefore unlikely to run into anytime soon.

A professionally organized and conducted campaign will proceed on two fronts:

I **Front one:** A carefully targeted rifle approach to a select group of companies. You first identified these 'superdesirable' places to work when you researched your long list of potential employers. You will continue to add to this primary target list as you unearth fresh opportunities in your day-to-day research efforts. While this may be your primary target list, at the beginning of the job hunt you are building both it and contacts within the company, so you may not be e-mailing to these companies initially. You will wait until you are comfortable with your developing skills – at least until you have finished reading the interview sections of this book.

I **Front two:** A carpet-bombing approach to every possible employer in your target area. After all, you won't know what opportunities exist unless you go and find out, and you need to start generating activity.

Here you begin with an e-mail/letter to one or two contacts within the company then repeat the mailings to other contacts when your initial follow-up calls result in referrals or dead ends. Remember, just because Harry in engineering says there are no openings in the company, that doesn't make it so. Besides, any one of the additional contacts you make could well be the person *who knows the person* who is anxious to meet you.

Once your campaign is in motion and you start to receive responses to your mailings and begin to schedule interviews from your calls (how to make the calls is covered in the next chapter), your emphasis will change. Those contacts and interviews will require follow-up letters and conversation, and you will be spending time preparing for the interviews.

This is the point at which most job hunts stall. We get so excited about the interview activity that we convince ourselves 'this will be the offer.' Experienced headhunters know that, thanks to Murphy's Law, the offer that can't fail usually does fail. The offer doesn't materialize, and we are left sitting with no interview activity. You have to keep that job search pump primed with ongoing activity to generate an ongoing flow of interviews, because you never know which one is going to generate the ideal opportunity.

The more contacts you make, the more follow-up calls you can make to schedule interviews. The more interviews you get, the more proficient you will become at them. The better you get at interviewing, the more offers you will get – and the *more* offers you get, the more choices you will have when making your decision.

Direct-marketing calls

You must be clear in your mind that at the same time you are e-mailing and posting CVs, you will pick up the phone and call people. This is the single most effective way of generating job interviews. I don't want you to think that you can execute a job hunt with just a letter and e-mail campaign; many people deceive themselves into thinking this is possible because they are terrified of picking up the phone to call strangers.

We have already talked about making networking presentations in person and networking calls over the telephone. Those discussions, however, focused on talking to peers and getting leads on job opportunities and the names of people to contact. There is a difference between a networking call to a peer and making a marketing presentation about the professional you to a potential employer. With your networking calls, getting leads on possible job openings and referrals or introductions to hiring managers were your primary objectives. With marketing calls, you directly target managers with the authority to hire you. As those leads on managers, directors, and department heads begin to pile up, the time comes to make contact and introduce the professional you.

I'm going to show you how to build simple, sophisticated, and productive presentations and how to navigate the ensuing conversations, recognizing and responding to the 'buy signals' that denote interest, and how best to overcome any objections. The result will be job interviews and live leads for additional opportunities.

Most job hunters have but a single goal when they pick up the phone: 'Get an interview.' Naturally, this approach offers only one chance of success, but many more for failure and feelings of inadequacy and depression. You will multiply your success rate when you have a multiple-goal strategy in place. When headhunters make calls, for example, they typically have these five basic goals in mind, to maximize the impact of every call they make:

- I will arrange an interview date and time.

- If my contact is busy, I will arrange another time to talk.

- I will develop leads on promising job openings elsewhere in this and other companies.

- I will leave the door open to talk with this person again in the future.

- I will send a CV for subsequent follow-up.

Try to keep these common-sense goals in mind every time you talk with someone during your job hunt, because every conversation holds the potential for turning into an interview or leading you toward one that will generate first a telephone interview then a face-to-face meeting. In the following sections you will learn to:

- develop a concise word picture of your professional strengths;

- be prepared for a telephone interview every time you pick up the phone;

■ recognize 'buy signals' and objections as they crop up in your conversations, and learn how to turn them into interviews;

■ turn apparent dead-end conversations into live leads for interviews.

As you still may feel that making calls is intimidating, let's take the sting out of them with an examination of their essential building blocks: what to say and how to say it.

The reason you might worry about calling people directly is that you are concerned they will be annoyed at the intrusion. This is a misconception. Remember, the first job of any manager is to get work done through others, so every smart manager is always on the lookout for talent. With a presentation that comes in at well under a minute, you can't be construed as wasting anybody's time. If that isn't enough to allay your fears, keep in mind that the person on the other end of the line has more than likely been in your position and is sensitive to how you feel.

Paint a word picture

The trick to turning calls into interviews is to paint a convincing word picture of yourself. The presentation you build should be short, to the point, and 'specifically vague' – specific enough to make the listener prick up his or her ears with interest, and at the same time vague enough to encourage the questions that will kick-start the conversation. Your aim is to paint a representation of your skills in broad-brush strokes with examples of achievements all managers like to hear. The need for brevity is to avoid giving irrelevant or inappropriate information that might rule you out of consideration.

Your presentation should possess four characteristics to be successful, best remembered by an acronym from the advertising world: *AIDA*. You can apply this to your job-hunting calls, and you can also use it at work when you have to present new ideas to colleagues or customers.

A – You must get the listener's **Attention**.
I – You must generate **Interest**.
D – You must create a **Desire** to know more.
A – You must encourage the employer to take **Action**.

When you apply the concepts of AIDA to creating and making a marketing presentation, you will get attention. The interest you generate will be displayed by a desire to know more, so you'll hear questions like, 'Do you have a degree?' 'How much experience do you have?' By giving the appropriate answers to these and other questions (covered shortly), you can then turn that desire into an interview.

The types of questions you are asked also enable you to identify the company's specific needs, and once they are identified, you can customize any ongoing conversation toward those needs.

Here are the steps in building a presentation. Notice the brevity as you read; this pitch can be made in well under a minute.

Step one

Your first step is to give the employer a snapshot of who you are and what you do; the intention is to give that person a reason to stay on the phone. You may sometimes have an introduction from a colleague, in which case you will build a bridge with that:

'Miss Hepburn? Good morning, my name is Martin Yate, and our mutual friend Spencer Tracy suggested I call...'

Or you may have got the name and contact information from, for example, a professional association directory, in which case you will use that as a bridge:

'Miss Hepburn? My name is Martin Yate. We haven't spoken before, but as we are both members of x association, I hoped I might get a couple of minutes of your time for some advice...'

Otherwise your introduction will cut right to the chase with a generalized job title (this increases the opportunity for positive response) and a brief description of your duties and problem-solving/ orientation.

Tell enough about yourself to whet the listener's appetite and ignite a desire to know more. This is where the concept of 'specifically vague' comes in, so for example, you would initially describe yourself as experienced, rather than identifying a specific number of years in your field. This encourages the listener to qualify your statement with a question: 'How much experience do you have?' If you describe yourself right off as having four years' experience, and the company is looking for seven, you are likely to be ruled out as underqualified before you are even aware that the company is hiring for a job that you have been doing in your sleep for the last two years. Therefore, never specify exact experience or list all your accomplishments during the initial presentation; your aim is just to open a dialogue:

'Good morning, Mr O'Shea. My name is Cary Grant. I am an experienced office equipment salesperson with a track record selling to corporations, institutions, and small business...'

By the way, if you want to ask the person on the other end of the line if he or she is free to talk, always ask, 'Have I caught you at a good time?' Never ask if you have caught someone at a bad time; you are offering your contact an excuse to say they are busy. On the other hand, asking whether you have caught someone at a good time will usually get you a positive response; then you can go into the rest of your presentation. If at any point your contact says or implies that he or she is harried, immediately ask when would be a good time to call back.

Step two

This is where you colour in your word picture. Pull out a couple of key features from your CV and follow your introductory sentence with a small selection. Keep them brief and to the point, without embellishments.

'Since joining my company, I have increased sales in my territory 15 percent, to over £1 million. In the last six months, I won three major accounts from my competitors – a hospital, a bank, and a technology start-up.'

Step three

You have made the company representative want to know more about you, so now you 'ask for the sale', stating the reason for your call and a request to meet.

'The reason I'm calling, Mr Grant, is that I'm looking for a new challenge, and as I know and respect your product, I felt we might have some areas of common interest. Are these the types of skills and accomplishments you look for in your sales staff?'

Notice that your presentation is constructed to finish with a nonthreatening question that encourages a positive response, and also that the entire pitch can be spoken aloud in a conversational tone in well under a minute.

You should never make calls without taking the time to construct a written presentation, because the self-analysis process involved makes you capture the essence of the 'professional you'. Read your presentation word for word the first few times until you have the meat of it by heart, then keep it to hand as a safety net. Remember, though, that writing for the spoken word is very different from writing for the written word; it is less formal in grammar and syntax and more casually structured. When you have written it out, speak it aloud a few times to make it sound conversational and relaxed.

Knowing what you are going to say and what you wish to achieve – in other words, having a clear strategy – is the best way to generate multiple interviews and multiple job offers. When your presentation is prepared and polished, practice with a friend or spouse, or use a tape recorder or recording capabilities on your computer to critique yourself.

Once you have made a marketing presentation over the telephone, there will likely be a silence on the other end of the line. Be patient, as the employer may need a few seconds to digest your words. When the employer does respond, it will either be with a question, denoting interest (a 'buy signal'), or with an objection.

Questions and buy signals

When the silence is broken by a question, you breathe a sigh of relief because any question denotes interest and is a buy signal. The employer can ask questions that show interest: 'Do you have a degree?' 'Have you done this kind of work?' 'Have you done that kind of work?' Any question, because it denotes interest, is considered a buy signal.

Now, conversation is a two-way street, and you are most likely to win an interview when you take responsibility for your half. Just as the employer's questions show interest in you, your questions should show your interest in the work done at the company. By asking questions of your own in the normal course of conversation – questions usually tagged on to the end of one of your answers – you will forward the conversation. Also, such questions help you find out what particular skills and qualities are important to the employer. Inquisitiveness will increase your knowledge of the opportunity at hand, and that knowledge will give you the power to arrange an interview. If you leave all the interrogation to the employer, it will place you on the defensive, and at the end of the talk, you will be as ignorant of the real parameters of the job as you were at the start. As a result, the employer will know less about you than you might want.

Apply the technique of giving a short reasonable answer and finishing your reply with a question to carry your call forward. In answer to your questions, the interviewer will explain the job's specifics, and as that happens, you will present your relevant skills and experiences; by asking questions of your own, you move the conversation toward an interview.

Joan Jones: 'Good morning, Mr Grant. My name is Joan Jones. I am an office equipment salesperson experienced in selling to corporations, institutions, and small business. As a salesperson in my company, I increased sales in my territory 15 percent, to over £1 million. In the last six months, I won three major accounts from my competitors.

'The reason I'm calling, Mr Grant, is that I'm looking for a new challenge, and as I know and respect your company, I felt we might have areas for discussion. Are these the types of skills and accomplishments you look for in your staff?'

[Pause]

Mr Grant: 'Yes, they are. What type of equipment have you been selling?' *[Buy signal!]*

Joan Jones: 'My company carries a comprehensive range from furniture to office machines and supplies; I sell according to my customers' needs. I have been noticing a considerable interest in _____ recently. Has that been your experience?'

Grant: 'Yes, I have actually.' *[Useful information for you.]* 'Do you have a degree?' *[Buy signal!]*

Joan Jones: 'Yes, I do.' *[Just enough information to keep the company representative chasing you.]* 'I understand your company prefers salespeople with a degree to deal with its more sophisticated clients.' *[Your research is paying off.]*

Grant: 'Our customer base is very sophisticated, and they expect a certain professionalism and competence from us.' *[An inkling of the kind of person the company wants to hire.]* 'How much experience do you have?' *[Buy signal!]*

Joan Jones: 'Well, I've worked in both operations and sales, so I understand both the sales and fulfilment process.' *[General but thorough.]* 'How many years of experience are you looking for?' *[Turning it around, but furthering the conversation.]*

Grant: 'Ideally, four or five for the position I have in mind.' *[More good information.]* 'How many do you have?' *[Buy signal!]*

Joan Jones: 'I have two with this company, and one and a half before that, so I fit right in with your needs, don't you agree?' *[How can Mr Grant say 'no' to Ms Jones?]*

Grant: 'What's your territory?' *[Buy signal!]*

Joan Jones: 'I cover the North West Region. Mr Grant, it sounds as if we might have something to talk about.' *[Remember, your first goal is the face-to-face interview.]* 'I am planning to take personal time off next Thursday or Friday. Can we meet then?' *[Make Mr Grant decide which day he can see you, rather than whether he will see you at all.]* 'Which would be best for you?'

Grant: 'How about Friday morning? Can you bring a CV?'

Your conversation should proceed with this kind of give-and-take. Your questions show interest, carry the conversation forward, and teach you more about the company's needs. By the end of the conversation you have an interview arranged and several key areas to promote when you arrive:

■ The company sees growth in a particular area, so be sure you research where they stand in this area.

■ They want both professional and personal sophistication.

■ They ideally want four or five years' experience.

■ They are interested in your contacts.

The previous is a simple scenario, to show you ways to gather information as you answer questions. Occasionally your calls will go this smoothly, but not always. The example doesn't show you any number of other tricky questions that, inadequately handled, can rule you out of consideration. These include questions that appear to be simple buy signals, yet are in reality a part of every interviewer's arsenal of 'knockout' questions – so called because they can save time by quickly ruling out certain types of candidates. Such questions often arise during a telephone interview, but can still occur during an initial face-to-face interview.

Buy signal: 'How much experience do you have?'

Too much or too little experience could easily rule you out. Be careful how you answer this question and try to gain time. It is a vague question, and you have a right to ask for qualifications. Employers typically define jobs by years' experience. At the same time there is a major move away from simple chronological experience, toward the more important concern about what you can deliver on the job. Managers and HR people are now more open to thinking in terms of 'performance requirements' and 'competencies' than ever before.

Here are a couple of ways to handle it:

'Could you help me with that question? If you give me a brief outline of the performance requirements, I can give you a more accurate answer.' Or, *'I have x years' experience, but they aren't necessarily typical. If you'd give me a few details on the performance requirements I'd be able to give you a more accurate answer.'*

The employer's response, while gaining you time, tells you what it takes to do the job and therefore what aspects of your experience are most relevant. Take mental notes as the employer talks – you can even write them down, if you have time. Then give an appropriate response

You can move the conversation forward by asking a follow-up question of your own. For example: 'The areas of expertise you require sound like a match to my experience, and it sounds as if you have some exciting projects at hand. What projects would I be involved with in the first few months?'

Buy signal: 'Do you have a degree?'

If your degree matches the stated needs for the position, by all means go ahead and state it. If you don't have a degree at all, but the position requires one, all is not lost. As Calvin Coolidge used to say, 'the world is full of educated derelicts.' You may want to use the 'university of Life' answer. For example: 'My education was cut short by the necessity of earning a living at an early age. My past managers have discovered that this in no way speaks of my lack of processing power. However, I am currently enrolled in classes to complete my degree.'

You could enrol in degree-relevant classes and make this an honest answer, and in the process you'd be doing the right thing by your career. Ongoing education is important for your long-term career survival and economic success, and dramatically improves your earning and promotional potential, so enrolment in any and all career-relevant classes is to your benefit.

In a security conscious world, an increasing percentage of employers are verifying educational credentials and references. Do not lie about this during the interviews or on your CV; it will cost you that job if you are found out, or if it comes out later, you could be fired – which can lead to further employment problems down the line.

Buy signal: 'How much are you making/do you want?'

This is a direct question looking for a direct answer, yet it is a knockout question. Earning either too little or too much could ruin your chances before you're given the opportunity to shine in person. There are a number of options that could serve you better than a direct answer. First, you must understand that questions about money at this point in the conversation are being used to screen you in or screen you out. The answers you give now should be geared toward getting you in the door and into a face-to-face meeting. (Handling the serious salary negotiations that are attached to a job offer are covered in Chapter 19, 'Negotiating the offer'.) For now, your main options are as follows:

▍ Direct answer: If you know the salary range for the position and there is a fit, give a straightforward answer.

▍ Indirect answer: 'Around thirty.' Or 'thirty-five thousand.'

▍ Put yourself above the money: 'I'm looking for an opportunity that will give me the opportunity to make a difference with my efforts. If I am the right person for the job, I'm sure you'll make me a fair offer. By the way, what is the salary range for this position?'

When you give a salary range rather than a single figure, you have more flexibility and have greater chance of 'clicking with' the employer's approved range for the position.

When you are pressed a second time for an exact figure, be as honest and forthright as circumstances permit. If you have the skills for the job and you are concerned that your current low salary will eliminate you before you have the chance to show your worth, you might add, 'I realize this is well below industry norms, but it does not reflect on my expertise or experience in any way. It speaks of the need for me to make a strategic career move, to where I can be compensated competitively and based on my skills.'

If your current earnings are higher than the approved range, you could say, 'Mr Smith, my current employers feel I am well worth the money I earn due to my skills, dedication, and honesty. Were we to meet, I'm sure I could demonstrate my value and my ability to contribute to your department. A meeting would provide an opportunity to make that evaluation, wouldn't it?'

Notice the 'wouldn't it?' at the end of the reply; this is known as *reflexive questioning.* A reflexive question such as this is a great conversation-forwarding technique because it encourages a positive response. Such questions are easy to create. Just conclude with 'wouldn't you?' 'didn't you?' 'won't you?' 'couldn't you?' 'shouldn't you?' or 'don't you?' as appropriate at the end of any statement, and the interviewer will be encouraged to answer 'yes.'

After you have answered one or two buy-signal questions, ask for a meeting. If you simply ask, 'Would you like to meet me?' there are only two possible responses – 'yes' or 'no' – and your chances of success are about 50/50. When you suggest, however, that you will be in the area on a particular date or dates ('I'm going to be in town on Thursday and Friday, Mr Grant. Which would be better for you?') your question gives the company representative the choice of meeting you on Thursday or Friday, rather than meeting you or not meeting you. By presuming the 'yes,' you reduce the chances of hearing a negative, and increase the possibility of a face-to-face meeting.

How to deal with objections

By no means will every presentation you make be met with a few simple questions and then an invitation to interview; sometimes the silence will be broken by the employer with an objection. This usually comes in the form of a statement, not a question: 'Send me a CV' or 'I don't have time to see you,' or 'You are earning too much,' or 'You'll have to talk to personnel,' or 'I don't need anyone like you right now.'

Although these seem like brush-off lines, they don't have to be; frequently, objections like these can be turned into interviews.

Notice that all the following suggested response models have a commonality with buy-signal responses. They all end with a question, one that helps you learn more about the reason for the objection, perhaps to overcome it, and lead the conversation toward a meeting.

In dealing with objections, nothing is gained by confrontation, while much is gained by appreciation of the other's viewpoint. Consequently, most objections you hear are best handled by first demonstrating your understanding of the other's viewpoint. Try to start your responses with phrases like 'I understand,' or 'I can appreciate your position,' or 'I see your point,' or 'Of course.' Follow up with statements like 'However,' or

'Also consider,' or a similar line that allows the opportunity for rebuttal and to gather further information.

It's not necessary to memorize these responses verbatim, only to understand the underlying concept then put together a response in words that are sympathetic to your character and style of speech.

Objection: 'Why don't you send me a CV?'

The employer may be genuinely interested in seeing your résumé as a first step in the interview cycle, or it may be a polite way of getting you off the phone. You should identify the real reason without causing antagonism, and at the same time open up the conversation. A good reply would be, 'Of course, Mr Grant. Would you give me your exact title and address? Thank you. So that I can be sure that my qualifications fit your needs, what skills are you looking for in this position?' or 'What specific job title should I refer to when I send it?'

Notice the steps:

▌ agreement to start;

▌ a demonstration of understanding;

▌ a question to further the conversation (in this instance to confirm that an opening actually exists).

Mr Grant will relay the aspects of the job that are important to him, and you can use the additional information to draw attention to your skills in:

▌ your executive briefing or covering letter;

▌ a precisely customized CV;

▌ your face-to-face meeting.

Following Mr Grant's response, you can recap the match between his company's needs and your skills; savvy headhunters follow this confirmation step with the following question, which you will also find very effective:

'Assuming my CV matches your needs, as I think we are both confident that it will, could we pencil in a date and time for an interview next week. I am available next Thursday and Friday; which would you prefer?'

A pencilled-in date and time very rarely gets cancelled.

Objection: 'I don't have time to see you.'

If the employer is too busy to see you, it indicates that he or she has work pressures, and by recognizing that, you can show yourself as the one to alleviate some of those pressures through your problem-solving skills. You should avoid confrontation, however; it is important that you demonstrate empathy for the person with whom you are speaking. Agree, empathize, and ask a question that moves the conversation forward:

'I understand how busy you must be; it sounds like a competent, dedicated, and efficient professional [whatever your title is] could be of some assistance. Perhaps I could call you back at a better time to discuss how I might make a contribution in easing the pressure at peak times. When are you least busy, in the morning or afternoon?'

The company representative will either make time to talk now or will arrange a better time for the two of you to talk further.

You could also try, 'Since you are so busy, what is the best time of day for you? First thing in the morning, or is the afternoon a quieter time?' Or you could suggest, 'If you give me your e-mail address, you could study my background at your leisure. What would be a good time of day to call to follow up on this?'

Objection: 'You are earning too much.'

If the company representative brought up the matter, that's a buy signal. If the job really doesn't pay enough, and there will be openings for which you are earning too much, you've come (as they say) 'close, but no cigar!'

How to make a success of this seeming dead end is handled shortly. You should, however, follow the process through: 'Oh, I'm sorry to hear that – what is the range for that position?' Depending on the degree of salary discrepancy you can reiterate your interest. You can also refer to Chapter 19 on, 'Negotiating the offer', where you will find further advice on dealing with this issue.

Objection: 'We only promote from within.'

Your response could be, 'I realize that, Mr Grant. Your development of employees is a major reason I want to get in! I am bright, conscientious, and motivated. When you do hire from outside, and it must happen on occasion, what assets do you look for?' or 'How do I get into consideration for such opportunities?'

The response finishes with a question designed to carry the conversation forward and to give you a new opportunity to sell yourself. Notice that the response logically assumes that the company does hire from the outside, even though Mr Grant has said otherwise. You have called his bluff, but in a professional and inoffensive manner.

Objection: 'You'll have to talk to Human Resources.'

In this case, you reply, 'Of course, Mr Grant. Whom should I speak to in HR, and what specific position should I mention?'

You cover a good deal of ground with that response. You establish whether there is a job there or whether you are being fobbed off to HR to waste their time and your own. Also, you move the conversation forward again while changing the thrust of it to your advantage. Develop a specific job-related question to ask while the employer is answering the first question. It can open a fruitful line for you to pursue. If you receive a non-specific reply, probe a little deeper. A simple phrase like, 'That's interesting. Please tell me more,' or 'Why's that?' will usually do the trick.

Or you can ask, 'When I speak to HR, will it be about a specific job you have, or is it to see whether I might fill a position elsewhere in the company?'

Armed with the resulting information, you can talk to HR about your conversation with Mr Grant; remember to get the name of a specific person in HR with whom to speak, and to quote this prior contact by name.

'*Good morning, Ms Johnson. Cary Grant, over in marketing, suggested we should speak to arrange an interview for the open Sales Associate position.*'

Don't look at the HR department as a roadblock; it may contain a host of opportunities for you. In many companies different departments could use your talents, and HR is probably the only department that knows all the openings. With a larger employer you might be able to arrange three or four interviews with the same company for three or four different positions!

Objection: 'I really wanted someone with a degree.'

You should have learned the proper response to 'Do you have a degree?' But in case you were abducted by aliens a few pages ago, you could respond by saying, 'Mr Smith, I appreciate your viewpoint. It was necessary that I start earning a living early in life. If we meet, I am certain you would recognize the value of my additional practical experience.' If you have been smart enough to enrol in a course to pursue that always-important qualification, you should add, 'I am currently enrolled in courses to complete my degree, which should demonstrate my professional commitment, and perhaps that makes a difference?'

You might then ask what the company policy is for support and encouragement of employees continuing their education. Your response will end with, 'If we were to meet, I am certain you would recognize the value of my practical experience, in addition to my ongoing professional commitment. I am going to be in your area at the end of next week, and I know you will find the time to meet well spent. Is there a day and time that would be best for you?'

Objection: 'I don't need anyone like you now.'

Short of suggesting that the employer fire someone to make room for you (which, incidentally, has been done successfully on a few occasions), the chances of getting an interview with this company are slim. With the right question, however, that person will give you a personal introduction to someone else who could use your talents.

You can ask, 'When do you anticipate new needs in your area?' or 'May I send you my CV and keep in touch for when the situation changes?' or 'Who else in the company might need someone with my background and skills?' or 'Can you think of anyone at other companies who might have a need for someone with my background?'

Live leads from dead ends

Not every company has an opening for you. It's up to you to create leads, though, and there are some excellent questions you can ask that will steer you to opportunities elsewhere.

There will be times when you have said all the right things on the phone, but hear, 'I can't use anyone like you right now.' Not every company has a job opening for you, nor are you right for every job. Sometimes you must accept a temporary setback and understand that the rejection is not one of you as a human being. By using the special interview development questions given here, though, you should be able to turn those setbacks into job interviews.

The person you are talking to is a professional and knows other professionals in his or her field, in other departments, subsidiaries and even other companies. If you approach the phone presentation in a professional manner, he or she, as a fellow professional, will be glad to advise you on who is looking for someone with your skills. Nearly everyone you call will be pleased to point you in the right direction, but only if you *ask*! And you'll be able to ask as many questions as you wish, because you will be recognized as a colleague intelligently using the professional network. The person also knows that his or her good turn in referring you to a colleague at another company will be returned in the future. As a general rule, companies prefer candidates to be referred this way over any other method.

Do not expect people to be clairvoyant, though. There are two sayings: 'You get what you ask for' and 'If you don't ask, you don't get.' Each is pertinent here.

When you are sure that no job openings exist within a particular department, ask one of the following questions:

- 'Who else in the company might need someone with my qualifications?'

- 'Does your company have any other divisions or subsidiaries that might need someone with my attributes?'

- 'Who do you know in the business community who might have a lead for me?'

- 'Which are the most rapidly growing companies in the area?'

- 'Who should I speak to there?'

- 'Do you know anyone at the ABC Electronics Company?'

- 'When do you anticipate there being an opening in your company?'

- 'Are you planning any expansion or new projects that might create an opening?'

- 'When do you anticipate change in your manpower needs?'

Each one of these interview development questions can gain you an introduction or lead to a fresh opportunity. The questions have not been put in any order of importance – that is for you to do. Take a sheet of paper and, looking at the list, figure out what question you would ask if you had time to ask only one. Write it down. Do that with the remaining questions on the list. As you advance, you will develop a comfortable set of prioritized questions. Add questions of your own. For instance, the type of computer or word-processing equipment a company has might be important to some professions but not to others, and the person you speak to might be able to lead you to companies that have your machines. Be sure that any question you add to your list is specific and leads to a job opening. When you're satisfied with your list of interview development questions, put them on a fresh sheet of paper and store it safely with your telephone presentation and CV.

Those interview development questions will lead you to a substantial number of jobs in the hidden job market. You are getting referrals from the 'in' crowd who know who is hiring whom long before that news is generally circulated. By being in with the 'in' crowd, you establish a very effective referral network.

When you get leads on companies and specific individuals to talk to, be sure to thank your benefactor and ask to use his or her name as an introduction. The answer, you will find, will always be 'yes', but asking shows you to be someone with manners – in this day and age, that alone will set you apart.

You might also suggest to your contact that you leave your telephone number in case he or she runs into someone who can use you. You'll be surprised at how many people call back with a lead.

With personal permission to use someone's name on your next networking call, you have been given the greatest of job search gifts: a personal introduction. Your call will begin with something like, 'Hello, Ms White, my name is Jack Jones. Joseph McDonald recommended I give you a call. By the way, he sends his regards.' [Pause for any response to this.] 'He felt we might have something valuable to discuss.'

Follow up on every lead you get. Too many people become elated at securing an interview for themselves and then cease all effort to generate additional interviews, believing a job offer is definitely on its way. Your goal is to have a choice of the best jobs in town and without multiple interviews, there is no way you'll have that choice. Asking interview development questions ensures that you are tapping all the secret recesses of the hidden job market.

Networking is a continuous cycle. Make a commitment to sell yourself, make telephone calls, make a referral network and recognize buy signals and objections for what they really are – opportunities to shine. Make a commitment to ask interview development questions at every seeming dead end – they will lead you to all the jobs in town.

Stay the course

No matter how many interviews your calls and mail campaigns are generating, you must continue to research potential job openings. While you have to maintain contact with interested companies, you must also make yourself maintain a daily marketing schedule, making calls and sending e-mails and CVs to both nurture your existing contact base and to expand it in each of the following areas:

∎ internet job postings, and the company websites you discover from them;

∎ newspaper ads, and the other leads you identify in your print research;

∎ members of all your professional and personal networks;

∎ leads developed from job fairs and other research efforts;

∎ headhunters;

∎ follow-up letters to phone calls and from meetings.

The balance you maintain is important because most job hunters are tempted to send the easy e-mails and make the easy calls (networking with old friends) but ignore the more challenging, yet more productive calls. Don't stop searching even when an offer for a dream job is pending, and your potential boss says, 'Robin, you've got the job and we're glad you can start on Monday. The offer letter is in the post.' Never accept any 'yes' as an absolute until you have it in writing, you have started work, and the first cheque has cleared at the bank! Until then, keep your momentum building. It is the professional and circum-spect thing to do.

It is no use posting tens or even hundreds of CVs without following up with phone calls. However, if you are not getting a response with one CV format, you might try changing from a chronological to a functional or combination format, just as you would change the bait if the fish weren't taking what you had on the hook.

Also, try to keep things in perspective. Although your 224th contact may not have an opening for you, with a few polite and judicious questions he or she may well have a good lead. In the job hunt there are only two 'yeses': Their 'yes, I want you to work for us' and your 'yes, I can start on Monday.' Every 'no' brings you closer to the big 'yes.' Never take rejections of your CV or your phone call as rejections of yourself; just as every job is not for you, you aren't right for every job, and there is a great opportunity right around the corner, as long as you turn that corner by maintaining your forward momentum.

Stacking the odds in your favour

We all have 168 hours a week to become refuse collectors or billionaires and to make our lives as fulfilling as they can be. For some of us this means a better job; for others it means getting back to work to keep a roof over our heads. How we manage these hours will determine our success. These job search commandments will see you successfully through the job change process and career transition:

- Those in the professional employment field believe hundreds of contacts are required per job placement. You should anticipate no better odds. In a 40-hour week these professionals average 35 to 50 contacts per day. Build to this momentum.

- Work at getting a new job. Work at least 40 hours per week at it. Divide your time between contacting potential employers and generating new leads; the internet, networking, and all the other job search tools will generate plenty of leads for you.

- Research the companies you contact. In a tightly run job race, the candidate who is most knowledgeable about the employer has a distinct advantage; again, the internet can be of immense help in becoming a knowledgeable candidate.

- Follow up on the CVs you send out with phone calls. Resubmit your CV to identified openings after six or seven weeks. Change the format of your CV and resubmit yet again. (See *The Ultimate CV Book* for specific ideas on how to do this.)

- Stay in telephone contact with your job leads on a regular basis to maintain top-of-the-mind awareness. If you find yourself needing to call existing contacts more than every couple of months, you should be putting more emphasis on building your networks and doing direct research.

■ Develop examples of your professional profile that make you special – and rehearse building these examples into your interview responses. You will learn all about developing a desirable professional profile in Chapter 10.

■ Send follow-up notes with relevant news cuttings, cartoons, and so on to those in your networks; it's a light-touch way to help people keep you in mind.

■ Work on your self-image. Use this time to get physically fit. Studies show that unfit, overweight people take longer to find suitable work. The more you do today, the better you will feel about yourself.

■ Maintain a professional demeanour during the workweek (clothing, posture, personal hygiene).

■ Use regular business hours for making contacts. Use the early morning, lunchtime, after 5pm, and Saturday for doing the ongoing research and writing projects to maintain momentum.

■ Don't feel guilty about taking time off from your job search. Just do it conscientiously. If you regularly spend Saturday morning in the library doing research, you can take Wednesday afternoon off to go to the cinema once in a while.

■ Keep records of your contacts. They will benefit not only this job search but also those in the future.

■ Never stop the research and job-hunting process until you have a written job offer in hand and you have accepted that job in writing with an agreed-upon start date; even then, continue with any ongoing interviews.

■ Remember: It's all up to you. There are many excuses not to make calls or send CVs on any given day. There are many excuses to get up later or knock off earlier. There are many excuses to back off because this one's in the bag. But there are no real *reasons*. There are no jobs out there for those who won't look, while there are plenty of opportunities for those who work at it.

▪ Take off the blinkers. We all have two specific skills: our professional/technical skills – say, computer programming; and our industry skills – banking, for example. Professional/technical skills can be transferable to other industries; and industry skills can open other opportunities in your industry. For example, that programmer, given decent communication skills, could become a technical trainer for programmers and/or technophobes.

Using a contact tracker

As you get your job hunt up to speed, the number of baited hooks you have in the water will grow dramatically. The CVs you send out will require follow-up calls, and the networking and research calls you make to potential employers will create the need to send out CVs, which in return will generate more follow-up calls.

Without tracking mechanisms in place this can quickly get out of hand. It would be insane to make this effort to get your job hunt and career management plan functioning, then let important opportunities fall through the cracks for lack of attention to detail.

You can create a contact tracker on a spreadsheet program, with columns for company name, telephone number, contact name, e-mail address; the date you sent a CV, and the date you should follow up with a call (or vice versa); and room for comments on the substance of conversations.

Follow-up: the key ingredient

In theory, the perfect letters or e-mails you send cold or as a result of phone calls will receive a response rate of 100 percent. Unfortunately, there is no perfect letter, e-mail, or call in this less-than-perfect world. If you sit like some fat Buddha waiting for the world to beat a path to your door, you may wait a long time.

An IT manager of my acquaintance once advertised for a programmer analyst. By Wednesday of the following week he had over 100 responses. Ten days later he was still ploughing through them when he received a follow-up call (the only one he received) from one of the respondents. The job hunter was in the office that afternoon, returned the following morning, and was hired before lunchtime.

The story? The candidate's paperwork was languishing in the pile, waiting to be discovered. The follow-up phone call got it discovered. The call made the interviewer sort through the enormous pile of paper, pull out the letter and CV, and act on it. He wanted to get on with his work, and the job hunter in question made it possible by making himself visible on the employer's radar. Follow-up calls, and follow-up calls on the follow-up calls, do work.

Make phone calls to initiate contact, and you'll get requests for CVs and requests to come for an interview. Make follow-up calls on mailed and e-mailed CVs and you will generate further interviews.

No one is ever hired without passing through one or a series of formal interviews, and that is where this book is headed next: understanding, strategizing, and executing the job interview conversations that will ultimately lead to job offers.

6 The telephone interview

Interviewers use the telephone to weed out applicants. Your goal is a face-to-face meeting, and here are the methods you must use to get it.

There are some aspects of job hunting that are not clear-cut. For instance, a telephone interview for a job might be arranged for a certain date and time, so you have plenty of time to prepare for it. Then again, a networking call can turn into a presentation in a flash when you realize that the person on the other end of the phone line is in a position to hire you. Likewise, when that presentation progresses past the initial 'buy signs' and objections, it can suddenly become a telephone interview.

Employers use the telephone as a time management tool; it is easier to cut to the chase on the telephone and weed out candidates quickly. Your goal is a face-to-face meeting, so all you must do is convince the employer he or she will not be wasting time meeting you in person. Here are the techniques you should use to turn the telephone conversation into a face-to-face meeting.

Be ready for calls and telephone interviews

Your first substantive contact with a potential employer will always be by telephone.

It happens in one of three ways:

■ The person you are calling goes into a screening process because you have aroused interest.

■ An employer calls unexpectedly as a result of a CV you have sent.

■ You have arranged a specific time for a telephone interview.

Odds are good that you will experience plenty of telephone interviews during your job search. Whichever activities generate a telephone interview, you must think and act clearly to turn the opportunity into the real thing – a face-to-face meeting; how you perform will determine whether you move ahead or bite the dust.

A few words about telephone services: call waiting might be nice to have for social use, but responding to its demands during a job hunt will only annoy the person you have on the line at the time. If you have call waiting, disconnect it or ignore it.

Perhaps the most important consideration about telephone interviews is that the employer has only his ears with which to judge you. If the call comes unexpectedly, and screaming kids or barking dogs surround you, stay calm, sound positive, friendly, and collected: 'Thank you for calling, Mr Wooster. Would you wait a moment while I close the door?' You can then easily take a minute to calm yourself, call up the company Web site, and get your paperwork organized without causing offence. If you need to move to another phone, say so; otherwise, put the caller on hold, take a few controlled, deep breaths to slow down your pounding heart, put a smile on your face (it improves the timbre of your voice), and pick up the phone again. Now you are in control of yourself and the situation.

If you are heading out of the door for an interview or some other emergency makes this a bad time for an unexpected call, say so straight away and re-arrange: 'I'm heading out of the door for an appointment, Ms Bassett. Can we arrange a time when I will call you back?' Beware of overfamiliarity: You should always refer to the interviewer by his or her surname until invited to do otherwise.

Allow the person calling to guide the conversation – and to ask most of the questions, but keep up your end of the conversation. This is especially important when the interviewer does not give you the openings you need to sell yourself. Always have a few intelligent questions prepared to save the situation. The following questions will give you an excellent idea of why the position is open, and exactly the kind of skilled professional the company will eventually hire:

- 'What are the three major responsibilities in this job?'
- 'What will be the first project(s) I tackle?'
- 'What are the biggest challenges the department faces this year and what will be my role as a team member in tackling them?'
- 'Which projects will I be most involved with during the first six months?'
- 'Who succeeds in this job and why?'
- 'Who fails in this job and why?'

When you get a clear understanding of an employer's needs with questions like these, you can seize the opportunity to sell yourself appropriately: 'Would it be useful if I described my experience in the area of office management?' or 'Then my experience in word processing should be a great help to you,' or 'I recently completed an accounting project just like that. Would it be relevant to discuss it?'

When you identify an employer's imminent challenges and demonstrate how your skills can lessen the load, you portray yourself as properly focused with a problem-solving mentality and move immediately closer to a face-to-face interview; everyone hires a problem solver.

You can also keep up your end of the conversation by giving verbal signals that you are engaged in the conversation; you do this with occasional short interjections that don't interrupt the employer's flow but let him know you are paying attention. Comments like 'uh-huh,' 'that's interesting,' 'yes,' 'great,' and 'I see' are verbal equivalents of the body language techniques you'll use to show interest during a face-to-face meeting.

Always speak directly into the telephone, with the mouthpiece about one inch from your mouth. Numbered among the mystical properties of telephone technology is its excellence at picking up and amplifying background noise. This is excelled only by its power to transmit the sounds of food and gum being chewed, or smoke being inhaled and exhaled. Smokers take note: non-smokers naturally discriminate; they will assume that even if you don't actually light up at the interview, you'll have been chain-smoking beforehand and will carry the smell with you as long as you are around. Taking no chances, they probably won't even give you a chance to get through the door once they hear you puffing away over the phone.

You should take notes when possible; they will be invaluable if the employer is interrupted. You can jot down the topic under discussion, then when he or she gets back on the line, you helpfully recap: 'We were just discussing ...' This will be appreciated and show that you are organized and paying attention; your notes will also help you prepare for the face-to-face meeting.

The employer may talk about the company, and from your research or the website on your screen, you may also know something about them. A little flattery goes a long way: admire a company's achievements, when you can, and by inference you admire the interviewer. Likewise, if any areas of common interest arise, comment on them, and agree with the interviewer when reasonably possible – people usually hire people like themselves.

On the 200 telephone interviews a year that I average, I've found that standing for the interview calms the adrenaline a little, helps my breathing, and allows me to sound confident and relaxed. It might work for you, so give it a try.

Answering questions

Beware of giving yes/no answers, as they give no real information about your abilities and do nothing to forward your agenda. At the same time, don't waffle; your answers need to be concise. Understanding someone over the telephone can sometimes be a challenge, so if you didn't hear or didn't understand a question, ask the speaker to repeat it. If you need time to think about your answer, say so: 'Let me think about that for a moment...'

Whenever possible, you should give real-world examples to illustrate your points: 'That's interesting. I was involved in an audit like that a couple months back and it presented some interesting challenges.'

It isn't a bad idea to prepare a brief potted history of your professional life, for when you are asked, 'Tell me a little about yourself.' At this point your answer can be fairly brief: 'I have a degree in communication studies, and I've been working in pharmaceutical sales for three years. I am currently ranked fourth in the region. I have long competed against your company and know and respect your products, and your position in Glasgow will help me get closer to my family.'

There are some 200 questions you are likely to be asked during an interview, which we'll cover in detail over the coming pages. Meanwhile there are a handful of questions often asked during telephone interviews, in addition to the ones that come after you make a presentation. Let's look at them in light of your probable lack of information about the company and the job.

'*What are you looking for?*' With so little real knowledge about the company at this point, you need to be careful about specificity. Don't say, 'I want to move into marketing,' unless you know such opportunity exists. Otherwise keep your answer general.

'*What are your strengths?*' If you know about specific skill requirements, emphasize them; if not, stick to a brief outline of your professional behaviours (discussed on pages 11–13)

'*What is your greatest weakness?*' Don't throw the opportunity away before you even get in the door and have a real understanding of the job. Mention a brand-new technology/skill you have just developed, and say you have been working on it and try to keep abreast of the latest approaches in all aspects of your profession.

'*I don't think you'll be suitable because you lack _____ skill.*' If the statement is true, acknowledge it, then follow with an example of a similar skill you picked up quickly and apply with consummate skill: 'Yes, I understand. When I joined my current company I knew nothing about _____, but I studied on my own and with the help of a mentor within the department I was up to speed in a matter of weeks. Given my proven ability to learn quickly and my willingness to invest my own time, would you consider talking to me in more detail about this topic when we meet face-to-face?' With this type of response you are putting a positive spin on your shortcoming, which gives you a good shot at overcoming the objection. If you are successful in arranging a face-to-face interview, you'll now have time to bone up on the subject and/or identify a sensible self-development programme before you meet with the employer.

Under no circumstances, though, should you ask about salary, benefits or holidays; that comes much later. Your single objective at this point is to meet face-to-face; money is not an issue. If the interviewer brings up money, you can't get around a direct question asking how much you are earning, so be honest. On the other hand, if you are asked how much you want, answer truthfully that at this point you don't know enough about the company or the job to answer that question.

The telephone interview has come to an end when you are asked whether you have any questions – perhaps, 'What would you like to know about us?' This is a wind-down question, so it is a good opening to get some specific questions of your own answered that can advance your candidacy:

I 'What are the most immediate challenges of the job?'

I 'What are the most important projects of the first six months?'

I 'What skills and behaviours are most important to success on the job?'

I 'Why do some people succeed and others fail doing this work?'

By discovering answers to these questions now, you will have time before the face-to-face meeting to package your skills to the needs at hand and to create an appropriate executive briefing for distribution with your CV to the different interviewers you meet.

If you have not already asked or been invited to meet the interviewer, now is the time to take the initiative.

'It sounds like a very interesting opportunity, Ms Bassett, and a situation where I could definitely make a contribution. The most pressing question I have now is when can we get together?' (*Note:* Even though the emphasis throughout has been on putting things in your own words, phrases like 'make a contribution' show pride in your work – a key professional behaviour – and work as shorthand for 'I'm a team player.')

When an invitation for an interview is extended, there are practical matters that you need to clarify with a handful of simple questions that address the when (date and time), and where (don't assume the interview will be at a place that you associate with the company). You will also want to inquire about the interview procedure:

I 'How many interviews typically occur before a decision is made?'

I 'Who else will be part of the selection process, and what are their roles within the department or company?'

I 'What is the time frame for filling this position and how many other people are being considered?'

Follow with a casual inquiry as to what direction the meeting will take. You might ask, 'Would you tell me some of the critical areas you will discuss on Thursday?' The knowledge gained will help you to package and present yourself, and it will allow you time to bone up on any weak or rusty areas. This is also a good time to establish how long the meeting is expected to last, which will give you some idea of how to pace yourself.

Once the details are confirmed, finish with this request: 'If I need any additional information before the interview, I would like to feel free to get back to you.' The interviewer will naturally agree. No matter how many questions you get answered in the initial conversation, there will always be something you forgot. This allows you to call again to satisfy any curiosity – it will also enable you to increase rapport. Don't take too much advantage of it, though: One well-placed phone call that contains two or three considered questions will be appreciated; four or five phone calls will not.

In closing your conversation, take care to ascertain the correct spelling and pronunciation of the interviewer's name. This shows your concern for the small but important things in life – and it will be noticed, particularly when the interviewer receives your follow-up thank-you note.

It is difficult to evaluate an opportunity properly over the telephone, so even if the job doesn't sound right, go to the interview; it will give you practice, and the job may look better when you have more facts. You might even discover a more suitable opening elsewhere within the company when you go to the face-to-face interview.

7 Dressing for interview success

Dress like a professional and you are likely to be treated as one. Here are guidelines to dressing for interview success.

The moment we set eyes on someone, our minds make evaluations and judgments with lightning speed. The same is true for the potential employers who must assess us.

What you see is what you get!

'If a candidate can't put himself together in a professional manner, why should you assume he can put it all together on the job? Unless you look the part, don't expect an offer!' It may sound harsh, but that's an accurate summary of most employers' feelings on this issue. It's a fair estimate that 9 out of 10 of today's employers will reject an unsuitably dressed applicant without a second thought. Similarly dispiriting odds confront those who expect promotions but wear less than appropriate attire on the job. Like it or not, your outward image, attitude, confidence level and overall delivery are all affected by the clothes you wear.

The respect you receive at the interview is in direct proportion to the respect your visual image earns for you before you have the chance to say a word. If you wear clothes that are generally associated with leisure activities, you may be telling those who see you that you do not take your career seriously and therefore are not committed to your work. By the same token, if you report for work the first day on a new job wearing clothes that undercut your perceived effectiveness, personal skills and professionalism, it will be hard for you to be seen as a major contributor – no matter what you do between nine and five.

Employers rarely make overt statements about acceptable dress codes to their employees, much less to interviewees; more often there is an unspoken dictum that those who wish to climb the professional career ladder will dress appropriately and those who don't, won't.

There are some areas of employment where on-the-job dress (as opposed to interview dress) is somewhat less conservative than in the mainstream – fashion, entertainment and advertising are three examples. In these and a few other fields, there is a good deal of leeway with regard to personal expression in workplace attire, but for most of us, our jobs and our employers require a certain minimal level of professionalism in our dress. Interviewees must exceed these standards. That is not to say that you must dress like the Chairman of the Board (although that probably won't hurt), but you should be aware that dressing for the Friday night party (or even 'dress down Friday') on the day of your interview is not in your best professional interests. For the interview, it is generally accepted that you should dress one or two levels up from the job you are applying for, while remaining consistent with the type of occupation it is within.

Dressing sharp: your interviewing advantage

Our appearance tells people how we feel about ourselves as applicants, as well as how we feel about the interviewer(s), the company and the process of interviewing itself. By dressing professionally, we tell people that we understand the niceties of corporate life and send a subtle 'reinforcing' message that we can, for example, be relied on to deal one-to-one with members of a company's prized client base.

More to the point, the correct image at an interview will give you a real edge over your competition. In fact, your overall appearance and presentation may even leave a more tangible impression than the words you say, as memory is rooted most strongly in pictures and impressions. At the very least, you can expect what you say to be strongly influenced in the mind of your interviewer by the way you present yourself – if he or she likes the look of you, he or she will listen to what you have to say.

Of course, the act of taking time to present an attractive professional image before your interview will add to your own sense of self-esteem and confidence, too. That is perhaps the greatest advantage of all. Therefore, it is important that your professional dress code matches your own personal flavour. You must feel comfortable and 'yourself' in what you wear in order to present a confident image. As G Bruce Boyer, fashion editor for *GQ* and *Esquire* magazines in the United States so aptly puts it, 'The whole idea of individualized clothing is devoted to personal comfort. But what we have always been conscious of is that individuality and comfort are not the enemies of propriety and appropriateness. In the end the clothes that make sense are the ones that bring together the public and private person. Individuality, propriety and comfort can be nicely brought together in a good-fitting, well-made suit.'

The look

The safest look for both men and women at interviews is traditional and conservative. Look at investing in a 'good-fitting, well-made' suit as your first step to a successful new career. Up until recent years, this was fairly easy for men, as their professional fashions tended not to change much from year to year. These days, men's fashions are experiencing a metamorphosis, with high-fashion designers offering affordable lines of updated, yet professionally acceptable looks. However, a man can always interview with confidence and poise in his three-year-old good-quality suit, provided that it isn't worn to a shine.

For women, the matter is a little more complicated. Appropriate female attire for the interview should ideally reflect the current fashion if the applicant is to be taken seriously. Moreover, in selecting her current professional look the female applicant must walk a fine line, combining elements of both conformity (to show she belongs) and panache (to show a measure of individuality and style).

The key for both sexes is to dress for the position you want, not the one you have. This means that the upwardly mobile professional might need to invest in the clothes that project the desired image. The employee who dresses like one of the corporate walking wounded is unlikely to move upwards. Positions of responsibility are awarded to those who demonstrate that they are able to shoulder the burden. Looking capable will inspire others with the confidence to give you the most visible challenges.

The correct appearance alone probably won't get you a job offer, but it will go a long way towards winning attention and respect. When you know you look right, you can stop worrying about the impression your clothes are making and concentrate on communicating your message.

To be sure, every interview and every interviewer is different; because of this, it isn't possible to set down rigid guidelines for exactly what to wear in each situation. There is, however, relevant broadly based counsel that will help you make the right decision for your interview.

As we have seen, much of what we believe about others is based on our perception of their appearance, and this chapter will help you ensure that you are perceived as practical, well-mannered, competent, ethical and professional.

General guidelines

Appropriate attire, as we have noted, varies from industry to industry. The university professor can sport tweed jackets with elbow patches on the job, but is, nevertheless, likely to wear a suit to an interview. The advertising executive may wear wild ties as a badge of creativity (that is what he is being paid for), but he, too, is likely to dress more conservatively for an interview. In all instances, our clothes are sending a message about our image, and the image we want to convey is one of reliability, trustworthiness and attention to detail.

Most of us are far more adept at recognizing the dress mistakes of others than at spotting our own sartorial failings. When we do look for a second opinion, we often make the mistake of asking only a loved one. It's not that spouses, lovers and parents lack taste; these people are, however, more in tune with our positive qualities than the rest of the world and so, frequently, they do not recognize how essential it is to reflect those qualities in our dress. Better candidates for evaluation of your interview attire are trusted friends who have proved their objectivity in such matters or even a colleague at work.

Whenever possible, find out the dress code of the company you are visiting. For example, if you are an engineer applying for a job at a high-tech company, a blue three-piece suit might be overpowering. It is perfectly acceptable to ask someone in HR about the dress code (written or informal) of the company. You may even want to make an anonymous visit to get a sense of the corporate style of the company. In the above example, you might be perfectly comfortable showing up *for work* in a jacket or blazer; nevertheless, you are advised to wear a suit for at least the first interview.

You may simply decide to change your look somewhat after learning that there is a more informal atmosphere with regard to dress at the firm you visit. If you are told that everyone works in shirt-sleeves and that there is never a tie in sight, a prudent and completely acceptable approach is to opt for your less formal suit, rather than dark blues, greys or pinstripes.

8 | *Body language*

Learn to control negative body movements and encourage positive ones. Discover the seven guidelines for good body language during your interview.

Given the awful choice of going either blind or deaf, which would you choose? If you're like most people, you would choose to go deaf. As human beings we rely to a remarkable degree on our ability to gather information visually. This really is not all that surprising, because while speech is a comparatively recent development, humans have been sending and receiving nonverbal signals since the dawn of the species.

In fact, the language of the body is the first means of communication we develop after birth. We master the spoken word later in life, and in so doing we forget the importance of nonverbal cues – but the signals are still sent and received (usually at a subconscious level).

It is common to hear people say of the body language they use, 'Take me or leave me as I am.' This is all very well if you have no concern for what others think of you. For those seeking professional employment, however, it is important to recognize that your body is consistently sending messages, and to make every effort to understand and control the information stream. If your mouth says, 'Employ me,' but your body says, 'I'm not being truthful,' you are likely to leave the interviewer confused. 'Well,' he or she will think, 'the right answers all came out, but there was something about that candidate that just rubbed me the wrong way.' Such misgivings are generally sufficient to keep a candidate from making the short list. The interviewer may or may not be aware of what causes the concern, but the messages will be sent, and your cause will suffer.

Of course, interviewers can be expected to listen carefully to what you say, too. When your body language doesn't contradict your statements, you will generally be given credence. When your body language complements your verbal statements, your message will gain a great deal of impact, but when your body language *contradicts* what you say, the interviewer will be sceptical. In short, learning to use positive body signals and control negative ones during an interview can have a significant impact on your job hunt and on the new job.

Under the microscope

The challenge for the interviewer is to determine, using every means at his or her disposal, what kind of an employee you would make. Your task as a candidate is to provide the clues most likely to prompt a decision to hire.

Let's begin at the beginning. When you are invited in to an interview, you are probably safe in assuming that your interviewer believes you meet certain minimum standards and could conceivably be hired.

In this context, the adage that actions speak louder than words appears to be something you should take quite literally. Studies done at the University of Chicago found that over 50 percent of all effective communication relies on body language. Since you can expect interviewers to respond to the body language you employ at the interview, it is up to you to decide what messages you want them to receive.

There are also studies that suggest the impression you create in the first few minutes of the interview is the most lasting. Since the first few minutes after you meet the interviewer is a time when he or she is doing the vast majority of the talking, you have very little control over the impression you create with your words – you can't say much of anything! It is up to your body to do the job for you.

The greeting

For a good handshake:

1.   Your hands should be clean and adequately manicured.

2.   Your hands should be free of perspiration.

It is best to allow the interviewer to initiate the handshake. If, through nerves, you find yourself initiating the handshake, don't pull back, as you will appear indecisive. Instead, make the best of it, smile confidently, and make good eye contact.

Your handshake should signal cooperation and friendliness. Match the pressure extended by the interviewer – never exceed it. A typical professional handshake lasts for between two and five seconds, just two or three reasonably firm up and down pumps accompanied by a smile. The parting handshake may last a little longer; smile and lean forward very slightly as you shake hands before departing.

Certain professional and cultural differences should also be considered as well. Many doctors, artists, and others who do delicate work with their hands can and do give less enthusiastic handshakes than other people. If you work in media you'll notice that quite frequently on-air personalities don't want to shake hands at all; it's the easiest way to catch a cold and they depend on their voices and appearance more than most. Similarly, the English handshake is considerably less firm than the American, while the German variety is typically firm.

Use only one hand and always shake vertically. Do not extend your hand parallel to the floor with the palm up, as this conveys submissiveness. By the same token, you may be seen as too aggressive if you extend your hand outward with the palm facing down.

While a confident and positive handshake helps break the ice and gets the interview moving in the right direction, proper use of the hands throughout the rest of the interview will help convey an above-board, 'nothing-to-hide' message.

Watch out for hands and fingers that take on a life of their own, fidgeting with themselves or other objects such as pens, paper, your tie, or your hair. Pen tapping is interpreted as the action of an impatient person; this is an example of an otherwise trivial habit that can take on immense significance in an interview situation. Rarely will an interviewer ask you to stop doing something annoying; instead, he'll simply make a mental note that you are an annoying person, and congratulate himself for picking this up before making the mistake of employing you.

Other negative hand messages include:

■ Clasping your hands behind your head: you'll expose perspiration marks, and you run the risk of appearing smug, superior, bored, and possibly withdrawn.

▋ Showing insecurity by constantly adjusting your tie: when inter-viewing with a woman, this gesture might be interpreted as displaying something beyond a businesslike interest in the interviewer.

▋ Slouching in your chair, with hands in pockets or thumbs in belt: this posture can brand you as insolent and aggressive (just recall any teenage boy). When this error is made in the presence of an inter-viewer of the opposite sex, it can carry sexually aggressive overtones as well.

▋ Pulling your collar away from your neck: this may seem like an innocent enough reaction to the heat of the day, but the interviewer might assume that you are tense and/or masking an untruth. The same goes for scratching your neck during, before, or after your response to a question.

▋ Moving your hands toward a personal feature that you perceive as deficient: this is a common unconscious reaction to stress. A man with thinning hair, for example, may thoughtlessly put his hand to his forehead when pondering how to respond to the query, 'Why aren't you earning more at your age?' This habit may be extremely difficult for you to detect in the first place, much less reverse, but make the effort. Such protective movements are likely to be perceived – if only on a subliminal level – as acknowledgments of low self-esteem.

▋ Picking at invisible bits of fluff on one's suit: this gesture looks exactly like what it is, a nervous tic. Keep your focus on the interviewer. If you do have some bit of lint somewhere on your clothing, the best advice is usually to ignore it until you can remove it discreetly.

By contrast, employing the hands in a positive way can further your cause:

▋ Subtly exposing your palms now and then as you speak can help demonstrate that you are open, friendly, and have nothing to hide. You can see this technique used to great effect by politicians and television talk show hosts.

▋ It can, very occasionally, be beneficial to 'steeple' your fingers for a few seconds as you consider a question or when you first start to talk. Unless you hold the gesture for long periods of time, it will be perceived as a neutral demonstration of your thoughtfulness. Of course, if you overuse this or hold the position for too long, you may be taken as condescending. Steepling also gives you something constructive to do with your hands; it offers a change from holding your pad and pen.

Taking your seat

Some thirty inches from my nose
The frontier of my person goes.
Beware of rudely crossing it,
I have no gun, but I can spit.
  – W. H. Auden

Encroaching on another's 'personal space' is a bad idea in any business situation, but it is particularly dangerous in an interview. The 30-inch (75cm) standard is a good one to follow: it is the distance that allows you to extend your hand comfortably for a handshake. Maintain this distance throughout the interview, and be particularly watchful of personal-space intrusions when you first meet, greet, and take a seat.

A person's office is an extension of sorts of his or her personal space; this is why it is not only polite but also sound business sense to wait until the interviewer offers you a seat.

It is not uncommon to meet an interviewer in a conference room or other supposedly 'neutral' site. Again, wait for the interviewer to motion you to a spot, or, if you feel uncomfortable doing this, tactfully ask the interviewer to take the initiative: 'Where would you like me to sit?'

The type of chair you sit in can affect the signals you send with your body during an interview. If you have a choice, go with an upright chair with arms. Deep armchairs can restrict your ability to send certain positive signals, and encourage the likelihood of slumping. They're best suited for watching television, not for projecting the image of a competent professional.

Always sit with your bottom well back in the chair and your back straight. Slouching, of course, is out, but a slight forward leaning posture will show interest and friendliness toward the interviewer. Keep your hands on the sides of the chair; if there are no arms on the chair, keep your hands in your lap or on your pad of paper.

Crossed legs, in all their many forms, send a mixture of signals; most of them are negative:

▌ Crossing one ankle over the other knee can show a certain stubborn and recalcitrant outlook (as well as the bottom of your shoe, which is not always a pretty sight). The negative signal is intensified when you grasp the horizontally crossed leg or – worst of all – cross your arms across your chest.

▌ Some body language experts feel crossed ankles indicate that the person doing the crossing is withholding information. Of course, since the majority of interviews take place across a desk, crossed ankles will often be virtually unnoticeable. This body signal is probably the most permissible barrier you can erect; if you must allow yourself one body language vice, this is the one to choose.

▌ When sitting in armchairs or on sofas, crossing the legs may be necessary to create some stability. In this instance, the signals you send by crossing your legs will be neutral, as long as your crossed legs point toward, rather than away from, the interviewer.

Facial/head signals

Once you take your seat, and the conversation begins, the interviewer's attention will be focused on your face.

Our language is full of expressions testifying to the powerful influence of facial expressions. When you say that someone is shifty-eyed, is tight-lipped, has a furrowed brow, flashes bedroom eyes, stares into space, or grins like a Cheshire cat, you are speaking in a kind of shorthand and using a set of stereotypes that enables us to make judgments – consciously or unconsciously – about that person.

Tight smiles and tension in the facial muscles often bespeak an inability to handle stress; little eye contact can communicate a desire to hide something; pursed lips are often associated with a secretive nature; and frowning, looking sideways, or peering over one's glasses can send signals of haughtiness and arrogance. Hardly the stuff of which winning interviews are made!

The eyes

Looking at someone means showing interest in that person, and showing interest is a giant step forward in making the right impression. Remember: we are all our own favourite subject!

Looking away from the interviewer for long periods while he is talking, closing your eyes while being addressed, and repeatedly shifting focus from the subject to some other point are all likely to leave the wrong impression.

Of course, there is a big difference between looking and staring at someone! Rather than looking at the speaker straight on at all times, create a mental triangle incorporating both eyes and the mouth; your eyes will follow a natural, continuous path along the three points. Maintain this approach for roughly three-quarters of the time; you can break your gaze to look at the interviewer's hands as points are emphasized or to refer to your notebook. This is the way we maintain eye contact in nonstressful situations, and it will allow you to appear attentive, sincere, and committed.

Be wary of breaking eye contact too abruptly and of shifting your focus in ways that will disrupt the atmosphere of professionalism. Examining the interviewer below the head and shoulders, for instance, is a sign of overfamiliarity. This is especially important when being interviewed by someone of the opposite sex.

The eyebrows send messages as well. Under stress, one's brows may wrinkle; this sends a negative signal about your ability to handle challenges in the business world. The best thing to do is take a deep breath and collect yourself. Most of the tension that people feel at interviews has to do with anxiety about how to respond to what the interviewer will ask.

The head

Nodding your head slowly shows interest, validates the comments of your interviewer, and subtly encourages her to continue. Tilting the head slightly, when combined with eye contact and a natural smile, demonstrates friendliness and approachability. The tilt should be momentary and not exaggerated, almost like a bob of the head to one side. (Do not overuse this technique unless you are applying for a job in a parrot shop!) Rapidly nodding your head can leave the impression that you are impatient and eager to add something to the conversation – if only the interviewer would let you.

The mouth

One guiding principle of good body language is to turn upward rather than downward. Look at two boxers after a fight: the victor's arms are raised high, his back is straight, and his shoulders are square. His smiling face is thrust upward and outward, and you see happiness, openness, warmth, and confidence. The loser, on the other hand, is slumped forward, brows knit and eyes downcast, and the signals you receive are those of anger, frustration, belligerence, and defeat.

Your smile is one of the most powerful positive body signals in your arsenal; it best exemplifies the up-is-best principle as well. Offer an unforced, confident smile as frequently as opportunity and circumstances dictate; *avoid* grinning idiotically, as this indicates that you may not be quite right in the head.

You should be aware that the mouth also provides a seemingly limitless supply of opportunities to convey weakness. This may be done by touching the mouth frequently; 'faking' a cough when confronted with a difficult question; and/or gnawing on one's lips absentmindedly. Employing any of these 'insincerity signs' when you are asked about, say, why you lost your last job, might instil or confirm suspicions about your honesty or openness.

Glasses

People who wear glasses sometimes leave them off when going on an interview in an attempt to project a more favourable image. There are difficulties with this approach. Long-sighted people who don't wear their glasses will (unwittingly) seem to stare long and hard at the people they converse with, and this is a negative signal. Also, pulling out glasses for reading and peering over the top of your glasses – even if you have been handed something to read and subsequently asked a question – carries professorial connotations that can be interpreted as critical. If you wear glasses for reading, you should remove them when conversing, replacing them only when appropriate.

Wearing dark glasses to an interview will paint you as secretive, cold, and devious. Even if your prescription glasses are tinted, the effect will be the same. You might consider un-tinted glasses for your interview, or contacts. At the same time, glasses on a younger-looking person can add an air of seriousness and might be considered a plus.

Body Signal Barricades

Folding or crossing your arms, or holding things in front of the body, sends negative messages to the interviewer: 'I know you're there, but you can't come in. I'm nervous and closed for business.'

It is bad enough to feel this way, but worse to express it with blatant signals. Don't fold your arms or 'protect' your chest with hands, clipboard, briefcase, or anything else during the interview. You can, however, keep a notebook and pen on your lap. It makes you look organized and gives you something to do with your hands.

Feet

Some foot signals can have negative connotations. Women and men wearing slip-on shoes should beware of dangling the loose shoe from the toes; this can be distracting, and, as it is a gesture often used to signal physical attraction, it has no place in a job interview. Likewise, avoid compulsive jabbing of floor, desk, or chair with your foot; this can be perceived as a hostile and angry motion, and is likely to annoy the interviewer.

Some people (your author included in the front ranks on this one) have an annoying habit of jiggling one leg up and down on the ball of the foot. Those of us who do this know it is a tic that says we are totally engaged and excited about some topic (and sometimes even the one under discussion); those forced to endure it find it distracting and can interpret it as impatience. If you are a dreaded jiggler, you must get this under control for your job interviews!

Walking

Many interviews will require that you walk from one place to the next – on a guided tour or, from one office to another. How long these walks last is not as important as how you use them to reinforce positive professional behaviours and impressions.

Posture is your main concern: keep your shoulders back and maintain an erect posture. Smile, and make eye contact as appropriate. Avoid fidgeting with your feet as you move, rubbing one shoe against the other, or kicking absentmindedly at the ground if you stand to talk; these signals will lead others to believe that you are anxious and/or insecure. Crossing your arms or legs while standing carries the same negative connotations as it does when you are sitting. Putting your hands in your pockets is less offensive – assuming you don't jangle keys or coins – but men must be careful not to employ the hands-on-hips or thumbs-in-belt postures discussed earlier. These send messages that you are aggressive and dominating.

Putting it all together

Now you have the big picture, and you can begin to be more aware of the signals your body can unwittingly send. Let's reduce all this information into a handful of simple recommendations. Positive signals reinforce one another; employing them in combination yields an overwhelming positive message that is truly greater than the sum of its parts.

So far you have focused primarily on the pitfalls to avoid; but what messages *should* be sent, and how? Here are seven general suggestions on good body language for the interview:

1. Walk slowly, and stand tall upon entering the room.

2. On greeting your interviewer, give a smile, make eye contact, and respond warmly to the interviewer's greeting and handshake.

3. Sit well back in the chair; this allows the chair back to help you sit upright. Increase the impression of openness ('I have nothing to hide!') by unbuttoning your jacket as you sit down. Keep your head up. Maintain eye contact a good portion of the time, especially when the interviewer begins to speak and when you reply. Smile naturally whenever the opportunity arises. Avoid folding your arms; it is better to hold a notebook and pen, or keep your arms on the arms of the chair, which will also help you avoid slouching. Remember to show one or both of your palms occasionally as you make points, but do not overuse this gesture.

4. Use mirroring techniques to reproduce the positive signals your interviewer sends. Say the interviewer leans forward to make a point; a few moments later, you too lean forward slightly, demonstrating that you don't want to miss a word. Perhaps the interviewer leans back and laughs; you 'laugh beneath' the interviewer's laughter, taking care not to overwhelm your partner by using an inappropriate volume level. This can seem contrived at first, but through observing those in your own social circle, you'll notice that this is natural behaviour for good communicators.

5. Keep your head up and your eyes front at all times – and don't slouch in your seat.

6. Try to remain calm and do not hurry your movements; you'll look harried and are more likely to knock things over. Most people are more clumsy when they are nervous, and consciously slowing your body movements will lessen the chances of disaster and give you a more controlled persona.

7. Remember to breathe. When we are nervous we can forget to do this, which leads to oxygen deprivation and obviously affects your cognitive processes.

Open for business

The more open your body movements during the interview, the more you will be perceived as open yourself. Understanding and directing your body language will give you added power to turn interviews into cooperative exchanges between two professionals.

Just as you interpret the body language of others, both positive and negative, your body language makes an indelible impression on those you meet. It tells them whether you like and have confidence in yourself, whether or not you are pleasant to be around, and whether you are more likely to be honest or deceitful. Like it or not, your body carries these messages for the world to see.

Job interviews are reliable in one constant: They bring out insecurities. All the more reason to consciously manage the impressions your body sends. You will absorb the lessons in this chapter quite quickly if you take the time to observe and interpret the body signals of friends and family. When you see and can understand body language in others, you'll be more aware of your own, and more capable of controlling it.

9 The curtain goes up on the job interview

First impressions are the strongest. Here are the preparations to make before heading out to the interview.

Backstage in the theatre, the announcement 'Places, please' is made five minutes before the curtain goes up. It's the performers' signal to psych themselves up, complete final costume adjustments, and make time to reach the stage. They are getting ready to go onstage and knock 'em dead. You should go through a similar process to get thoroughly prepared for your time in the spotlight.

Winning a job offer depends not only on the things you do well but also on the mistakes you avoid. As the interview approaches, settle down with your CV and immerse yourself in your past successes and the professional behaviours that made them possible. Interview nerves are to be expected; the trick is to use them to your benefit by harnessing that nervous energy to your physical and mental preparation.

▌ **The company dossier**: Always take a few copies of your CV and executive briefing: one for you and the others for the interviewers you might meet. Your main interviewer will invariably have a copy of your CV, but you can't be certain of that with other people you meet. It is perfectly acceptable to have your CV in front of you at the interview; it shows you are organized, and it will remind you of essential facts. It is not unusual to hear, 'Mr Jones wasn't hired because he didn't pay attention to detail and couldn't even remember his employment dates' – just the kind of thing you are likely to forget in the nervousness of the moment.

I **A pad of paper and writing instruments**: They demonstrate your preparedness, and they give you something constructive to do with your hands during the interview.

I **A list of job-related questions**: The details of the job you already know are likely to be general in nature. Asking questions that give you the practical details of the activities you will be involved with in the first few months will make you think about your experience with a focus complementary to that of your interviewers. You might ask:

> 'What are the most immediate challenges of the job?'
> 'What are the most important projects of the first six months?'
> 'What skills and behaviours are most important to success on the job?'
> 'Why do some people succeed and others fail doing this work?'
> 'Why is the position open?'
> 'What is the job's relationship to other departments?'
> 'How do the job and the department relate to the company?'
> You can find more questions to ask at the end of Chapter 11, 'How to knock 'em dead'.
> *Note*: In the early rounds of interviewing stay away from questions about where the job can lead and what the pay and benefits are. It's not that these questions aren't important to you; it is just that the timing is wrong. It won't do you any good to know what a job pays when you aren't going to get a job offer. Instead, ask the questions that will lead to a job offer being extended then ask the questions you need to evaluate it. For questions to ask during the negotiation phase, see Chapter 19, 'Negotiating the offer'.

I **Any additional information you have about the company or the job**: If time permits, visit the company website, review any company literature and research you might have, and do a Google search for news articles mentioning the company by name, and for articles that relate to your profession.

I **Directions to the interview**: Decide on your form of transport and finalize your time of departure, leaving enough time to accommodate travel delays. Check the route, distance, and travel time. If you forget to verify date, time, and place (including floor and room number), you might not even arrive at the right place, or on the right day, for your interview. Write it all down legibly and put it with the rest of your interview kit.

To arrive at an interview too early indicates overanxiousness and to arrive late is inconsiderate, so arrive at the interview on time, but at the location early. This allows you time to visit the restroom (usually your only private sanctuary at an interview) and make the necessary adjustments to your appearance, to review any notes, and to put on your 'professional face'. Remember to add contact telephone numbers to your interview kit, so if you are delayed on the way to the interview, you can call and let the interviewer know.

■   Dress conservatively. As you could be asked to appear for an interview at a scant couple of hours notice, keep your best outfit freshly cleaned, your shirts or blouses wrinkle-free, and your shoes polished, and reserve them exclusively for interviews.

■   Visit the hairdresser once a month, so you always look groomed, and keep your nails clean and trimmed at all times, even if you work with your hands.

■   While you will naturally shower or bath prior to an interview, and the use of an unscented deodorant is advisable, you should avoid wearing after-shave or perfume; you are trying to get a job, not a date. Never drink alcohol the day before an interview. It affects eyes, skin tone, and your wits.

When you get to the interview site, visit your private sanctuary to check your appearance and take a couple of minutes to do the following:

■   Review the company dossier.

■   Recall your commitment to the profession and the team, and the professional behaviours that help you succeed.

■   Breathe deeply and slowly for a minute to dispel your natural physical tension.

■   Review the questions you will need to identify first projects and initial needs.

▌ Smile and head for the interview – you are as ready as you are ever going to be.

Afterward you will review your performance to make sure the next one goes even better.

Under no circumstances should you back out because you do not like the receptionist or the look of the office – that would be allowing those interview nerves to get the better of you. As you are shown into the office, you are on!

Do:

▌ Give a firm handshake – respond to the interviewer's grip and duration.

▌ Make eye contact and smile. Say, 'Hello, Ms Larsen. I am John Jones. I have been looking forward to meeting you.'

Do not:

▌ Use first names (unless asked).

▌ Smoke (even if invited).

▌ Sit down (until invited).

▌ Show anxiety or boredom.

▌ Look at your watch.

▌ Discuss equal rights, sex, race, national origin, religion, or age.

▌ Show samples of your work (unless requested).

▌ Ask about benefits, salary, or vacation.

Now you are ready for anything – except for the tough questions that are going to be thrown at you next. We'll handle those over the next pages.

Part III

Great Answers to Tough Interview Questions

This section tells you not only what to answer but also how to answer. It provides the real preparation for getting the job you want and deserve.

'Like being on trial for your life' is how many people look at a job interview. They are probably right. With the interviewer as judge and jury, you are at least on trial for your livelihood. Therefore, you must lay the foundation for a winning defence. F Lee Bailey, one of the United States' most celebrated defence attorneys, attributes his success in the courtroom to preparation. He likens himself to a magician going into court with 50 rabbits in his hat, not knowing which one he'll really need, but ready to pull out any single one. Bailey is successful because he is ready for any eventuality. He takes the time to analyse every situation and every possible option. He never underestimates his opposition. He is always prepared. F Lee Bailey usually wins.

Another famous attorney, Louis Nizer, successfully defended all of his 50-plus capital offence clients. When lauded as the greatest courtroom performer of his day, Nizer denied the accolade. He claimed for himself the distinction of being the *best prepared*.

You won't win your day 'in court' just based on your skills. As competition for the best jobs increases, employers are comparing more and more applicants for every opening and asking more and more questions. To win against stiff competition, you need more than just your merits. When the race is close, the final winner is, as often as not, picked for a comparative lack of negatives when ranged against the other contenders. Like Bailey and Nizer, you can prove to yourself that the prize always goes to the best prepared.

During an interview, employers ask you dozens of searching questions – questions that test your confidence, poise and desirable personality traits. Questions that trick you into contradicting yourself. Questions that probe your quick thinking and job skills. They are all designed so that the interviewer can make decisions regarding some critical areas.

∎ Can you do the job?

∎ Are you professional in your behaviour?

∎ Are you willing to take the extra step?

∎ Are you a manageable team player?

∎ Are you a problem solver?

Notice that only one of the critical areas has anything to do with your actual job skills. Being able to do the job is only a small part of getting an offer. Whether you will fit in and make a contribution or not and if you are manageable are just as important to the interviewer. Those traits that companies probe for during the interview are the same that will mark a person for professional growth when on board. In this era of high specialization, companies become more critical in the selection process and look more actively for certain traits, some of which cannot be ascertained by a direct question or answer. Consequently, the interviewer will seek a pattern in your replies that shows your possession of such traits – I discuss them in detail in the next chapter.

The time spent 'in court' on trial for your livelihood contains four deadly traps:

- failing to listen to the question;

- answering a question that was not asked;

- providing superfluous, inappropriate or irrelevant information;

- attempting the interview without preparing for it.

The effect of such blunders is cumulative, and each reduces your chances of receiving a job offer.

The number of offers you win in your search for the ideal job depends on your ability to answer a staggering array of questions in terms that have value and relevance to the employer, such as 'Why do you want to work here?', 'What are your biggest accomplishments?', 'How long will it take you to make a contribution?', 'Why should I employ you?', 'What can you do for us that someone else cannot do?', 'What is your greatest weakness?', 'Why aren't you earning more?' and 'What interests you least about this job?' are just some of the questions you are likely to be asked.

The examples of answers to these kinds of questions in the following chapters come from across the job spectrum. Though the examples of answers might come from the mouth of an administrator, while you are a scientist or in one of the service industries, the commonality of all job functions in contributing to the bottom line will help you draw the correct parallel for your job.

You will also notice that each example teaches a small yet valuable lesson in good business behaviour – something you can use both to get the job and make a good impression when you are on board.

Remember, the answers provided in the following chapters should not be repeated word for word, exactly as they come off the page. You have your own style of speech (not to mention your own kind of business experience), so try to put the answers in your own words.

10 The five secrets of securing a job offer

Knowing how an interviewer thinks is a critical element of the job search that is too frequently overlooked.

Every job offer in every profession and every company, at every level, ever made, anywhere in the world, was made based on the five criteria I unfold in this chapter; you might well want to read it twice – it's really that important. Understanding these five secrets will revolutionize the way you perform at job interviews.

An employer never wakes up in the morning and says, 'It's a wonderful day; I think I'll go and hire an accountant.' Employees never get added to the payroll for the fun of it; rather, they get added to the payroll to make a difference with their presence, to make a contribution to the bottom line (make £, save £, save time), and to both solve and prevent problems in their area of expertise. You get hired to prevent problems and, when prevention isn't an option, to solve them as they arise in the daily discharge of your duties. In the process, you are also expected to make a contribution by either contributing to revenue generation or productivity. The following five criteria that employers apply to each and every job offer they make all relate to this overriding 'problem identification and solution' concern that gave rise to the job opening in the first place.

The first secret: ability and suitability

Saying, 'Hey, I can do this job – give me a shot and I'll prove it to you' is not enough any more. Today you have to *prove* your ability and suitability.

Every working professional has a combination of skills that broadly defines his or her ability and suitability. How well you program that computer, service that client or sew up that appendix is part of the picture; knowing the steps involved well enough *to be able to explain them clearly and simply to others* is another part.

Itemize your technical/professional skills as they parallel the requirements of the job. Then recall an incident to illustrate each of those skills. When you have done this, and not before, you will be in a position to begin justifying your ability and suitability to an employer.

If you are applying for a job in an industry with which you are familiar, you should also consider highlighting your industry sensibilities. Industry sensibilities means knowing 'how we do things here'. For example, a good computer programmer working in a bank has technical and professional skills – that is, the ability to program a computer is required by the employer. That same programmer has knowledge of how to get things done in the industry in which he or she operates – that is, the ability to work well with bankers, which is quite different from being able to work well with, say, television fundraisers.

Demonstrating both professional/technical *and* industry skills will set you apart from the vast majority of candidates. Show that you understand these combinations and you will stand out from the pack.

The second secret: willingness

You may find your interviewer asking you such questions as, 'Are you willing to make tea and coffee?' or, if you are in a small office, 'Are you willing to wash up or answer the phones?' You may want to ask if these duties are part of your job description, but doing so may lose you the opportunity to demonstrate your readiness to pitch in with any task. These questions are being used more and more by potential employers who want to gauge *willingness* – and have no intention of having you brew the perfect cup of tea or coffee.

The issue isn't whether or not you are prepared to do demeaning tasks. It is whether or not you are the kind of person who is prepared to do whatever it takes to help the team survive and prosper. Can you take the rough with the smooth? Are you prepared to go that extra mile? You are? Great. Think of a time when you did. Work out how your doing so helped the company. Now rehearse the story until you can tell it in about 90 seconds.

The third secret: manageability and teamwork

There isn't a manager in the world who enjoys a sleepless night caused by an unmanageable employee. Avoiding such nights is a major concern for managers, who develop, over time, a remarkable sixth sense when it comes to spotting and weeding out mavericks.

Manageability is defined in different ways:

■ the ability to work alone;

■ the ability to work with others;

■ a willingness to work with others regardless of their sex, age, religion, physical appearance, abilities or disabilities, skin colour or national origin;

■ the ability to take direction and criticism when it is carefully and considerately given;

■ last, but perhaps dearest to the manager's heart, the ability to take direction when it _isn't_ carefully and considerately given, often because of a crisis.

Such 'manageability' considerations make a job interview tricky. Yes, you should certainly state your strongly held convictions – after all, you don't want to appear wishy-washy – but you should do so _only_ as long as they are professional in nature and relate to the job at hand.

Let me give you an example of what I mean. A number of people have asked me about what they perceive as discrimination as a result of their religious beliefs. However, each discussion invariably ends in the conclusion that a job interview is simply no place to bring up personal beliefs. Today's managers will usually go well out of their way to avoid even the perception of intolerance towards sincerely held spiritual beliefs, especially as this is now illegal. Yet, by the same token, they are deeply suspicious of any strident religious rhetoric that surfaces in a professional setting. (This also holds true of political, ethnic or other inappropriate issues raised by a candidate during an interview.) The potential employer's caution in these circumstances, far from representing discrimination, is a sign of concern that the candidate might not be tolerant of the views of others and might thereby become an obstacle to a harmonious work group.

The rules here are simple. Don't bring up religious, political or racial matters during the job interview. Even a casual reference to such topics can put a potential employer on the spot as he or she could subject the company to a lawsuit if a racial or religious topic is perceived as having influenced an employment decision. The interview is a potential payslip; don't mess with it.

You're a team player, someone who gets along well with others and has no problem tolerating other opinions or beliefs. Demonstrate that with your every word and action.

The fourth secret: professional behaviour

I emphasize *professional* behaviour throughout this book because, to a large extent, the behaviours that are most desirable to employers are learned and developed as a result of our experiences in the workplace, not the behaviours we developed growing up. Remember that first day on your first job, when you eventually got up the courage to go and forage for a cup of coffee? You found the coffee machine, and there stuck on the wall was a handwritten sign reading:

YOUR MOTHER DOESN'T WORK HERE
CLEAR UP AFTER YOURSELF

You thought to yourself, 'Clear up after myself? I've got to learn a whole new way of behaving.' So you started to observe and emulate the more successful professionals around you, and you slowly developed a whole range of learned behaviours that help you succeed throughout your professional life.

An important part of your interview weaponry is the ability to show employers you are in possession of a full slate of professional behaviours universally sought by all employers. These are the very behaviours that get you hired, get you noticed, land plum assignments, and generate promotions and pay rises – in short they enable you to succeed in all your professional endeavours.

Showing possession of these universally admired professional behaviours, and showing them in action with illustrative examples you give in answers to tough interview questions, is your passport to success at any interview. They will give your answers substance and a ring of truth. Going through the list of learned professional behaviours, you probably recognize that you apply many of them on a regular basis in your work; if not, they are readily learnable and you'll be able to begin developing these valuable career assets as soon as you recognize their importance. As you read through the list of behaviours, you'll see, for example, 'determination', and think, 'Yes, I'm determined.' When this happens, try to come up with times when you used determination in the execution of your duties. You might also come across 'time management and organization', and say, 'now there's something I have to work on!' In this instance you have identified a key behaviour that needs work, and you can immediately set about an improvement programme.

The examples you generate can be used in your CV, in your covering letters, and as illustrative answers to questions in interviews. Then when you get asked, 'So why are you different?' you will have something meaningful to say, and the illustrations that you provide will give that aura of truth to your claims. Absorbing this list of learnable professional behaviours, and making them part of the professional you, will win you interviews and job offers and provide the backbone of your long-term career success.

▮ **Communication and listening skills:** The ability to communicate effectively to people at all levels in a company is a key to success. It refers to verbal and written skills along with technological adaptedness, dress, and body language. This is an especially important consideration when it comes to your covering letter and CV, because these written documents are the first means an employer has of judging your communication skills. It means you must take the time to craft, edit, and re-edit your letter until it communicates what you want it to, and at the same demonstrates that you do have adequate communication skills.

I recently counselled someone in the 500K a year range, and he was having problems getting in front of the right people. The first paragraph of his CV stated that he was an executive with 'superior communication skills'; unfortunately, the last 12 words of the sentence gave the lie to his claims – they contained two spelling errors! In an age of spell checkers this sloppiness isn't acceptable at any level.

Communication embraces *listening skills*: listening and understanding, as opposed to just waiting your turn to talk. Consciously develop your 'listening to understand' skills, and the result will be improved and more persuasive communication abilities.

I **Goal-orientation:** All employers are interested in goal-orientated professionals: those who achieve concrete results with their actions and who constantly strive to get the job done, rather than just filling the time allotted for a particular task. You might be able to use an example or reference to this behaviour or others in your letters and CV.

I **Willingness to be a team player:** The highest achievers (always goal-orientated) are invariably *team players*: employers look for employees who work for the common good and always with the group's goals and responsibilities in mind. Team players take pride in group achievement over personal aggrandizement; they look for solutions rather than someone to blame.

I **Motivation and energy:** Employers realize a motivated professional will do a better job on every assignment. Motivation expresses itself in a commitment to the job and the profession, an eagerness to learn and grow professionally and a willingness to take the rough with the smooth.

Motivation is invariably expressed by the *energy* someone demonstrates in their work, as shown by always giving that extra effort to get the job done and to get it done right.

I **Analytical skills:** Being able to weigh the short- and long-term benefits of proposed course of action against all its possible negatives. We see these skills demonstrated in the way a person identifies potential problems and so is able to minimize their occurrence. Successful application of analytical skills at work requires understanding how your job and the role of your department fits into the overall goal for profitability. It also means thinking things through and not jumping at the first or easiest solution.

I **Dedication and reliability:** Dedication to your profession and the role it plays in the larger issues of company success, and the empowerment that comes from knowing how your part contributes to the greater good. Dedication to your professionalism is also a demonstration of enlightened self-interest. The more you are engaged in your career the more likely you are to join the inner circles that exist in every department and company enhancing opportunities for advancement; at the same time this dedication will repay you with better job security and improved professional horizons.

Your dedication will also express itself in your _reliability_: Showing up is half the battle; the other half is your performance on the job. This requires following up on your actions, not relying on anyone else to ensure the job is done well, and keeping management informed every step of the way.

▌ **Determination:** Someone who does not back off when a problem or situation gets tough. It's the person who chooses to be part of a solution rather than standing idly by and being part of the problem. Determined professionals have decided to make a difference with their presence every day and are willing to do whatever it takes to get a job done, even if that includes duties that might not appear in a job description.

▌ **Confidence:** As you develop desirable professional behaviours your confidence grows in the skills you have and in your ability to develop new ones, and with this comes confidence in taking on new challenges. You have the confidence to ask questions, the confidence to look at challenges calmly, the confidence to look at mistakes squarely, and the confidence to make changes to eradicate them. In short, you develop a quiet confidence in the ability of the professional you to deliver the goods.

▌ **Pride and integrity:** Pride in yourself as a professional means always making sure the job is done to the best of your ability; this means paying attention to the details and to the time and cost constraints. Integrity means taking responsibility for your actions, both good and bad; it also means treating others, within and outside the company, with respect at all times and in all situations. With pride in yourself as a professional with integrity, your actions will always be in the best interests of the company, and your decisions will never be based on whim or personal preference.

When it comes down to it, companies have very limited interests: making money, saving money (the same as making money), and saving time, which saves money and makes time to make more money. Actually, you wouldn't want it any other way, as it is this focus that delivers your payslip come payday. Developing these professional behaviours and maintaining sensitivity to the profit interests of any business endeavour is the mark of a true professional. To this end, behaviour that demonstrates an awareness of the need for procedures, efficiency and economy rounds out the profile of the consummate professional:

I **Efficiency:** Always keeping an eye open for wasted time, effort, resources, and money.

I **Economy:** Most problems have two solutions: and the expensive one isn't always the best. Ideas of efficiency and economy engage the creative mind in ways other workers might not consider; they are an integral part of your analytical proficiency.

I **Ability to follow procedures:** Procedures exist to keep the company profitable, so you don't work around them. Following the chain of command, you don't implement your own 'improved' procedures or organize others to do so.

Now understanding what the desirable professional behaviours are, and seeing that you possess them, is only part of the secret let's talk about the importance of illustrating these behaviours at work.

Harry works in Import and Export. He reads the list of learned professional behaviours, comes across the category labelled 'Determination' and thinks, 'Yes, that's me. I'm determined.'

It's good for Harry to know this and be able to mention it at the interview, but how much better if he could give illustrate his claim with a real-life work experience. So Harry recalls the time he came in over the weekend to clear the warehouse in time to make room for the 20-ton press due in Monday morning at seven. When he tells this story to the interviewer, he gets a lot further than he would if he simply said, 'Employ me; I'm determined' – a bland, unsubstantial claim that would be forgotten almost the instant it left Harry's mouth. Instead, the interviewer gets a mental image of Harry coming in over the weekend to make room for that press. Actually, the interviewer sees something much more important – namely, Harry applying the same level of determination and extra effort on behalf of the interviewer's company.

Simple statements don't leave any lasting impression on employers. Anecdotes that prove a point do.

The fifth secret: everyone employs people for the same job

Surprised? Here's another: No one in the history of industry and commerce has ever been added to a payroll for the love of mankind.

Regardless of job or profession, we are all, at some level, _problem solvers_. That's the first and most important part of the job description for anyone who has ever been taken on for any job, at any level, in any organization, anywhere in the world. This fifth secret is absolutely key to job hunting and career success in any field.

Think of your profession in terms of its problem-solving responsibilities. Once you have identified the particular problem-solving business you are in, you will have gone a long way towards isolating what the interviewer will want to talk about. Identify and list for yourself the typical problems you tackle for employers on a daily basis. Come up with plenty of specific examples. Then move on to the biggest and dirtiest problems you've been faced with. Again, recall specifically how you solved them.

Here's a technique used by HR professionals to help people develop examples of their problem-solving skills and the resultant achievements:

▌ **State the problem** What was the situation? Was it typical of your job or had something gone wrong? If the latter, be wary of apportioning blame.

▌ **Isolate relevant background information** What special knowledge or education were you armed with to tackle this dilemma?

▌ **List your key qualities** What professional skills and personal behaviour traits did you bring into play to solve the problem?

▌ **Recall the solution** How did things turn out in the end? (If the problem did not have a successful resolution, do not use it as an example.)

▌ **Determine what the solution was worth** Quantify the solution in terms of money earned, money saved or time saved. Specify your role as a team member or as a lone gun, as the facts demand.

With an improved understanding of what employers seek in employees, you will have a better understanding of yourself and what you have to offer in the way of specific problem-solving abilities. If you follow the steps outlined above, you will develop a series of illustrative stories for each key area. Remember, stories help interviewers visualize you solving *their* problems, as a paid member of the team.

Here's a story for you. It's based on a real-life interview pattern, although the names are fictional.

Mr Wanton Grabbit, 80-year-old senior partner at the revered law firm of Sue, Grabbit, and Runne, ran a 'wanted' advertisement in the paper for a word processing specialist. He was looking for someone with five years' experience in word processing and the same amount working in a legal environment. He also wanted someone with experience in using the office computer system.

Grabbit interviewed 10 candidates with exactly the experience the advertisement demanded. Each of them came away from the interview convinced that a job offer was imminent. None of them got the job. The person who did get the job had *three* years of experience and had never before set foot inside a law office.

Sue Sharp, the successful candidate, understood the fifth secret and asked a few intelligent questions of her own during the interview. Specifically, she asked, 'What are the first projects I will be involved with?' This led Mr Grabbit to launch into a long discourse on his desire to see the law firm rush headlong into the modern world. The first project, he explained, would be to load the firm's approximately 4,000 manual files on to the computer system.

Now, although Sue had never worked in a law firm before, she had, at her last job, automated a cumbersome manual filing system. Having faced the *problem* before, even though she had done so in the 'wrong' setting, she was able to demonstrate an understanding of the challenges the position presented. Furthermore, she was able to tell the illustrative stories from her last job that enabled Mr Grabbit to see her, in his mind's eye, tackling and solving his immediate, specific, short-term problems successfully.

We get two very special benefits when we understand and apply the fifth secret. First, we show that we possess the problem-solving abilities of a first-rate professional in the field. Second, when we ask about the problems, challenges, projects, deadlines and pressure points that will be tackled in the early months, we show that we will be able to hit the ground running on those first critical projects.

Integrate the five secrets as you read the following chapters. You will reap the rewards, while your competition will have to resign themselves to harvesting sour grapes.

11 **How to knock 'em dead**

There are a couple of handfuls of specific learned professional behaviours that are catnip to all employers. Learn how to apply them during the interview process.

If you are like most people, you are terrified of job interviews, partly because you don't know exactly what questions are going to be asked. Even though there are questions you think the interviewer might ask, you have no idea of how best to answer them. Even if you have an arsenal of rehearsed answers to likely questions, you know slick answers are going to make you sound like a used-car salesperson. Take a look at these scary questions: do you know how to answer them?

■ 'Describe a situation where your work or an idea was criticized.'

■ 'Have you done the best work you are capable of doing?'

■ 'What problems do you have getting along with others?'

■ 'How long will you stay with the company?'

■ 'I'm not sure you're suitable for the job.'

■ 'Tell me about something you are not very proud of.'

■ 'What are some of the things your supervisor did that you disliked?'

■ 'What aspects of your job do you consider most crucial?'

Can you answer all these questions off the top of your head? Can you do it in a way that will set your worth above the other job candidates? I doubt it – but after you have read this section you will be thoroughly prepared for these questions and hundreds more like them. You know it isn't enough to have slick answers ready because each answer you give must help satisfy one of those five secrets of the job offer that employers apply to each candidate.

As you learned in the last few pages, an employer is looking for more than just the ability to flip a burger, write code, or balance a departmental budget.

Use those professional behaviours

Every question is a chance for you to demonstrate those desirable professional behaviours that we covered at in the last chapter and that all employers are looking for. They are, to recap:

▊ communication and listening skills

▊ goal orientation;

▊ willingness to be a team player;

▊ motivation and energy;

▊ analytical skills;

▊ dedication and reliability;

▊ determination;

▊ confidence;

▊ pride and integrity.

When you have these desirable professional behaviours, make sure that the interviewer not only knows about them but that they can picture you using them for their benefit. Presenting them in action by illustrating your answers with meaningful anecdotes is the key to success in every interview that you undertake.

The reason that these learnable behaviours are so universally admired is that they relate to profit and the ongoing competitiveness of a company. Using examples of them in your answers to interview questions (as well as in your CV and covering letters) will make you stand out as someone worthy of special consideration.

Get ready for the tough questions

We are now going to look at all those sneaky, dirty, mean, low-down trick questions that can be thrown at you in the course of an interview. I will help you understand what is behind each question, the kind of information an employer is likely to be seeking, and give an example of the kind of points you might want to make in your answers. The examples should be used as a starting point; you'll look within your own experience for the responses to use at an actual interview.

As the requirements of the job are unfolded for you at the interview, meet them point by point with your qualifications. If your experience is limited, stress the appropriate professional behaviour (such as energy, determination, motivation), your relevant interests, and your desire to learn. If you are weak in a particular area, keep your mouth shut – perhaps that dimension will not arise. If the area is probed, stress skills that compensate and/or demonstrate that you will experience a fast learning curve.

Do not show discouragement if the interview appears to be going poorly. You have nothing to gain by showing defeat, and it could merely be an interview tactic to test your self-confidence by putting you under stress (we'll be handling stress techniques in Chapter 14).

If for any reason you need time to think, say, 'Let me think about that for a moment....' If you get flustered or lost, gain time to marshal your thoughts by asking, 'Could you help me with that?' or 'Would you say that again?' or 'That's a good question; I want to be sure I understand. Could you please explain it again?'

When studying the tough questions that follow, remember to use the information you have gathered about your professional self earlier in the book to create the examples and explanations that reflect your skills, experiences, and professional behaviours.

'What are the reasons for your success in this profession?'

With this question, the interviewer is not so much interested in examples of your success – he or she wants to know what makes you tick. Keep your answers short, general and to the point. Using your work experience, personalize and use key items from your personal, professional and business profiles. For example, 'I attribute my success to three things. First, I've always received support from colleagues, which encourages me to be cooperative and look at my specific job in terms of what we as a department are trying to achieve. That gives me great pride in my work and its contribution to the department's efforts, which is the second factor. Finally, I find that every job has its problems and, while there's always a costly solution, there's usually an economical one as well, whether it's in terms of time or money.' Then give an example from your experience that illustrates those points.

'What is your energy level like? Describe a typical day'

You must demonstrate good use of your time, that you believe in planning your day beforehand and that, when it is over, you review your own performance to make sure you are reaching the desired goals. No one wants a part-time employee, so you should sell your energy level. For example, your answer might end with, 'At the end of the day when I'm ready to go home, I make a rule always to type one more letter [make one more call, etc], clear my desk, review the day's achievements and plan for the next day.'

In many of the discussions about how to answer questions, you will learn valuable lessons that will help you be a more successful professional. For example, in the previous question you might pick up some useful, and proven successful, ideas about the 'Plan, Do, Review' cycle that successful people apply every day to keep themselves organized and on track.

'Why do you want to work here?'

To answer this question, you must have researched the company and built a dossier about it. Your research work earlier is now rewarded. Reply with the company's attributes as you see them. Cap your answer with reference to your belief that the company can provide you with a stable and happy work environment – the company has that reputation – and that such an atmosphere would encourage your best work.

'I have a degree in communication studies, and I've worked in pharmaceutical sales for three years. I am currently ranked fourth in the region. I have long competed against your company, and I know and respect your products [you'll add plenty of specific details to show you really know the company]. Your location will also help me get closer to my family.'

'What kind of experience do you have for this job?'

This is a golden opportunity to sell yourself, but, before you do, be sure you know what is most critical to the company. The interviewer is not just looking for a competent engineer, typist or what-have-you, but looking for someone who can contribute quickly to the current projects. When interviewing, companies invariably give everyone a broad picture of the job, but the person they employ will be a problem solver, someone who can contribute to the specific projects in the first six months. Only by asking will you identify the areas of your interviewer's greatest urgency and therefore interest.

If you do not know the projects you will be involved with in the first six months, you must ask. Level-headedness and analytical ability are respected and the information you get will naturally let you answer the question more appropriately. For example, a company experiencing shipping problems might appreciate this answer, 'My high-speed machining background and familiarity with your equipment will allow me to contribute quickly. I understand deadlines, delivery schedules and the importance of getting the product shipped. Finally, my awareness of economy and profit has always kept reject parts to a bare minimum.'

'What are the broad responsibilities of a ...?'

This is suddenly becoming a very popular question with interviewers and rightly so. There are three layers to it. First, it acknowledges that all employees nowadays are required to be more efficiency and profit-conscious and need to know how individual responsibilities fit into the big picture. Second, the answer provides some idea of how much you will have to be taught or reoriented if and when you join the company. Third, it is a very effective knock-out question – if you lack a comprehensive understanding of the job, that's it! You'll be knocked out then and there.

To answer effectively you need to understand the small role your job plays in the bigger picture of departmental responsibilities (including your responsibilities as a team player) and how the department's role in turn helps contribute to the bottom line. Whatever your job, you have customers, or end users, of your service; they are always front and centre in your considerations. Explain your day-to-day responsibilities, who you are serving with your presence, and how your function serves the profit motive of the organization.

While your answer must reflect an understanding of the responsibilities, be wary of falling foul of differences in corporate jargon. A systems analyst in one company, for instance, may be only a trainee programmer in another. With this in mind, you may wish to preface your answer with, 'While the responsibilities of my job title vary somewhat from company to company, at my current/last job, my responsibilities include/included…' Then, in case your background isn't an exact match, ask, 'Which areas of relevant expertise haven't I covered?' That will give you the opportunity to recoup.

'Describe how your job relates to the overall goals of your department and company'

This can be a stand-alone question or a follow-up to the previous one. This not only probes your understanding of departmental and corporate missions, but also obliquely checks into your ability to function as a team member to get the work done. Consequently, whatever the specifics of your answer, include words to this effect: 'The quality of my work directly affects the ability of others to do their work properly. As a team member, one has to be aware of the other players and our common goals.'

'What aspects of your job do you consider most crucial?'

A wrong answer here can knock you out of the running very quickly. The executive who describes expenses reports as the job's most crucial aspect is a case in point. The question is designed to determine time management, prioritization skills and any inclination for task avoidance. It demands that you have a clear awareness of the role of your job in contributing to the overall success of the company.

'Are you willing to go where the company sends you?'

Unfortunately with this one, you are, as the saying goes, damned if you do and damned if you don't. What is the real question? Do they want you to relocate or just travel on business? If you simply answer 'no', you will not get the job offer, but if you answer 'yes', you could end up anywhere. So, play for time and ask, 'Are you talking about business travel or is the company relocating?' In the final analysis, your answer should be 'yes'. You don't have to accept the job, but without the offer you have no decision to make. Your single goal at an interview is to sell yourself and win a job offer. Never forget, only when you have the offer is it possible to make a decision about that particular job.

'What did you like/dislike about your last job?'

The interviewer is looking for incompatibilities. If a trial lawyer says he or she dislikes arguing a point with colleagues, such a statement will only weaken – if not immediately destroy – his or her candidacy.

Most interviews start with a preamble by the interviewer about the company. Pay attention: that information will help you answer this question. In fact, any statement the interviewer makes about the job or company can be used to your advantage.

So, in answer, you liked everything about your last job. You might even say your company taught you the importance of certain key areas of your business, achievement or professional profile. Criticizing a prior employer is a warning flag that you could be a problem employee. No one intentionally hires trouble and that's what's behind the question. Keep your answer short and positive. You are allowed only one negative about past employers and then only if your interviewer has a 'hot button' about his or her department or company; if so, you will have written it down on your notepad. For example, the only thing your past employer could not offer might be something like 'the ability to contribute more in different areas in the smaller environment you have here.' You might continue with, 'I really liked everything about the job. The reason I want to leave it is to find a position where I can make a greater contribution. You see, I work for a large company that encourages specialization of skills. The smaller environment you have here will, as I said, allow me to contribute far more in different areas.' Tell them what they want to hear – replay the hot button.

Of course, if you interview with a large company, turn it around. 'I work for a small company and don't get the time to specialize in one or two major areas.' Then replay the hot button.

'What is the least relevant job you have held?'

If your least relevant job is not on your CV, it shouldn't be mentioned. Some people skip over those six months between jobs when they worked as waiting staff just to pay the bills and would rather not talk about it, until they hear a question like this one. However, mention of a job that, according to all chronological records, you never had, will throw your integrity into question and your candidacy out the door.

Apart from that, no job in your profession has been a waste of time if it increases your knowledge about how the business works and makes money. Your answer will be along the lines, 'Every job I've held has given me new insights into my profession and the higher one climbs, the more important the understanding of the lower-level, more menial jobs. They all play a role in making the company profitable. Anyway, it's certainly easier to schedule and plan work when you have first-hand knowledge of what others will have to do to complete their tasks.'

'What have you learnt from jobs you have held?'

Tie your answer to your business and professional profile. The interviewer needs to understand that you seek and can accept constructive advice, and that your business decisions are based on the ultimate good of the company, not your personal whim or preference. 'More than anything, I have learnt that what is good for the company is good for me. So I listen very carefully to directions and always keep my boss informed of my actions.'

'How do you feel about your progress to date?'

This question is not geared solely to rating your progress; it also rates your self-esteem. Be positive, yet do not give the impression you have already done your best work. Make the interviewer believe you see each day as an opportunity to learn and contribute and that you see the environment at this company as conducive to your best efforts.

'Given the parameters of my job, my progress has been excellent. I know the work, and I am just reaching that point in my career when I can make significant contributions.'

'Have you done the best work you are capable of doing?'

Say 'yes' and the interviewer will think you're a has-been. As with all these questions, personalize your work history. For this particular question, include the essence of this reply: 'I'm proud of my professional achievements to date, especially [give an example]. However, I believe the best is yet to come. I am always motivated to give of my best and in this job there are always opportunities to contribute when you stay alert.'

'How long would you stay with the company?'

The interviewer might be thinking of offering you a job, so you must encourage him or her to sell you on the job. With a tricky question like this, end your answer with a question of your own that really puts the ball back in the interviewer's court. Your reply might be, 'I would really like to settle down with this company. I take direction well and love to learn. As long as I am growing professionally, there is no reason for me to make a move. How long do you think I would continue to be challenged here?'

'How long would it take you to make a contribution to our company?'

Again, be sure to qualify the question – in what area does the interviewer need rapid contributions? You are best advised to answer this with a question, such as 'That is an excellent question. To help me answer, what do you anticipate my responsibilities will be for the first six or seven months?' or 'What are your greatest areas of need right now?' You give yourself time to think while the interviewer concentrates on images of you working for the company. When your time comes to answer, start with, 'It would take me a few weeks to settle down and learn the ropes. I'd be earning my keep very quickly, but making a real contribution... [give a hesitant pause]. Do you have a special project in mind you would want me to get involved with?' That response could lead directly to a job offer, but, if not, you already have the interviewer thinking of you as an employee.

'What would you like to be doing five years from now?'

The safest answer contains a desire to be regarded as a true professional and team player. As far as promotion goes, that depends on finding a manager with whom you can grow. Of course, you will ask what opportunities exist within the company before being any more specific: 'From my research and what you have told me about growth here, it seems that operations is where the heavy emphasis is going to be. It seems that's where you need the effort and where I could contribute towards the company's goals.' Alternatively, you could say, 'I have always felt that first-hand knowledge and experience open up opportunities that one might never have considered, so while, at this point in time, I plan to be a part of [for example] operations, it is reasonable to expect that other exciting opportunities will crop up.'

'What are your qualifications?'

Be sure you don't answer the wrong question. Does the interviewer want job-related or academic job qualifications? Ask. If the question concerns job-related information, you need to know what problems must be tackled first before you can answer adequately. If you can determine this, you will also know what is causing the manager most concern. Then, if you can show yourself as someone who can contribute to the solution of those projects or problems, you have taken a dramatic step ahead in the race for the job offer. Ask for clarification, then give your relevant skills and achievements. You might say, 'I can give you a general answer, but I feel my answer might be more valuable if you could tell me about specific work assignments in the early months.' Another good answer is, 'If the major task right now is to automate the filing system, I should tell you that, in my last job, I was responsible for creating a computerized database for a previously uncomputerized firm.'

'What are your biggest accomplishments?'

Keep your answers job-related – from earlier exercises, a number of achievements should spring to mind. If you exaggerate contributions to major projects, you will be accused of suffering from 'coffee machine syndrome', the affliction of a junior clerk who claimed success for an Apollo space mission based on his relationships with certain scientists, established at the coffee machine. You might begin your reply with, 'Although I feel my biggest achievements are still ahead of me, I am proud of my involvement in... I made my contribution as part of that team and learnt a lot in the process. We did it with hard work, concentration and an eye for the bottom line.'

'How do you organize and plan for major projects?'

Effective planning requires both forward thinking – 'Who and what am I going to need to get this job done?' – and backwards thinking – 'If this job must be completed by the 20th, what steps must be made, and at what time, to meet that deadline?' Effective planning also includes contingencies and budgets for time and cost overruns. Show that you cover all the bases.

'How many hours a week do you find it necessary to work to get your job done?'

There is no absolutely correct answer here, so, again, you have to cover all the bases. Some managers pride themselves on working nights and weekends or never taking their full holiday quota. Others pride themselves on their excellent planning and time management that allows them never to work more than the usual office hours. You must pick the best of both worlds: 'I try to plan my time effectively and usually can. Our business always has its rushes, though, so I put in whatever effort it takes to get the job finished.' It is rare that the interviewer will then come back and ask for a specific number of hours. If that does happen, turn the question around: 'It depends on the projects. What is typical in your department?' The answer will give you the right cue, of course.

'Tell me how you've moved up through the organization'

A fast-track question, the answer to which tells a lot about your personality, goals, past, future and whether or not you still have any steam left in you. The answer might be long, but try to avoid rambling. Include a fair sprinkling of your key professional behaviours in your stories (because this is the perfect time to do it). As well as listing the promotions, you will want to demonstrate that they came as a result of dedicated, long-term effort, substantial contributions and flashes of genius.

'Can you work under pressure?'

You might be tempted to give a simple 'yes' or 'no' answer, but don't. It reveals nothing and you lose the opportunity to sell your skills and professional behaviours. Actually, this common question often comes from an unskilled interviewer, because it is closed. (How to handle different types of interviewers is covered in Chapter 13, 'The other side of the desk'.) As such, the question does not give you the chance to elaborate. Whenever you are asked a closed question, mentally add, 'Please give me a brief yet comprehensive answer.' Do that and you will give the information requested and seize an opportunity to sell yourself. For example, you could say, 'Yes, I usually find it stimulating. However, I believe in planning and proper management of my time to reduce panic around deadlines within my area of responsibility.'

'What is your greatest strength?'

This is a chance to make some serious points about your application; you want to make points in two distinct categories.

First, you should talk about your job-specific skills. For example, a lawyer might talk about his or her research skills, if possible giving an answer that shows that skill being put to good use in the job. Second, you will want to talk about some aspect of your professional behaviour. For example, that same lawyer might talk about the roles that planning, organization and time management play when carrying a heavy caseload.

The best answer is a balance between the job-specific skills and the behavioural skills of any serious professional.

'What are your outstanding qualities?'

This is essentially the same as an interviewer asking you what your greatest strengths are. While in the former question you might choose to pay attention to job-specific skills, this question asks you to talk about your professional behaviours. Now, while you are fortunate enough to have a list of the business world's most desirable professional behaviours in the previous chapter, try to do more than just list them. In fact, rather than offering a long 'shopping list', you might consider picking out just two or three and giving an illustration of each.

'What interests you most about this job?'

Be straightforward, unless you haven't been given adequate information to determine an answer, in which case you should ask a question of your own to clarify. Perhaps you could say, 'Before answering, could I ask you to tell me a little more about the role this job plays in relation to departmental goals?' or 'Where is the biggest vacuum in your department at the moment?' or 'Could you describe a typical day for me?' The additional information you gather with these questions provides the appropriate slant to your answer – that is, what is of greatest benefit to the department and the company. Career-wise, that obviously has the greatest benefit to you, too. Your answer then displays the professional behaviours that support the existing need. Your answer in part might include, 'I'm looking for a challenge and an opportunity to make a contribution, so if you feel the biggest challenge in the department is X, I'm the one for the job.' Then, include the behaviour and experience that support your statements. Perhaps, 'I like a challenge, my background demonstrates excellent problem-solving abilities [give some examples] and I always see a project through to the finish.'

'What are you looking for in your next job?'

You want a company where your personal and professional profile will allow you to contribute to the business. Avoid saying what you want the company to give you; you must say what you want in terms of what you can give to your employer. The key word in the following example is 'contribution': 'My experience at XYZ Limited has shown me I have a talent for motivating people. That is demonstrated by my team's absenteeism rate dropping by 20 per cent, turnover steadying at 10 per cent and production increasing by 12 per cent. I am looking for an opportunity to continue that kind of contribution and a company and supervisor who will help me develop in a professional manner.'

'Why should I give you the job?'

Your answer will be short and to the point. It will highlight areas from your background that relate to current needs and problems. Recap the interviewer's description of the job, meeting it point by point with your skills. Finish your answer with 'I have the qualifications you need [itemize them], I'm a team player, I take direction and I have the desire to make a thorough success of it.'

'What can you do for us that someone else cannot?'

This question should come only after a full explanation of the job has been given. If not, qualify the question with, 'What voids are you trying to fill when you appoint someone to this position?' Then recap the interviewer's job description, followed with, 'I can bring to this job a determination to see projects through to a proper conclusion. I listen and take direction well. I am analytical and don't jump to conclusions. Finally, I understand we are in business to make a profit, so I keep an eye on costs and returns.' End with, 'How do these qualifications fit your needs?' or 'What else are you looking for?'

You finish with a question that asks for feedback or a powerful answer. If you haven't covered the interviewer's hot buttons, he or she will cover them now and you can respond accordingly.

'Describe a difficult problem you've had to deal with'

This is a favourite tough question. It is not so much the difficult problem that's important, it's the approach you take to solving problems in general. It is designed to probe your professional skills – specifically, your analytical skills.

'Well, I always follow a five-step format with a difficult problem. One, I stand back and examine the problem. Two, I recognize the problem as the symptom of other, perhaps hidden, factors. Three, I make a list of possible solutions to the problem. Four, I weigh both the consequences and costs of each solution and determine the best solution. Five, I go to my boss, outline the problem, make my recommendation and ask for my superior's advice and approval.'

Then give an example of a problem and your solution. Here is a thorough example: 'When I joined my present company, I filled the shoes of a manager who had been fired. Staff turnover was very high. My job was to reduce turnover and increase performance. Sales of our new copier had slumped for the fourth quarter in a row, partly due to ineffective customer service. The new employer was very concerned and he even gave me permission to sack any or all of the sales team. The cause of the problem? The customer service team had never had any training. All my people needed was some intensive training. My boss gave me permission to speak to a training specialist. With what I learnt from her, I turned the department around. Sales continued to slump in my first quarter. Then they skyrocketed. Management was pleased with the sales and felt my job in customer service had played a real part in the turnaround. My boss was pleased because the solution was effective and cheap. I only had to replace two customer service people.'

'What would your references say?'

You have nothing to lose by being positive. If you demonstrate how well you and your boss got along, the interviewer does not have to ask, 'What do you dislike about your current manager?'

It is a good idea to ask past employers to give you a letter of recommendation. That way, you know what is being said. It reduces the chances of the interviewer checking up on you and, if you are asked this question, you can pull out a sheaf of rousing accolades and hand them over. If you are unable to obtain references in advance of a job offer, and the interviewer wishes to see them, he or she should ask your permission before writing to your referees. All that said, never offer references or written recommendations unless they are requested.

'Can we check your references?'

This question is frequently asked as a stress question to catch the too smooth candidate off-guard. It is also one that occasionally is asked in the general course of events. Comparatively few managers or companies ever check references – this astounds me, yet it's a fact of life. On the other hand, the higher up the corporate ladder you go, the more likely it is that your references will be checked. There is only one answer to this question if you ever expect to get an offer: 'Yes'.

Your answer may include, 'Yes, of course you can check my references. However, at present, I would like to keep matters confidential, until we have established a serious mutual interest [an offer]. At such time I will be pleased to furnish you with whatever references you need from prior employers. I would expect you to wait to check my current employer's references until you have extended an offer in writing, I have accepted, we have agreed on a start date and I have had the opportunity to resign in a professional manner.' You are under no obligation to give references from a current employer until you have a written offer in hand. You are also well within your rights to request that reference checks of current employers wait until you have started your new job.

Most people only ever talk to their references immediately before they are to be checked, if at all. I suggest you contact the people who you think will speak well of you at the beginning of your job search (or as soon as you read this). They might also be able to come up with job leads and introductions.

'What type of decisions did you make on your last job?'

If you have taken the time to deconstruct the target job in the way we discussed in Chapter 10, on the secrets of the job offer, you will have a clear understanding of the job's expected deliverables and the decision-making events that typically accompany that job. You might expect the interviewer to follow with a question about 'how you reached those decisions', so this will often be a two-part question:

I the level and application of your decision making;

I the analytical processes applied.

This is an opportunity, however humble your position, to demonstrate your professional behaviours.

For example: 'Being in charge of the postroom, my job is to make sure people get information in a timely manner. The job is well defined, and my decisions aren't that difficult. I noticed a year or two ago that when I took internal post around at 10am, everything stopped for 20 minutes. I had an idea and gave it to my boss. She got it cleared by the MD, and ever since, we take any post around just before lunch. Mr Gray, the MD, told me my idea improved productivity, saved time, and that he wished everyone was as conscientious.'

'What was the last book you read/film you saw? How did it affect you?'

It doesn't really matter what you say about the latest book or film, just as long as you have read or seen it. Don't be like the interviewee who said the name of the first book that came to mind – *In Search of Excellence* – only to be caught by the follow-up question, 'To what extent do you agree with Peters' simultaneous loose/tight pronouncements?' Also, by naming such a well-known book, you have managed only to say that you are like millions of others, which doesn't make you stand out in the crowd. Better that you should name something less faddish – that helps to avoid nasty follow-up questions. You needn't mention the most *recent* book or film you've seen either. Your answer must simply make a statement about you as a potential employee. Come up with a response that will set you apart and demonstrate your obvious superiority. Ideally you want to mention a work that in some way has helped you improve yourself – anything that has honed any of the admired professional behaviours will do.

'How do you handle tension?'

This question is different from 'Can you handle pressure?' It asks _how_ you handle it. You could reply, 'Tension is caused when you let things pile up. It is usually caused by letting other areas of responsibility slip by for an extended period. For instance, if you have a difficult presentation coming up, you may procrastinate in your preparations for it. I've seen lots of people do things like that – a task seems so overwhelming they don't know where to begin. I find that if you break those overwhelming tasks into little pieces, they aren't so overwhelming any more. So I suppose I don't so much handle tension as handle the causes of it, by not letting things slip in areas that can give rise to it.'

'How long have you been looking for another position?'

If you are employed, your answer isn't that important – a short or long time is irrelevant to you in any follow-up probes because you are just looking for the right job, with the right people and company that offers you the right opportunities.

If, on the other hand, you are unemployed at the time, how you answer becomes more important. If you say, 'Well, I've been looking for two years now', this isn't going to score you any points. The interviewer thinks, 'Two years? No one else wanted him in that time, so I certainly don't.' So, if you must talk of months or more, be careful to add something like, 'Well, I've been looking for about a year now. I've had a number of offers in that time, but I have determined that, as I spend most of my waking hours at work, the job I take and the people I work with have got to be people with values I can identify with.'

'Have you ever been fired?'

Say 'no' if you can; if not, act on the advice given regarding the next question. Many people confuse being made redundant, being downsized, having their jobs automated out of existence or exported overseas with getting fired. So if you were laid off as part of general work force reduction, be straightforward, short, and then shut up. Do not over-talk; it makes you sound guilty.

'Why were you fired?'

If you have been terminated with cause this is a very difficult question to answer. Like it or not, termination with cause is usually justified because the most loathed responsibility of any manager is to take away someone's livelihood. Virtually no one fires an employee just for the sake of it.

Looking at that painful event objectively, you will probably find the cause of your dismissal rooted in the absence of one or more of the professional behaviours. Having been fired also creates instant doubt in the mind of the interviewer and greatly increases the chances of your references being checked. So, if you have been fired, the first thing to do is bite the bullet and call the person who fired you, find out why it happened, if you don't know already, and learn what he or she would say about you today.

Your aim is to clear the air, so, whatever you do, don't be antagonistic. Reintroduce yourself, explain that you are looking (or, if you have been unemployed for a while, say you are 'still looking') for a new job. Say that you appreciate that the manager had to do what he or she did and that you learnt from the experience. Then, ask, 'If you were asked as part of a pre- or post-employment references check, how would you describe my leaving the company? Would you say that I was fired or that I simply resigned? You see, every time I tell someone about my termination, whoosh, there goes another chance of getting another job!' Most managers will plump for the latter option, describing your departure as a resignation. After all, even testy managers tend to be humane after the fact and such a response saves them potential headaches and even lawsuits.

Whatever you do, don't advertise the fact you were fired. If you are asked, be honest, but make sure you have packaged the reason in the best light possible. Perhaps, 'I'm sorry to say, but I deserved it. I was having some personal problems at the time and I let them affect my work. I was late to work and lost my motivation. My supervisor (who, by the way, I still speak to) had directions to trim the workforce anyway and, as I was hired only a couple of years previously, I was one of the first to be let go.'

If you can find out the staff turnover figures, voluntary or otherwise, you might add, 'Fifteen other people have left so far this year.' A combination answer of this nature minimizes the stigma. You have even managed to demonstrate that you take responsibility for your actions, which shows your analytical and listening skills. If one of your past managers will speak well of you, there is nothing to lose and everything to gain by finishing with, 'Jill Johnson, at the company, would be a good person to check for a reference on what I have told you.'

I would never advise you to be anything but honest in your answers to any interview question. If, however, you have been terminated by a manager who is still vindictive, take heart: only about 10 per cent of all successful job candidates ever find that their references have been checked.

'Have you ever been asked to resign?'

When someone is asked to resign, it is a gesture on the part of the employer: 'You can quit or we will sack you, so which do you want it to be?' Because you were given the option, though, that employer cannot later say, 'I had to ask him to resign' – that is tantamount to firing and could lead to legal problems. In the final analysis, it is safe to answer 'no'.

'Were you ever dismissed from your job for a reason that seemed unjustified?'

Another sneaky way of asking, 'Were you ever fired?' The sympathetic phrasing is geared to getting you to reveal all the sordid details. The cold hard facts are that hardly anyone is ever fired without cause and you're kidding yourself if you think otherwise. With that in mind, you can quite honestly say 'no' and move on to the next topic.

'In your last job, what were some of the things you spent most of your time on and why?'

Employees come in two categories: goal-oriented (those who want to get the job done) and task-oriented (those who believe in 'busy' work). You must demonstrate good time management and that you are, therefore, goal-oriented, for that is what this question probes for.

You might reply, 'I work on the telephone, like a lot of businesspeople; meetings also take up a great deal of time. What is more important to me is effective time management. I find more gets achieved in a shorter time if a meeting is scheduled, say, immediately before lunch or at the close of business. I try to block my time in the morning. At 4 pm, I review what I've achieved, what went right or wrong and plan adjustments and my main thrust of business for tomorrow.'

'In what ways has your job prepared you to take on greater responsibility?'

This is one of the most important questions you will have to answer. Only the context of the question can tell you if it is focused on your ability to do well in the new, more responsible, job, or whether it is to determine your potential for future growth; this determination will affect the particular slant of your answer. Again, your careful job description deconstruction will help you determine the kinds of specific information the employer seeks. Regardless of context and other considerations, the interviewer is always hoping to see you take personal responsibility for your professional development, so your answer in part needs to demonstrate this. This simple example shows self-awareness, growth, planning and listening skills and ethical behaviour. Parts of it, perhaps the then-and-now aspect of the answer, can be adapted to your personal experience.

'When I started my job, my boss would brief me morning and evening. I made some mistakes, learned a lot, and got the work in on time. As time went by I took on greater responsibilities *[list some of them]*. Now, I meet with her every Friday to discuss the week and proposed directional changes, so that she can keep management informed. I think this demonstrates not only my growth but also the confidence management has in my judgment and ability to perform consistently above standard.' The exact nature of your answer should reflect your ability to meet the deliverables of the target job.

'In what ways has your job changed since you originally joined the company?'

You can use the same answer here as for the previous question.

'What skills are most critical to this job?'

The question examines your practical understanding of the day-to-day responsibilities of the job, and the skills required to execute them. If your answer fails to demonstrate a clear grasp, you can kiss a job offer goodbye. Even if you know your job well, take a few minutes to deconstruct it into component parts and identify the skill sets necessary to execute each part of the job. As you identify each skill, try to come up with an illustration of your application of that skill.

Apart from skills unique to your job, your answer should also integrate one or more of the professional behaviours I talk about throughout this book. You might reply, 'With high-end marketing of product launches into new territories I think there are two overwhelming skills needed. First, there are strategic marketing skills: the identifying, prioritizing and penetration of the new market – something I have done in the Bristol area in both my prior jobs. Second, I'd have to say negotiating skills. And here I'm not just talking about negotiation tactics, along with written and verbal communication skills – all of which are ongoing areas of study for me. But I'm also talking about skills in regulatory analysis, which have given me an edge in countless deals.'

If, however, you are trying to break into a new profession, you need to do a little research to see if that profession is suitable for you; in the process you will learn to answer the question in a convincing manner. Talk to people already doing the job, through your personal contacts and through membership in a professional association, and read whatever you can about it – on the internet and at your library.

Don't shy away from making this effort; the rewards can include job offers and better understanding of what it takes to be successful in your chosen profession.

'What skills would you like to develop in this job?'

Behind the question is an interest in your motivation to do the work on offer. The interviewer is looking for a fit between your dreams and his or her reality. All worthwhile jobs require hard work and an attitude of learning – an awareness sometimes noticeable by its absence.

It is helpful to gather as much information about the job, the department and their entwined futures as you can. The more information you have, the better you will be able to customize your answers to an employer's specific needs.

As most interviews start with a quick overview of the job and the department, try to turn this overview into an information-gathering conversation, by showing an interest in the role of the department within the company, and how this might affect the responsibilities of department members. These insights will help ensure the compatibility of your answers with the job's future. If this is not possible, fall back on the further development of core skills and professional behaviours you know are pivotal to your profession. It's important to stress the future here; you don't want to give the impression of inadequacy in the basics.

'Why do you want to work in this industry?' *or* 'Why do you think you will shine in this profession?'

These are both questions most likely to be asked either when you are at the entry level or perhaps as an experienced professional in the midst of a strategic career shift. Your answer should speak both to your pragmatism and to your motivation. An answer along the following lines will work in both instances: 'At this point in my career I am looking at the industry because I believe it offers stability and professional growth potential over the years [explain why]. Also, I'll be using skills [itemize strong skill sets that are relevant to the job] that are areas of personal strength, from which I derive great personal satisfaction. So I think that my carefully considered choice of profession, the skills I can bring to the table, and my interest in _____ means I feel confident in being able to make a contribution.'

'How resourceful are you?'

This is a question about creativity and initiative; it is also asking you to talk about how things went wrong and how you, like Mighty Mouse, came to save the day. The problem you wrestled with doesn't need to be of planetary proportions to show you in a positive light, because the question is really examining your professional behaviour. The interviewer wants to know about how you handled a problem, not the problem itself. Talk about your analytical skills, your determination in the face of daunting odds and your ability to stay with a difficult task until completion, and you'll be thinking along the right lines.

Your answer should follow a simple sequence: the problem, your approach and solution, the result, and its value to the company... the old PSRV we talked about before.

As always, having an illustrative story ready enables the interviewer to 'watch' you being resourceful. Also, you never know when an interviewer will ask, 'Can you give me an example of that?' as a follow-up question.

'How does this job compare with others you have applied for?'

This is a variation on more direct questions, such as 'How many other jobs have you applied for?' and 'Who else have you applied to?', but it is a slightly more intelligent question and therefore more dangerous. It asks you to compare. Answer the question and sidestep at the same time: 'No two jobs are the same and this one is certainly unlike any other I have applied for.'

If you can highlight some of the interviewer's stated pluses about the job so much the better. Remember that first and foremost you are there to get a job offer. You have nothing to evaluate until then.

If you are pressed further, say, 'Well, to give you a more detailed answer, I would need to ask you a number of questions about the job and the company.' Ask about major projects, who succeeds and who fails and why, how the company encourages professional growth and so on; for more on good questions to ask you should read the negotiation chapter.

'What makes this job different from your current/last one?'

Such questions might address responsibilities, the deliverables of the job, extent of authority, perceived role of the job within the company structure; see the chapter on negotiation for many good questions to ask.

If you don't have enough information to answer the question, say so, and ask some of your own. Behind the question is the interviewer's desire to uncover experience you are lacking – your answer could be used as evidence against you. Focus on the positive: 'From what I know of the job, I seem to have all the experience required to make a thorough success of it (itemize here as it's a good opportunity to re-enforce the match). I would say that the major differences seem to be…' and here you play back the positive attributes of the department and company as the interviewer gave them to you, either in the course of the interview or in answer to your specific questions.

'Do you have any questions?'

A good question. Almost always, this is a sign that the interview is drawing to a close and that you have one more chance to make an impression. Remember the adage: people respect what you inspect, not what you expect. Most people ask questions about money and benefits. These are nice-to-know questions, which the interviewer is not really interested in discussing at this point. As your goal at the interview is to bring the interviewer to the point of offering you the job, these questions are really irrelevant at this point. Better that you concentrate on gathering information that will help you further your candidacy.

Create questions from any of the following:

▌ Find out why the job is open, who had it last and what happened to him or her. Was he or she promoted or fired? How many people have held this position in the last couple of years? What happened to them subsequently?

▌ Why did the interviewer join the company? How long has he or she been there? What is it about the company that keeps him or her there?

▌ To whom would you report? Will you get the opportunity to meet that person?

▌ Where is the job located? What are the travel requirements, if any?

▌ What type of training is required and how long is it? What type of training is available?

▌ What would your first assignment be?

▌ What are the realistic chances for growth in the job? Where are the opportunities for greatest growth within the company?

▌ What are the skills and attributes most needed to get ahead in the company?

▌ Who will be the company's major competitor over the next few years? How does the interviewer feel the company stacks up against them?

▌ What has been the growth pattern of the company over the last five years? Is it profitable? How profitable?

▌ If there is a written job description, could you see it?

▌ How regularly do performance evaluations occur? What model do they follow?

Skills

If the job calls for you to be able to type 75 words a minute, then you may be given a typing test. If you are a programmer, you may be asked to take an objective test of programming skills or asked to debug a program. There are tests to measure every possible skill – filing, bookkeeping, mechanical comprehension, specific computer programs, mathematical ability and so on. Some of them are typical paper and pencil written tests. Newer tests present the information using a software program. Typing tests, for instance, have largely been replaced by keyboarding tests; you are still typing but there's no paper or correction fluid involved.

It's hard to argue against some of these tests. After all, if the job calls for you to type letters and reports all day, the boss wants to employ the best typist who applies. If you're supposed to use particular software on the PC all day, the employer will look for the person with the best knowledge of that program. As long as the employer is measuring an important skill, testing skills makes sense.

12 'What kind of person are you really, Mr Jones?'

Learn the techniques an interviewer uses to find out if you will fit into the company and the department and, most important, whether or not you are a good person to work with.

Will you reduce your new employer's life expectancy? The interviewer wants to know! If you are offered the job and accept, you will be working together up to 50 weeks of the year. Every employer wants to know whether or not you will fit in with the rest of the staff, if you are a team player and, most of all, are you manageable?

There are several questions the interviewer might use to probe this area. They will mainly be geared to your behaviour and attitudes in the past. Remember, it is universally believed that your past actions predict your future behaviour.

'How do you take direction?'

The interviewer wants to know if you are open-minded and can be a team player. Can you follow directions or are you a difficult, high-maintenance employee? It is hoped that you are a low-maintenance professional who is motivated to ask clarifying questions about a project before beginning and then gets on with the job at hand, coming back to initiate requests for direction as circumstances dictate.

This particular question can also be defined as 'How do you accept criticism?' Your answer should cover both points: 'I take direction well and recognize that it can come in two varieties, depending on the circumstances. There is carefully explained direction, when my boss has time to lay things out for me in detail; then there are those times when, as a result of deadlines and other pressures, the direction might be brief and to the point. While I have seen some people get upset with that, personally I've always understood that there are probably other considerations I am not aware of. As such, I take the direction and get on with the job without taking offence, so my boss can get on with his or her job. It's the only way.'

'Would you like to have your boss's job?'

It is a rare boss who wants his or her livelihood taken away. On my own very first job interview, my future boss said, 'Mr Yate, it has been a pleasure to meet you. However, until you walked in my door, I wasn't out on the street looking for a new job.'

The interviewer wants to know if you are the type of person who will be confrontational, challenging, undermining or too ambitious or arrogant. He or she also seeks to determine how goal-oriented and motivated you are in your work life, so you may also want to comment on your sense of direction. However, remember that, while ambition is admired, it is admired most by the ambitious. Be cautiously optimistic, saying perhaps, 'Well, if my boss were promoted over the coming years, I would hope to have made a consistent enough contribution to warrant his recommendation. It is not that I am looking to take anyone's job; rather, I am looking for a manager who will help me develop my capabilities and grow with him.'

'What do you think of your current/last boss?'

Short, sweet and shut up. People who complain about their employers are recognized to be the same people who cause the most disruption in a department. This question means the interviewer has no desire to take on trouble. 'I liked her as a person, respected her professionally and appreciated her guidance.' This question is often followed by one that tries to validate your answer.

'Describe a situation where your work or an idea was criticized'

A doubly dangerous question. You are being asked to say how you handle criticism *and* detail your faults. If you are asked this question, describe a poor *idea* that was criticized, not poor work. Poor work can cost money and is a warning sign, obviously, to the interviewer.

One of the wonderful things about a new job is that you can leave the past entirely behind, so it does not matter how you handled criticism in the past. What does matter is how the interviewer would like you to handle criticism, if and when it becomes his or her unpleasant duty to dish it out – that's what the question is really about. So, relate one of those it-seemed-like-a-good-idea-at-the-time ideas; you will want to put this situation in the past, address how you handled the criticism, and just as importantly what you learned from the experience. You might say something that captures the essence of this example: '*[after describing the situation]*... I listened carefully and asked a couple of questions for clarification. Then I fed back what I heard to make sure the facts were straight. I asked for advice, we bounced some ideas around, then I came back later and represented the idea in a more viable format. My super-visor's input was invaluable.' The steps you go through to become maximally productive in these situations? Listen for understanding (not just waiting for your turn to speak), confirm the understanding, ask guidance for the desired solution, confirm the path/outcome expected, show a satisfactory resolution was ultimately reached, recognize the positive impact of the manager, then demonstrate what you learned and how your thinking/approach has changed as a result.

'Tell me about yourself'

This is invariably one of the first questions we all face. It helps the inter-viewer get a picture of you, and it helps you get used to talking; it is not an invitation to ramble. Your interviewers are meeting you to see if you are the right person to fill a position that has been carefully defined by a job description. You will study the job ad and the job description so that you have a very clear picture of the issues an employer is likely to want to discuss. Make sure you have a clear idea of what the interviewer wants to hear about: how your professional life experiences have qual-ified you to be at this meeting, throwing your hat in the ring for this particular job. This question will come up with some frequency at the beginning of interviews, so it is worthwhile spending a few minutes preparing a succinct statement that says who you are today and how you got here. For example:

'I'm the Area Director of Marketing for the X area. I oversee all aspects of marketing to acquire and retain basic, digital and online customers through tactics such as mass media and direct mail, as well as launch new products/services like VOD. I have a team of 46 employees, which also includes 26 door-to-door sales reps.

'I rose to this position year by year, climbing through the ranks based on my performance, achievement and every growing frame of reference for the business. As we get into the nuts and bolts I'm sure that you'll see that I have a real understanding of communications convergence and the role of a manager on the front lines of the consumer interface.'

This isn't a question that you can answer effectively without thought and preparation. Take some time in advance to think about your career to date and how it has prepared you for the position at hand.

'How do you get along with different kinds of people?'

You don't have to talk about respect for others, the need for diversity or how it took you 10 years to realize Jane was a different sex and Charlie a different colour, because that is not what this question is about. If you do respect others, then you will demonstrate this by explaining to your interviewer how you work in a team environment (because this is, in reality, a 'team player' question) and how you solicit and accept input, ideas, and viewpoints from a variety of sources. If you can give a quick, honest illustration of learning from a colleague who is obviously different from you in some way, it won't hurt.

'Rate yourself on a scale of 1 to10'

A stupid question. That aside, bear in mind that this is meant to plumb the depths of your self-esteem. If you answer 10, you run the risk of portraying yourself as insufferable. On the other hand, if you say less than 7, you might as well get up and leave. You are probably best claiming to be an 8 or 9, saying that you always give of your best, but that, in doing so, you always increase your skills and therefore always see room for improvement.

'What kinds of things do you worry about?'

Some questions, such as this one, can seem so off-the-wall that you might start treating the interviewer as a father confessor in no time flat. Your private phobias have nothing to do with your job and revealing them can get you labelled as unbalanced. It is best to confine your answer to the sensible worries of a conscientious professional: 'I worry about deadlines, staff turnover, lateness, back-up plans for when the computer crashes or that one of my auditors burns out or defects to the competition – just the normal stuff. It goes with the territory, so I don't let it get me down.' Whatever you identify as a worry might then be the subject of a follow-up question, so think through what you identify as worrying and in turn what you do to eradicate the worry.

'What is the most difficult situation you have faced?'

This question looks for information on two fronts: how you define and how you handled the situation. You must have a story ready for this one in which the situation was both tough and allows you to show yourself in a good light. Avoid talking about problems that have to do with colleagues. As we have talked about the importance of problem solving throughout the book and steps you can take to identify proper approaches and solutions, you should have numerous examples with which to illustrate your answer; just remember the sequence: *Problem, Solution, Result, Value.*

'What are some of the things that bother you?' 'What are your pet hates?' 'Tell me about the last time you felt anger on the job'

These questions are so similar that they can be treated in the same way. It is tremendously important that you show you can remain calm. Most of us have seen a colleague lose his or her cool on occasion – not a pretty sight and one that every sensible employer wants to avoid. This question comes up more and more often the higher up the corporate ladder you climb and the more frequent your contact with clients and the general public. To answer it, find something that angers conscientious workers: 'I enjoy my work and believe in giving value to my employer. Dealing with clock-watchers and the ones who regularly get sick on Mondays and Fridays really bothers me, but it's not something that gets me angry or anything like that.' An answer of this nature will help you much more than the kind given by one engineer who went on for some minutes about how he hated the small-mindedness of people who don't like pet rabbits in the office.

'What have you done that shows initiative?'

This question probes whether or not you are a doer, someone who will look for ways to increase sales and save time or money – the kind of person who gives a manager a pleasant surprise once in a while, who makes life easier for colleagues. Be sure, however, that your example of initiative does not show a disregard for company policies and procedures.

'My boss has to organize a lot of meetings. That means developing agendas, letting employees around the country know the dates well in advance, getting materials printed and so on. Most people in my position would wait for the work to be given to them. I don't. Every quarter, I sit down with my boss and find out the dates of all his meetings for the next six months. I immediately make the hotel and flight arrangements and then work backwards. I ask myself questions like, "If the agenda for the July meeting is to reach the field at least six weeks before the meeting, when must it be finished by?" Then I come up with a deadline. I do that for all the major activities for all the meetings. I put the deadlines in his diary and mine, only two weeks earlier in mine. That way I remind the boss that the deadline is getting close. My boss is the best-organized, most relaxed manager in the company. None of his colleagues can understand how he does it.'

'What are some of the things about which you and your supervisor disagreed?'

It is safest to state that you did not disagree.

'In what areas do you feel your supervisor could have done a better job?'

The same goes for this one. You could reply, though, 'I have always had the highest respect for my supervisor. I have always been so busy learning from Mr Jones that I don't think he could have done a better job. He has really brought me to the point where I am ready for greater challenges. That's why I'm here.'

'What are some of the things your supervisor did that you disliked?'

If you and the interviewer are both non-smokers, for example, and your boss isn't, use it. Apart from that, say something like, 'You know, I've never thought of our relationship in terms of like or dislike. I've always thought our role was to get along together and get the job done.'

'How well do you feel your boss rated your job performance?'

This is one very sound reason to ask for written evaluations of your work before leaving a company. Some performance review procedures include a written evaluation of your performance   perhaps your company employs it. If you work for a company that asks you to sign your formal review, you are quite entitled to request a copy of it. You should also ask for a letter of recommendation whenever you leave a job – you have nothing to lose. While I don't recommend thrusting recommendations under unwilling interviewers' noses (they smell a rat when written endorsements of any kind are offered unrequested), the time will come when you are asked and can produce them with a flourish. If you don't have written references, perhaps say, 'My supervisor always rated my job performance well. In fact, I was always rated as being capable of accepting further responsibilities. The problem was, there was nothing available in the company – that's why I'm here.'

If your research has been done properly, you can also quote verbal appraisals of your performance from prior jobs. 'In fact, my boss said only a month ago that I was the most valuable [for example] engineer in the work group, because…'

'How did your boss get the best out of you?'

This is a manageability question, geared to probing whether or not you are going to be a pain in the neck. Whatever you say, it is important for your ongoing happiness that you make it clear you don't appreciate being treated like a doormat. You can give a short, general answer: 'My last boss got superior effort and performance by treating me like a human being and giving me the same personal respect with which she liked to be treated herself.' This book is full of answers that get you out of tight corners and make you shine, but this is one instance in which you really should tell it like it is. You don't want to work for someone who is going to make life miserable for you.

'How interested are you in sports?'

A recently completed survey of middle and upper management personnel found that the executives who listed group sports/activities among their extracurricular activities made quite a bit more money per year more than their sedentary colleagues. Don't you just love football suddenly? The interviewer is looking for your involvement in groups, as a signal that you know how to get along with others and pull together as a team.

'I really enjoy most team sports. Don't get a lot of time to indulge myself, but I am a regular member of my company's five-a-side team.' Apart from team sports, endurance sports are seen as a sign of determination – swimming, running, and cycling are all OK. Games of skill (bridge, chess, and the like) demonstrate analytical skills.

'What personal characteristics are necessary for success in your field?'

You know the answer to this one: it's a brief recital of your key professional behaviours.

You might say, 'To be successful in my field? Drive, motivation, energy, confidence, determination, good communication and analytical skills. Combined, of course, with the ability to work with others.'

'Do you prefer working with others or alone?'

This question is usually used to determine whether or not you are a team player. Before answering, however, be sure you know whether or not the job requires you to work alone. Then answer appropriately. Perhaps, 'I'm quite happy working alone when necessary – I don't need much constant reassurance – but I prefer to work in a group as so much more is achieved when people pull together.'

'Explain your role as a group/team member'

You are being asked to describe yourself as either a team player or a loner. Think for a moment why the job exists in the first place: it is there to contribute to the bottom line in some way; as such it has a specific role in the department to help make that contribution and in turn your department has a similar, but larger, role in the company bottom line. Your ability to link your small role to that of the department's larger responsibilities to the overall success of the company, will demonstrate a developed professional awareness. Most departments depend on harmonious teamwork for their success, so describe yourself as a team player, by all means: 'I perform my job in a way that helps others to do theirs in an efficient fashion. Beyond the mechanics, we all have a responsibility to make the workplace a friendly and pleasant place to be. That means everyone working for the common good and making the necessary personal sacrifices towards that good.'

'How would you define a conducive work atmosphere?'

This is a tricky question, especially because you probably have no idea what kind of work atmosphere exists in that particular office. So, the longer your answer, the greater your chances of saying the wrong thing. Keep it short and sweet: 'One where the team has a genuine interest in its work and desire to turn out a good product/deliver a good service.'

'Do you make your opinions known when you disagree with the views of your supervisor?'

If you can, state that you come from an environment where input is encouraged when it helps the team's ability to get the job done efficiently. 'If opinions are sought in a meeting, I will give mine, although I am careful to be aware of others' feelings. I will never criticize a colleague or a superior in open forum; besides, it is quite possible to disagree without being disagreeable. However, my past manager made it clear that she valued my opinion by asking for it. So, after a while, if there was something I felt strongly about, I would make an appointment to sit down and discuss it one-to-one.' You might choose to end by turning the tables with a question of your own: 'Is this a position where we work as a team to solve problems and get the job done or one where we are meant to get on independently and speak when spoken to?'

'What would you say about a supervisor who was unfair or difficult to work with?'

For this job, you'll definitely want to meet your potential supervisor – just in case you have been earmarked for the company ogre without warning. The response, 'Do you have anyone in particular in mind?'

will probably get you off the hook. If you need to elaborate, try: 'I would make an appointment to see the supervisor and diplomatically explain that I felt uncomfortable in our relationship, that I felt he or she was not treating me as a professional colleague and therefore that I might not be performing up to standard in some way – that I wanted to right matters and ask for his or her input as to what I must do to create a professional relationship. I would enter into the discussion in the frame of mind that we were equally responsible for whatever communication problems existed and that this wasn't just the manager's problem.'

'Do you consider yourself a natural leader or a born follower?'

Ow! How you answer depends a lot on the job offer you are chasing. If you are a recent graduate, you are expected to have high aspirations, so go for it. If you are already on the corporate ladder with some practical experience in the school of hard knocks, you might want to be a little more cagey. Assuming you are up for (and want) a leadership position, you might try something like this: 'I would be reluctant to regard anyone as a natural leader. Hiring, motivating and disciplining other adults and, at the same time, moulding them into a cohesive team involves a number of delicately tuned skills that no honest people can say they were born with. Leadership requires, first of all, the desire; then it is a lifetime learning process. Anyone who reckons they have it all under control and have nothing more to learn isn't doing the employer any favours.'

Of course, a little humility is also in order because just about every leader in every company reports to someone and there is a good chance that you are talking to such a someone right now. So, you might consider including something like, 'No matter how well developed any individual's leadership qualities, an integral part of the skills of a leader is to take direction from his or her immediate boss and also to seek the input of the people being supervised. The wise leader will always follow good advice and sound business judgement wherever it comes from. I would say that, given the desire to be a leader, the true leader in the modern business world must embrace both.' How can anyone disagree with that kind of wisdom?

'Why do you feel you are a better [for example] assistant than some of your colleagues?'

If you speak disparagingly of your colleagues, you will not put yourself in the best light. That is what the question asks you to do, so it poses some difficulties. The trick is to answer the question but not accept the invitation to show yourself in anything other than a flattering light. 'I think that question is best answered by a manager. It is so difficult to be objective and I really don't like to slight my colleagues. I don't spend my time thinking about how superior I am because that would be detrimental to our working together as a team. I believe, however, some of the qualities that make me an outstanding assistant are...' and you can go on to illustrate job-related personal qualities that make you a beacon of productivity.

'You have a doctor's appointment arranged for noon. You've waited two weeks to get in. An urgent meeting is scheduled at the last moment, though. What do you do?'

'What a crazy question,' you mutter. It's not. It is even more than a question, it is what I call a question shell. The question within the shell – in this instance, 'Will you sacrifice the appointment or your job?' – can be changed at will. This is a situational interviewing technique that poses an on-the-job problem to see how the prospective employee will respond. A company I know of asks this question as part of its initial screening and if you give the wrong answer, you never even get a face-to-face interview. So, what is the right answer to this or any similar shell question?

Fortunately, once you understand the interviewing technique, it is quite easy to handle – all you have to do is turn the question around: 'If I were the manager who had to schedule a really important meeting at the last moment and someone on my staff chose to go to the doctor's instead, how would I feel?'

It is unlikely that you would be an understanding manager unless the visit were for a triple bypass. To answer, you start with an evaluation of the importance of the problem and the responsibility of everyone to make some sacrifices for the organization and finish with: 'The first thing I would do is reschedule the appointment and save the doctor's office inconvenience. Then I would immediately make sure I was properly prepared for the emergency meeting.'

'How do you manage to interview while still employed?'

As long as you don't say that you faked a dentist appointment to make the interview you should be all right. Beware of revealing anything that might make you appear at all underhanded. Best to make the answer short and sweet and let the interviewer move on to richer areas of enquiry. Just explain that you had some holiday time due or took a day off in lieu of overtime pay. 'I had some holiday time, so I went to my boss and explained I needed a couple of days off for some personal business and asked her what days would be most suitable. Although I plan to change jobs, I don't in any way want to hurt my current employer in the process by being absent during a busy time.'

'How have your career motivations changed over the years?'

This question only crops up when you have enough years under your belt to be regarded as a professional. The interviewer's agenda is to examine your emotional maturity and how realistic you are about future professional growth.

Your answer requires self-awareness. While the desire to rule the world can be seen as motivation in young professionals, it may not be interpreted so positively coming from a mature professional, where more realism is expected.

Your answer should reflect a growing maturity as well as a desire to do a good job for its own reward, and for making a contribution as part of the greater whole. Here's an example you can use as a starting point in crafting your own: 'In earlier years I was more ego-driven, with everything focused on becoming a star. Over the years I've come to realize that nothing happens with a team of one – we all have to function as part of a greater whole if we are to make meaningful contributions with our professional presence. Nowadays I take great pleasure in doing a job well, in seeing it come together as it should, and especially in seeing a group of professionals working together in their different roles to make it happen. Maybe the best way to say this is that I've discovered that the best way to stand out is to be a real team player, and not worry about standing out.'

'How do you regroup when things haven't gone as planned?'

We can all react to adversity in pretty much the same way we did as kids, but that isn't always productive. Here's a way you can deal with setbacks in your professional life and wow your interviewer in the process: 'I pause for breath and reflection for as long as the situation allows – this can be a couple of minutes or overnight. I do this to analyse what went wrong and why. I'm also careful to look for the things that went right too. I'll examine alternate approaches and, time allowing, I'll get together with a peer or my boss and review the whole situation and my proposed new approaches, to get a second opinion.'

You can go on to explain that the next time you face the same kind of problem you'll know what to avoid, what to do more of, and other new approaches as well.

You might consider finishing your answer with a statement about the beneficial effects of experiencing problems: 'Over the years I've learnt just as much from life's problems as from its successes.'

'What would your colleagues tell me about your attention to detail?'

Say that you are shoddy and never pay attention to the details, and you'll hear a *whoosh* as your job offer flies out the window.

Your answer obviously lies in the question. You pay attention to detail, your analytical approach to projects helps you identify all the component parts of a given job, and your time management and organizational skills make sure you get the job done in a timely manner without anything falling through the cracks.

'When do you expect a promotion?'

Tread warily – show that you believe in yourself and have both feet firmly planted on the ground. 'That depends on a few criteria. Of course, I cannot expect promotions without the performance that marks me as deserving of promotion. I also need to join a company that has the growth necessary to provide the opportunity. I hope that my manager believes in promoting from within and will help me grow so that I will have the skills necessary to be considered for promotion when the opportunity comes along.'

If you are the only one doing a particular job in the company or are in management, you need to build another factor into your answer. For example, 'As a manager, I realize that part of my job is to have done my succession planning and that I must have someone trained and ready to step into my shoes before I can expect to step up. That way I play my part in preserving the chain of command.' To avoid being caught off-guard with queries about your having achieved that in your present job, you can finish with 'Just as I have done in my present job, where I have a couple of people capable of taking over the reins when I leave.'

'Tell me a story'

Wow. What on earth does the interviewer mean by this question? You don't know until you get him or her to elaborate. Ask, 'What would you like me to tell you a story about?' To make any other response is to risk making a fool of yourself. Very often the question is asked to see how analytical you are. People who answer the question without qualifying show that they do not think things through carefully. The subsequent question will be about either your personal or professional life. If it is about your personal life, tell a story that shows you like people and are determined. Do not discuss your love life. If the subsequent question is about your professional life, tell a story that demonstrates your willingness and manageability.

'What have your other jobs taught you?'

Talk about the professional skills you have learnt and the professional behaviours you have polished. Many interviewees have had success finishing their answer with 'There are two general things I have learnt from past jobs. First, if you are confused, ask – it's better to ask a silly question than make a stupid mistake. Second, it's better to promise less and produce more than to make unrealistic forecasts.'

'Define cooperation'

This question asks you to explain how to function as a team player in the workplace. Your answer could be, 'Cooperation is a person's ability to sacrifice personal wishes and beliefs whenever necessary to assure that the department reaches its goals. It is also a person's desire to be part of a team and, by hard work and goodwill, make the department greater than the sum of its parts.'

'What difficulties do you have tolerating people with different backgrounds and interests from yours?'

Another 'team player' question with the awkward implication that you do have problems. Give the following answer: 'I don't have any.'

'In hindsight, what have you done that was a little harebrained?'

You are never harebrained in your business dealings and you haven't been harebrained in your personal life since you left school, right? The only safe examples to use are ones from your deep past that ultimately turned out well. One of the best to use, if it applies to you, is this one: 'Well, probably the time I bought my house. I had no idea what I was letting myself in for and, at the time, I really couldn't afford it. Still, I managed to make the payments, though I had to work like someone possessed. Yes, my first house – that was a real learning experience.' Not only can most people relate to this example, but it also gives you the opportunity to sell one or two of your very positive professional behaviours.

If you think the interview is only tough for the interviewee, it's time to take a look at things from the other side of the desk. Knowing what's going on can really help you shine.

13 *The other side of the desk*

Two types of interviewers can spell disaster for the unprepared: the highly skilled and the unconsciously incompetent. Find out how to recognize and respond to each one.

There are two terrible places to be during an interview – sitting in front of the desk wondering what on earth is going to happen next and sitting behind the desk asking the questions. The average interviewer dreads the meeting almost as much as the interviewee, yet for opposite reasons.

Many businesses frequently yield to the mistaken belief that any person, on being promoted to the ranks of management, becomes mystically endowed with all necessary managerial skills. That is a fallacy. Comparatively few management people have been taught to interview; most just bumble along and pick up a certain proficiency over a period of time.

There are two distinct types of interviewers who can spell disaster for you if you are unprepared. One is the highly skilled interviewer, who has been trained in systematic techniques for probing your past for all the facts and evaluating your potential. The other is the totally incompetent interviewer, who may even lack the ability to phrase a question adequately. Both are equally dangerous when it comes to winning a job offer.

The skilful interviewer

Skilled interviewers understand that a manager's first job is to get work done through others, so they recognize that making the right choice is a serious task.

They know exactly what they want to discover, having taken exhaustive steps to learn the strategies that will help them employ only the best for their company. They follow a set format for the interview process to ensure objectivity in selection and a set sequence of questions to ensure the facts are gathered. They will definitely test your mettle.

There are many ways for a manager to build and conduct a structured interview, but all have the same goals, which are to:

▌ ensure systematic coverage of your work history and applicable job-related skills;

▌ provide a technique for gathering all the relevant facts;

▌ provide a uniform strategy that objectively evaluates all job candidates;

▌ determine ability, willingness and manageability.

Someone using structured interview techniques will usually follow a standard format to help maintain objectivity. The interview will begin with small talk and a brief introduction to relax you. Following close on the heels of that chit-chat comes a statement geared to assure you that baring your faults is the best way to get the job. It's not, but neither is it necessary to lie. Your interviewer will then outline the steps in the interview. That will include you giving a chronological description of your work history, then the interviewer asking specific questions about your experience. Then, prior to the close of the interview, you will be given an opportunity to ask your own questions.

Sounds pretty simple, huh? Well, watch out! The skilled interviewer knows exactly what questions to ask, why they will be asked, in what order they will be asked and what the desired responses are. He or she will interview and evaluate every applicant for the job in exactly the same fashion. You are up against a pro.

Like the hunter who learns to think like his or her prey, you will find that the best way to win over the interviewer is to think like the interviewer in order to understand what he or she is likely to ask and why. In fact, take that idea a little further – you must win, but you don't want the other guys to realize you beat them at their own game. To do that, you must learn how the interviewer has prepared for you; and by going through the same process you will beat your competitors to the job offer.

The dangerous part of this type of structured interview is called 'skills evaluation'. The interviewer has analysed all the different skills it takes to do the job and all the professional behaviours that complement those skills. Armed with that data, he or she has developed a series of carefully sequenced questions to draw out your relative merits and weaknesses.

Graphically, it looks like this:

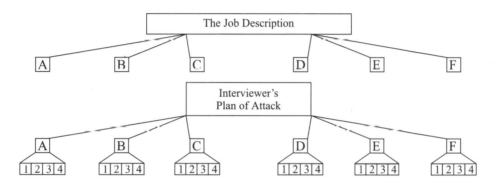

Letters A–F are the separate skills necessary to do the job; numbers 1–4 are questions asked to identify and verify each particular skill. This is where many of the tough questions will arise. The only way to prepare for them effectively is to take the interviewer's viewpoint and complete this exercise in its entirety. The effort requires a degree of objectivity, but will generate multiple job offers.

■ Look at the position you seek. What role does it play in helping the company achieve its corporate mission and make a profit?

■ What are the five most important duties of that job?

■ From a management viewpoint, what are the skills and attributes necessary to perform each of these tasks?

Write it all down. Now, put yourself in the interviewer's shoes. What topics would you examine to find out if a person can really do the job? If, for some reason, you get stuck in the process, just use your past experience. You have worked with good and bad people and their work habits and skills will lead you to develop both the potential questions and the correct answers.

Each job skill you identify is fertile ground for the interviewer's questions. Don't forget the intangible skills that are so important to many jobs, like self-confidence and creativity, because the interviewer won't. Develop a number of questions for each job skill you identify.

Again, looking back at colleagues (and still wearing the manager's hat), what are the personal characteristics that would make life more comfortable for you as a manager? These are also dimensions that are likely to be probed by the interviewer. Once you have identified the questions you would ask in the interviewer's position, the answers should come easily.

If you are entering the world of work for the first time, or making a substantial career shift, you might not have the knowledge to analyse the skills required. In this case go back to your networks and call people already in the profession to identify the skill sets and behaviours necessary to succeed in your new career.

That's the way managers are trained to develop structured interview questions – I just gave you the inside track. Complete the exercise by developing the answers you would like to hear as a manager. Take time to complete the exercise conscientiously, writing out both the questions and the appropriate answers.

These sharks have some juicy questions to probe your skills, attitude and personality. Would you like to hear some of them? Notice that these questions tend to lay out a problem for you to solve, but in no way lead you towards the answer. They are often two- and three-part questions as well. The additional question that can be tagged on to them all is, 'What did you learn from this experience?' Assume it is included whenever you get one of these questions – you'll be able to sell different aspects of your success profile.

'You have been given a project that requires you to interact with different levels within the company. How do you do this? What levels are you most comfortable with?'

This is a two-part question that probes communication and self-confidence skills. The first part asks how you interact with superiors and motivate those working with and for you on the project. The second part of the question is asking, 'Who do you regard as your peer group – help me categorize you.' To cover those bases, you will want to include the essence of this: 'There are essentially two types of people I would interact with on a project of this nature. First, there are those I report to, who bear the ultimate responsibility for its success. With them, I determine deadlines and how they will evaluate the success of the project. I outline my approach, breaking the project down into component parts, getting approval on both the approach and the costs. I would keep my supervisors up to date on a regular basis and seek input whenever needed. My supervisors would expect three things from me: the facts, an analysis of potential problems and that I will not be intimidated, as that would jeopardize the project's success. I would comfortably satisfy those expectations.

'The other people to interact with on a project like this are those who work with and for me. With those people, I would outline the project and explain how a successful outcome would benefit the company. I would assign the component parts to those best suited to each and arrange follow-up times to assure completion by deadline. My role here would be to facilitate, motivate and bring the different personalities together to form a team.

'As for comfort level, I find this type of approach enables me to interact comfortably with all levels and types of people.'

'Tell me about an event that really challenged you. How did you meet the challenge? In what way was your approach different from others'?'

This is a straightforward two-part question. The first probes your problem-solving abilities. The second asks you to set yourself apart from the herd. First of all, outline the problem. The blacker you make the situation, the better. Having done that, go ahead and explain your solution, its value to your employer and how it was different from other approaches.

'My company has offices all around the country; I am responsible for 70 of them. My job is to visit each office on a regular basis and build market penetration strategies with management and train and motivate the sales and customer service force. When the recession hit, the need to service those offices was more important than ever, yet the travelling costs were getting prohibitive.

'Morale was an especially important factor – you can't let outlying offices feel defeated. I reapportioned my budget and did the following: I dramatically increased telephone contact with the offices. I instituted a monthly sales technique letter – how to prospect for new clients, negotiate difficult sales and so forth. I bought and rented sales training and motivational tapes and sent them to my managers with instructions on how to use them in a sales meeting. I stopped visiting all the offices. Instead, I scheduled weekend training meetings in central locations throughout my area: one day of sales training and one day of management training, concentrating on how to run sales meetings, early termination of low producers and so on.

'While my colleagues complained about the drop in sales, mine increased, albeit by a modest 6 per cent. After two quarters, my approach was officially adopted by the company.'

'Give me an example of a method of working you have used. How did you feel about it?'

You have a choice of giving an example of either good or bad work habits. Give a good example, one that demonstrates your understanding of corporate goals, your organizational skills, analytical ability or time management skills.

You could say, 'I believe in giving an honest day's work for a day's pay. That requires organization and time management. I do my paperwork at the end of each day, when I review the day's achievements. With this done, I plan for tomorrow. When I come to work in the morning, I'm ready to get going without wasting time. I try to schedule meetings right before lunch – people get to the point more quickly if it's on their time. I feel that is an efficient and organized method of working.'

'When you joined your last company and met the group for the first time, how did you feel? How did you get on with them?'

Your answer should include: 'I naturally felt a little nervous, but I was excited about the new job. I shared that excitement with my new friends and told them that I was enthusiastic about learning new skills from them. I was open and friendly and, when given the opportunity to help someone myself, I jumped at it.'

'In your last job, how did you plan for the interview?'

That's an easy one. Just give a description of how the skilled interviewer prepares.

'How have you benefited from your disappointments?'

Disappointments are different from failures. It is an intelligent – probably trained – interviewer who asks this one. It is also an opportunity for the astute interviewee to shine. The question itself is very positive – it asks you to show how you benefited. Note also that it doesn't ask you to give details of specific disappointments, so you don't have to open your mouth and insert your foot. Instead, be general. Edison once explained his success as an inventor by claiming that he knew more ways not to do something than anyone else living; you can do worse than quote him. In any event, sum up your answer with, 'I treat disappointments as a learning experience – I look at what happened, why it happened and how I would do things differently in each stage should the same set of circumstances appear again. That way, I put disappointment behind me and am ready with renewed vigour and understanding to face the new day's problems.'

Incidentally, a person with strong religious beliefs may be tempted to answer a question like this in terms of religious values. If you benefit from disappointments in a spiritual way, remember that not everyone feels the same as you do. More importantly, the interviewer cannot discuss your religion with you as it may contravene anti-discrimination legislation, and making an interviewer feel awkward in any way is not the way to win a job offer.

'What would you do when you have a decision to make and no procedure exists?'

This question probes your analytical skills, integrity and dedication. Most of all, the interviewer is testing your manageability and adherence to procedures – the 'company way of doing things'. You need to cover that with: 'I would act without my manager's direction only if the situation were urgent and my manager was unavailable. Then, I would take command of the situation, make a decision based on the facts and implement it. I would update my boss at the earliest opportunity.' If possible, tell a story to illustrate.

'That is an excellent answer. Now to give me a balanced view, can you give me an example that didn't work out so well?'

There are two techniques that every skilled interviewer will use, especially if you are giving good answers. In this question, the interviewer looks for negative balance – that is, in the follow-up, the person will look for negative confirmation. Here, you are required to give an example of an inadequacy. The trick is to pull something from the past, not the present, and finish with what you learnt from the experience. For example, 'That's easy. When I first joined the workforce, I didn't really understand the importance of systems and procedures. There was one time when I was too anxious to contribute and didn't have the full picture. There was a sales visit report everyone had to fill out after visiting a customer. I always put a lot of effort into it until I realized it was never read – it just went in the files. So, I stopped doing it for a few days to see if it made any difference. I thought I was gaining time to make more sales for the company. I was so proud of my extra sales calls I told the boss at the end of the week. My boss explained that the records were for the long term, so that, should my job change, the next salesperson would have the benefit of a full client history. It was a long time ago, but I have never forgotten the lesson: there's always a reason for systems and procedures. I've had the best-kept records in the company ever since!'

To look for negative confirmation, the interviewer may then say something like, 'Thank you. Now, can you give me another example?' He or she is trying to confirm a weakness. If you help, you could well do yourself out of a job. Here's what your reaction should be: you sit deep in thought for a good 10 seconds, then look up and say firmly, 'No, that's the only occasion when anything like that happened.' Then shut up and refuse to be enticed further.

The unconscious incompetent

Now you should be ready for almost anything a professional interviewer could throw at you. Your foresight and strategic planning will generate multiple offers of employment for you in all circumstances except one – when you face the unconsciously incompetent interviewer. He or she is probably more dangerous to your job offer status than everything else combined.

The problem is embodied in the experienced manager who is a poor interviewer, but who does not know it. He or she, consciously or otherwise, bases employment decisions on 'experience' and 'knowledge of humankind' and 'gut feeling'. In any event, he or she is an unconscious incompetent. You have probably been interviewed by one in your time. Remember leaving an interview and, upon reflection, feeling the interviewer knew absolutely nothing about you or your skills? If so, you know how frustrating that can be. Here, you'll see how to turn that difficult situation to your advantage. In the future, good managers who are poor interviewers will be offering jobs with far greater frequency than ever before. Understand that a poor interviewer can be a wonderful manager – interviewing skills are learnt, not inherited or created as a result of a mystical corporate blessing.

The unconscious incompetents abound. Their heinous crime can only be exceeded by your inability to recognize and take advantage of the proffered opportunity.

As in handling the skilled interviewer, it is necessary to imagine how the unconsciously incompetent thinks and feels. There are many manifestations of the poor interviewer. Each of the next examples is followed by instructions for appropriate handling of the unique problems posed for you.

Example 1

The interviewer's desk is cluttered and the CV or application that was handed to him or her a few minutes before cannot be found.

Response

Sit quietly through the bumbling and searching. Check out the surroundings. Breathe deeply and slowly to calm any natural interview nerves. As you bring your adrenaline under control, you bring a certain calming effect to the interviewer and the interview. This example, by the way, is the most common sign of the unconscious incompetent.

Example 2

The interviewer experiences constant interruptions from the telephone or people walking into the office.

Response

This provides good opportunities for selling yourself. Make notes on your pad of where you were in the conversation and refresh the interviewer on the point when you start talking again. He or she will be impressed with your level head and good memory. The interruptions also give time, perhaps, to find something of common interest in the office, something you can compliment. You will also have time to compose the suitable follow-up to the point made in the conversation prior to the interruption.

Example 3

The interviewer starts with an explanation of why you are both sitting there and then allows the conversation to degenerate into a lengthy diatribe about the company.

Response

Show interest in the company and the conversation. Sit straight, look attentive (the other applicants probably fall asleep), make appreciative murmurs and nod at the appropriate times until there is a pause. When it occurs, comment that you appreciate the background on the company, because you can now see more clearly how the job fits into the general scheme of things and that you see, for example, how valuable communication skills would be for the job. Could the interviewer please tell you some of the other job requirements? Then, as the job's functions are described, you can interject appropriate information about your background with 'Would it be of value, Mr Smith, if I described my experience with…?'

Example 4

The interviewer begins with, or quickly breaks into, the drawbacks of the job. The job may even be described in totally negative terms. That is often done without giving a balanced view of the duties and expectations of the position.

Response

An initial negative description often means that the interviewer has had bad experiences of employing people for the position. Your course is to empathize (not sympathize) with his or her bad experiences and make it known that you recognize the importance of (for example) reliability, especially in this particular type of job. Illustrate your proficiency in that particular aspect of your profession with a short example from your work history. Finish your statements by asking the interviewer what some of the biggest problems to be handled in the job are. The questions demonstrate your understanding and the interviewer's answers outline the areas of your background and skills to which you should draw attention.

Example 5

The interviewer spends considerable time early on in the interview describing 'the type of people we are here at XYZ Limited'.

Response

Very simple. You have always wanted to work for a company with that atmosphere. It creates the type of work environment that is conducive to a person really giving his or her best efforts.

Example 6

The interviewer asks closed questions, which are ones that demand no more than a yes or no answer, such as, 'Do you pay attention to detail?' Such questions are hardly adequate to establish your skills, yet you must handle them effectively to secure the job offer.

Response

A 'yes' or 'no' answer to a closed question will not get you that offer. The trick is to treat each closed question as if the interviewer has added, 'Please give me a brief yet thorough answer.' Closed questions also are often mingled with statements followed by pauses. In those instances, agree with the statement in a way that demonstrates both a grasp of your job and the interviewer's statement. For example, 'That's an excellent point, Mr Smith. I couldn't agree more that the attention to detail you describe naturally affects cost containment. My track record in this area is...'

Example 7   ·

The interviewer asks a continuous stream of negative questions (as described in the next chapter, 'The stress interview').

Response

Use the techniques and answers described earlier. Give your answers with a smile and do not take the questions as personal insults as they are not intended that way. The more stressful the situations the job is likely to place you in, the greater the likelihood of your having to field negative questions. The interviewer wants to know if you can take the heat.

Example 8

The interviewer has difficulty looking at you while speaking.

Response

The interviewer is someone who finds it uncomfortable being in the spotlight. Try to help him or her to be a good audience. Ask specific questions about the job responsibilities and offer your skills in turn.

Often, the manager interviewing will arrange for you to meet two or three other people as well. Frequently, the other interviewers have been neither trained in appropriate interviewing skills nor told the details of the job for which you are interviewing. So, take additional copies of your executive briefing with you to the interview to aid them in focusing on the appropriate job functions.

When you understand how to recognize and respond to these different types of interviewers, you will leave your interview having made a favourable first impression. No one forgets first impressions.

14 The stress interview

Your worst nightmare can come true at a stress interview, but, once you learn that these questions are just amplified versions of much simpler ones, you can remain cool and calm. Also, a vital discussion on handling illegal interview questions.

To all intents and purposes, every interview is a stress interview – the interviewer's negative and trick questions can act as the catalyst for your own fear. The only way to combat this fear is to be prepared, to know what the interviewer is trying to do and anticipate the various directions he or she will take. Whenever you are ill-prepared for an interview, no one will be able to put more pressure on you than you do on yourself. Remember, a stress interview is just a normal interview with the volume turned all the way up – the music is the same, just louder. Only preparation will keep you cool and collected.

You've heard the horror stories. An interviewer demands of a hapless applicant, 'Sell me this pen' or asks, 'How would you improve the design of a teddy bear?' The candidate is faced with a battery of interviewers, all demanding rapid-fire answers to questions like, 'You're giving a dinner party. Which 10 famous people would you invite and why?' When the interviewee offers evidence of foot-in-mouth disease by asking, 'Living or dead?' he receives his just desserts in reply: 'Ten of each.'

Such awful-sounding questions are thrown in to test your poise, see how you react under pressure and plumb the depths of your confidence.

Many people ruin their chances by reacting to them as personal insults rather than the challenges and opportunities to shine that they really are.

Previously restricted to the executive suite for the selection of high-powered executives, stress interviews are now widespread throughout the professional world. They can come complete with all the intimidating and treacherous tricks your worst nightmare can devise. Yet, a good performance at a stress interview can mean the difference between a job in the fast lane and a stalled career. The interviewers in a stress interview are invariably experienced and well organized and have developed tightly structured procedures and advanced interviewing techniques. The questions and tension they generate have the cumulative effect of throwing you off balance and revealing the 'real' you – rather than someone who can respond with last night's rehearsed answers to six or seven stock questions.

Stress questions can be turned to your advantage or merely avoided with nifty footwork. Whichever approach you choose, you will be among a select few who understand this line of questioning. As always, when addressing the questions in this chapter, remember to develop personalized answers that reflect your experience and profession. Practise your responses out loud – by doing that, they will become more natural and will help you feel more confident during an interview. You might even consider making a tape of tough questions, spacing them at intervals of 30 seconds to a couple of minutes. You can then play the tape back and answer the questions in real time.

As we will see in this chapter, reflexive questions can prove especially useful when the heat is on. Stress questions are designed to sort out the doers from those who freeze under pressure. Used with discretion, the reflexives – ' …don't you think?' – will demonstrate to the interviewer that you are able to function well under pressure. At the same time, of course, you put the ball back in the interviewer's court.

One common stress interview technique is to set you up for a fall: a pleasant conversation, one or a series of seemingly innocuous questions to relax your guard, then a dazzling series of jabs and body blows that leave you gibbering. For instance, an interviewer might lull you into a false sense of security by asking some relatively stress-free questions: 'What was your initial starting salary at your last job?' then, 'What is your salary now?' then, 'Do you receive bonuses?' and so on. To put you on the ropes, he or she might then completely surprise you with, 'Tell me what sort of troubles you have living within your means' or 'Why aren't you earning more at your age?' Such interviewers are using stress in an intelligent fashion, to simulate the unexpected and sometimes tense events of everyday business life. Seeing how you handle simulated pressure gives a fair indication of how you will react to the real thing.

The sophisticated interviewer talks very little, perhaps only 20 per cent of the time, and that time is spent asking questions. Few comments and no editorializing on your answers means that you get no hint, verbal or otherwise, about your performance.

The questions are planned, targeted, sequenced and layered. The interviewer covers one subject thoroughly before moving on. Let's take the simple example of 'Can you work under pressure?' As a reader of this book, you will know to answer that question with an example and thereby deflect the main thrust of the stress technique. The interviewer will be prepared for a simple yes or no answer. What follows will keep the unprepared applicant reeling.

'Can you work under pressure?'

A simple, closed question that requires just a yes or no answer, but you won't get off so easy.

'Good, I'd be interested to hear about a time when you experienced pressure in your job'

An open-ended request to tell a story about a pressure situation. After this, you will be subjected to the layering technique – six layers in the following instance. Imagine how tangled you could get without preparation.

'Why do you think this situation arose?'

It's best if the situation you describe is not a peer's or manager's fault.

'When exactly did it happen?'

Watch out! Your story of saving thousands from the burning skyscraper may well be checked with your references.

'What in hindsight were you most dissatisfied with about your performance?'

Here we go. You're trying to show how well you perform under pressure, then suddenly you're telling tales against yourself.

'How do you feel others involved could have acted more responsibly?'

An open invitation to criticize peers and superiors, which you should diplomatically decline.

'Who holds responsibility for the situation?'

Another invitation to point the finger of blame.

'Where in the chain of command could steps be taken to avoid that sort of thing happening again?'

This question probes your analytical skills and whether or not you are the type of person who always goes back to the scene of the crime to learn for the next time.

You have just been through an old reporter's technique of asking why, when, who, what, how and where. The technique can be applied to any question you are asked and is frequently used to probe those success stories that sound just too good to be true. You'll find them suddenly tagged on to the simple closed questions, as well as to the open-ended ones. Typically, they'll start with something like 'Share with me' 'Tell me about a time when' or 'I'm interested in finding out about' and then request specific examples from your work history.

After you've survived that barrage, a friendly tone may conceal another zinger: 'What did you learn from the experience?' This question is geared to probing your judgement and emotional maturity. Your answer should emphasize whichever of the key professional behaviours your story was illustrating.

When an interviewer feels you were on the edge of revealing something unusual in an answer, you may well encounter 'mirror statements'. Here, the last key phrase of your answer will be repeated or paraphrased and followed by a steady gaze and silence. For example, 'So, you learnt that organization is the key to management.' The idea is that the quiet and an expectant look will work together to keep you talking. It can be disconcerting to find yourself rambling on without quite knowing why. The trick is knowing when to stop. When the interviewer gives you an expectant look in this context, expand your answer (you have to), but by no more than a couple of sentences. Otherwise, you will get that creepy feeling that you're digging yourself into a hole.

There will be times when you face more than one interviewer at a time. When that happens, remember the story of a female attorney who had five law partners all asking questions at the same time. As the poor interviewee got halfway through one answer, another question would be shot at her. Pausing for breath, she smiled and said, 'Hold on, ladies and gentlemen. These are all excellent questions and, given time, I'll answer them all. Now who's next?' In so doing, she showed the interviewers exactly what they wanted to see and what, incidentally, is behind every stress interview and every negatively phrased question – finding the presence of poise and calm under fire, combined with a refusal to be intimidated.

You never know when a stress interview will raise its ugly head. Often it can be that rubber-stamp meeting with the senior manager at the end of a series of gruelling meetings. This is not surprising. While other interviewers are concerned with determining whether or not you are able, willing and a good fit for the job in question, the senior executive who eventually throws you for a loop may be probing you for potential promotability.

The most intimidating stress interviews are recognizable before the interviewer speaks – no eye contact, no greeting, either silence or a non-committal grunt and no small talk. You may also recognize such an interviewer by his or her general air of boredom, lack of interest or thinly veiled aggression. The first words you hear could well be, 'OK, so go ahead. I don't have all day.' In these situations, forewarned is forearmed, so here are some of the questions you can expect to follow such openings.

'What is your greatest weakness?'

This is a direct invitation to put your head in a noose. Decline the invitation.

This is perhaps one instance where the need for continuing education in the modern world of work can come to your rescue in a sticky situation. The changes in technology give everyone an ongoing challenge in getting up to speed with new skills. Your answer can address these very issues, and in the process show you as someone capable of staying on top of a rapidly changing workplace.

'With all the legal and technological changes impacting finance these days, staying up to date is a real challenge. Then, of course, there's working out how this affects the job and developing new knowledge or skills the changes demand' is an honest answer to which anyone can relate. It's all the better if you complete it with a course of action such as: 'I'm currently reading about…'; 'I just attended a weekend workshop where…'; or 'I'm signed up for classes at…'.

With this type of answer you identify your weakness as something that is only of concern to the most dedicated and forward-looking professionals in your field.

If there is a minor part of the job at hand where you lack knowledge – but knowledge you will obviously pick up quickly – use that. For instance, 'I haven't worked with this type of spreadsheet program before, but, given my experience with six other types, I don't think it should take me more than a couple of days to pick it up.' Here you remove the emphasis from a weakness and put it on to a developmental problem that is easily overcome. Be careful, however – this very effective ploy must be used with discretion.

Another good option is to design the answer so that your weakness is ultimately a positive characteristic. For example, 'I enjoy my work and always give each project my best shot. So, when sometimes I don't feel others are pulling their weight, I find it a little frustrating. I am aware of that weakness and, in those situations, I try to overcome it with a positive attitude that I hope will catch on.'

Also, consider the technique of putting a problem in the past. Here you take a weakness from way back and show how you overcame it. It answers the question but ends on a positive note. An illustration: 'When I first got into this field, I always had problems with my paperwork – you know, leaving an adequate paper trail. To be honest, I let it slip once or twice. My manager sat me down and explained the potential troubles such behaviour could cause. I really took it to heart and I think you will find my paper trails some of the best around today. You only have to tell me something once.' With that kind of answer, you also get the added bonus of showing that you accept and act on criticism.

Congratulations! You have just turned a pig of a question into an opportunity to sell yourself. In deciding on the particular answer you will give, remember that the interviewer isn't really concerned about your general weaknesses – no one is a saint outside of the interview room. He or she is simply concerned about any red flags that might signal your inability to perform the job or work well under supervision.

'With hindsight, how could you have improved your progress?'

Here's a question that demands, 'Tell me your mistakes and weaknesses.' If you can mention ways of improving your performance without damaging your candidacy, do so. The end of your answer should contain something like, 'Other than that, I don't know what to add. I have always given it my best shot.' Then shut up.

'What kinds of decisions are most difficult for you?'

You are human, admit it, but be careful what you admit. If you have ever had to fire someone, you are in luck, because no one likes to do that. Emphasize that, having reached a logical conclusion, you act. If you are not in management, tie your answer to your professional behaviours: 'It's not that I have difficulty making decisions – some just require more consideration than others. A small example might be holiday time. Now, everyone is entitled to it, but I don't believe you should leave your boss in a bind at short notice. I think very carefully at the beginning of the year when I'd like to take my holidays and then think of alternative dates. I go to my supervisor, tell him what I hope to do and see if there is any conflict. I wouldn't want to be out of the office for the two weeks prior to a project deadline, for instance. So, by carefully considering things far enough in advance, I don't procrastinate and make sure my plans fit in with my boss and the department for the year.'

Here you take a trick question and use it to demonstrate your consideration, analytical abilities and concern for the department – and for the company's bottom line.

'Tell me about the problems you have living within your means'

This is a twister to catch you off-guard. Your best defence is, first of all, to know that it exists and, second, give it short shrift. 'I know few people who are satisfied with their current earnings. As a professional, I am continually striving to improve my skills and improve my standard of living. My problems, though, are no different from those of this company or any other – making sure all the bills get paid on time and recognizing that every month and year there are some things that are prudent to do and other expenses that are best deferred.'

'What area of your skills/professional development do you want to improve at this time?'

Another 'tell me all your weaknesses' question. You should try to avoid damaging your candidacy by tossing around careless admissions. One effective answer to this is to say, 'Well, from what you told me about the job, I seem to have all the necessary skills and background. What I would really find exciting is the opportunity to work on a job where…' At this point, you replay the interviewer's hot buttons about the job. You emphasize that you really have all the job-related skills and also tell the interviewer what you find exciting about the job. It works admirably.

Another safe response is to reiterate one or two areas that combine personal strengths and the job's most crucial responsibilities, then finish by saying, 'These areas are so important that I don't think anyone can be too good or should ever stop trying to polish their skills.'

'Your application shows you have been with one company a long time without any appreciable increase in rank or salary. Tell me about this'

Ugh. A toughie. To start with, you should analyse why this state of affairs exists (assuming the interviewer's assessment is accurate). Then, when you have determined the cause, practise saying it out loud to yourself as you would say it during an actual interview. It may take a few tries. Chances are that, no matter how valid your explanation really is, it will come off sounding a little tinny or vindictive without some polishing. Avoid the sour grapes syndrome at all costs.

Here are some tactics you can use. First of all, try to avoid putting your salary history on application forms. No one is going to deny you an interview for lack of a salary history if your skills match those the job requires. Of course, you should never put such trivia on your CV.

If the interviewer is intent and asks you outright for this information, you'll find a great response in the section on salary histories in Chapter 19.

Now then, next we'll address the delicate matter of 'Why no promotions?' This is one case where saying the wrong thing can get you in just as much trouble as failing to say the right thing. The interviewer has posed a truly negative enquiry. The more time either of you spend on it, the more time the interviewer gets to devote to concentrating on negative aspects of your candidacy. Make your answer short and sweet, then shut up. For instance, 'My current employer is a stable company with a good working environment, but there's minimal growth there in my area – in fact, there hasn't been any promotion in my area since _____. Your question is the reason I am here meeting you; I have the skills and ability to take on more responsibility and I'm looking for a place to do that.'

'If you had to stay in your current job, what would you spend more time on, and why?'

Without a little self-control you could easily blurt out what you consider to be your greatest weaknesses. Tricky question, but with a little fore-knowledge your answer will shine.

Practically speaking, each of your job changes should occur within the context of an overall career management strategy. Now, while sensible career management blends personal fulfilment with ongoing solvency, an employer is only concerned with the latter. It's your continued employability that determines solvency, which is achieved by a growing competence in profession-critical skills that make you desirable to employers.

Enlightened self-interest means that an ongoing career management concern is for you to identify and develop the skills demanded in an ever-changing work environment. So your answer might begin in part, 'In the modern world of work, existing skills always need to be improved and new skills learnt, to handle the changing nature of our work. For instance, in this job [now give a job-specific example] I think the organizational software now available can have a major impact on personal productivity so…'.

With an answer along these lines you show foresight instead of weakness, and turn a tough question into an opportunity to shine.

'How do you keep up with new developments?'

The age of technological innovation in which we live means that the nature of every job is changing about as quickly as you turn these pages. Continual changes in the nature of your professional work mean that you must look at ongoing professional education as the price of sustained employability. In your answer, talk about your appreciation of this and the importance of keeping abreast of changes in the profession, and then illustrate with the following:

- courses you have taken and are planning to take;

- books you have read, or book clubs you belong to;

- membership of professional associations;

- subscriptions to professional journals.

Such an answer will identify you as an aware, connected and dedicated professional.

'Are you willing to take calculated risks when necessary?'

First, qualify the question: 'How do you define calculated risks? What sorts of risks? Give me an example of a risk you have in mind; what are the stakes involved?' That will show you exactly the right analytical approach to evaluating a calculated risk and, while the interviewer is rattling on, you have bought time to come up with an answer. Whatever your answer, you will include, 'Naturally, I would never take any risk that would in any way jeopardize the safety or reputation of my company or colleagues. In fact, I don't think any employer would appreciate an employee at any level taking risks of any nature without first having a thorough briefing and chance to give input.'

'See this pen I'm holding? Sell it to me'

Not a request, as you might think, that would only be asked of a salesperson. In today's professional workplace, everyone is required to communicate effectively and sell appropriately – sometimes products, but more often ideas, approaches and concepts. As such, you are being examined about your understanding of features and selling of benefits, how quickly you think on your feet and how effective your verbal communication is. For example, the interviewer holds up a yellow highlighter. First, you will want to establish the customer's needs with a few questions such as, 'What sort of pens do you currently use? Do you use a highlighter? Do you read reports and need to recall important points? Is comfort important to you?' Then you will proceed calmly, 'Let me tell you about the special features of this pen and show you how they will satisfy your needs. First of all, it is tailor-made for highlighting reports and that will save you time in recalling the most important points. The case is wide for comfort and the base is flat so it will stand up and be visible on a cluttered work area. It's disposable and affordable enough to have a handful for desk, briefcase, car and home. Also, the bright yellow means you'll never lose it.' Then close with a smile and a question of your own that will bring a smile to the interviewer's face 'How many boxes of these shall we deliver?'

'How will you be able to cope with a change in environment after [say] five years with your current company?'

Another chance to take an implied negative and turn it into a positive. 'That's one of the reasons for my wanting to make a change. After five years with my current employer, I felt I was about to get stale. Everyone needs a change of scene once in a while. It's just time for me to make some new friends, face some new challenges and experience some new approaches; hopefully, I'll have the chance to contribute from my experience.'

'Why aren't you earning more at your age?'

Accept this as a compliment to your skills and accomplishments. 'I have always felt that solid experience would stand me in good stead in the long run and that earnings would come in due course. Also, I am not the type of person to change jobs just for the money. At this point, I have a solid background that is worth something to a company.' Now, to avoid the interviewer putting you on the spot again, finish with a question: 'How much should I be earning now?' The figure could be your offer.

'What is the worst thing you have heard about our company?'

This question can come as something of a shock. As with all stress questions, your poise here is vital and if you can carry off a halfway decent answer as well, you are a winner. The best response to this question is simple. Just say with a smile, 'You're a tough company to get into because your interviews and interviewers are so rigorous.' It's true, it's flattering, and it shows that you are not intimidated.

'How would you define your profession?'

With questions that solicit your understanding of a topic, no matter how good your answer, you can expect to be interrupted in mid-reply with 'That has nothing to do with it' or 'Whoever put that idea into your head?' While your response is a judgement call, 999 times out of a thousand these comments are not meant to be taken as serious criticisms. Rather, they are tests to see how well you would be able to defend your position in a no-holds-barred conversation with the chairman of the Board, who says exactly what he or she thinks at all times. So, go ahead and defend yourself, without taking or showing offence.

Your first response will be to gain time and get the interviewer talking. 'Why do you say that?' you ask, answering a question with a question. Turning the tables on your aggressor displays your poise, calm and analytical skills better than any other response.

'Why should I take on an outsider when I could fill the job with someone inside the company?'

The question isn't as stupid as it sounds. Obviously, the interviewer has examined existing employees with an eye towards their promotion or reassignment. Just as obviously, the job cannot be filled from within the company. If it could be, it would be and for two very good reasons: it is cheaper for the company to promote from within and it is good for employee morale.

Hiding behind this intimidating question is actually a pleasant invitation: 'Tell me why I should give you the job.' Your answer should include two steps. The first is a simple recitation of your skills and strengths, tailored to the specific requirements of the job.

For the second step, realize first that whenever a manager is filling a position, he or she is looking not only for someone who can do the job but also for someone who can benefit the department in a larger sense. No department is as good as it could be – each has weaknesses that need strengthening. So, in the second part of your answer, include a question of your own: 'Those are my general attributes. However, if no one is promotable from inside the company, that means you are looking to add strength to your team in a special way. In what ways do you hope the final candidate will be able to benefit your department?' The answer to this is your cue to sell your applicable qualities.

'Have you ever had any financial difficulties?'

The potential employer wants to know if you can control not only your own finances but also finances in general. If you are in the insurance field, for example – in claims, accounting, supervision or management – you can expect to hear this one. The question, though, is not restricted to insurance – anyone, especially a person who handles money in day-to-day business, is fair game.

The interviewer does not want to hear sob stories. If your credit history is not too good, concentrate on the information that will damage your candidacy the least and enhance it the most. You might find it appropriate to bring the matter up yourself if you work in an area where your credit history is likely to be checked. If you choose to wait until the interviewer brings it up, you might say (if you had to file for bankruptcy, for instance), 'I should tell you that some years ago, for reasons beyond my control, I was forced into personal bankruptcy. That has been behind me for some time. Today, I have a sound credit rating and no debts. Bankruptcy is not something I'm proud of, but I did learn from the experience and I feel it has made me a more proficient account supervisor.' The answer concentrates on today, not past history.

'How do you handle rejection?'

This question is common if you are applying for a job in sales, including face-to-face sales, telemarketing, public relations and customer service. If you are after a job in one of these areas and you really don't like the heavy doses of rejection that are any salesperson's lot, consider a new field. The anguish you will experience will not lead to a successful career or a happy life.

With that in mind, let's look behind the question. The interviewer simply wants to know if you take rejection as rejection of yourself or simply accept it as a temporary rejection of a service or product. Here is a sample answer that you can tailor to your particular needs and background: 'I accept rejection as an integral part of the sales process. If everyone said 'yes' to a product, there would be no need for the sales function. As it is, I see every rejection as bringing me closer to the customer who will say 'yes'.' Then, if you are encouraged to go on, 'I regard rejection as simply a fact of life, that the customer has no need for the product today. I can go on to my next call with the conviction that I am a little closer to my next sale.'

'Why were you out of work for so long?'

You must have a sound explanation for any and all gaps in your employment history. If not, you are unlikely to receive a job offer. Emphasize that you were not just looking for another pay cheque, you were looking for a company with which to settle and make a long-term contribution.

'I made a decision that I enjoy my work too much just to accept another pay cheque. So, I determined that the next job I took would be one where I could settle down and do my best to make a solid contribution. From everything I have heard about this company, you are a group that expects people to pull their weight, because you've got a real job to do. I like that and I would like to be part of the team. What do I have to do to get the job?'

You answer the question, compliment the interviewer and shift the emphasis from your being unemployed to how you can get the job offer.

'Why have you changed jobs so frequently?'

If you have jumped around, blame it on youth (even the interviewer was young once). Now you realize what a mistake your job-hopping was and, with your added domestic responsibilities, you are now much more settled. Alternatively, you may wish to impress on the interviewer that your job-hopping was never as a result of poor performance and that you grew professionally as a result of each job change.

You could reply, 'My first job involved a long journey to and from work. It was hard, but I knew it would give me good experience in a very competitive field. Subsequently, I found a job much closer to home where commuting was only half an hour each way. I was very happy at my second job. However, I got an opportunity to really broaden my experience base with a new company that was just starting up. With the wisdom of hindsight, I realize that move was a mistake – it took me just six months to see that I couldn't make a contribution there. I've been with my current company a reasonable length of time. So, I have broad experience in different environments. I didn't just job-hop, I have been following a path to gain this broad experience. So, you see, I have more experience than the average person of my years and a desire to settle down and make it pay off for me and my employer.'

Alternatively, you can say, 'Now I want to settle down and make my diverse background pay off in my contributions to my new employer. I have a strong desire to contribute and am looking for an employer that will keep me challenged. I think this might be the company to do that – am I right?'

'Tell me about a time when you put your foot in your mouth'

Answer this question with caution. The interviewer is examining your ability and willingness to interact pleasantly with others. The question is tricky because it asks you to show yourself in a poor light. Your answer should downplay the negative impact of your action and end with positive information about your candidacy. The best thing to do is start with an example outside of the workplace and show how the experience improved your performance at work.

'About five years ago, I let the cat out of the bag about a surprise birthday party for a friend, a terrific *faux pas*. It was a mortifying experience and I promised myself not to let anything like that happen again.' Then, after this fairly innocuous statement, you can talk about communications in the workplace. 'As far as work is concerned, I always regard employer/employee communications on any matter as confidential unless expressly stated otherwise. So, putting my foot in my mouth doesn't happen to me at work.'

'Why do you want to leave your current job?' *or* 'Why did you leave your last job?'

This is a common trick question. You should have an acceptable reason for leaving every job you have held, but, if you don't, pick one of the six acceptable reasons from the employment industry formula, the acronym for which is CLAMPS:

■ *C*hallenge – you weren't able to grow professionally in that position;

■ *L*ocation – the journey to work was unreasonably long;

■ *A*dvancement – there was nowhere for you to go, you had the talent, but there were too many people ahead of you;

■ *M*oney – you were underpaid for your skills and contribution;

■ *P*ride or *P*restige – you wanted to be with a better company;

■ *S*ecurity – the company was not stable.

For example, 'My last company was a family-owned affair. I had gone as far as I was able. It just seemed time for me to join a more prestigious company and accept greater challenges.'

Under no circumstances should you be negative about a manager – even if she was a direct descendant of Attila the Hun. Doing so will only raise a red flag in the interviewer's mind: 'Oh, will he be complaining about me like this in a few months?'

'What interests you least about this job?'

This question is potentially explosive, but easily defused. Regardless of your occupation, there is at least one repetitive, mindless duty that everyone groans about and that goes with the territory. Use that as your example in a statement of this nature: 'Filing is probably the least demanding part of the job. However, it is important to the overall success of my department, so I try to do it with a smile.' This shows that you understand that it is necessary to take the rough with the smooth in any job.

'What was there about your last company that you didn't particularly like or agree with?'

You are being checked out as a potential fly in the ointment. If you have to answer, you might say something about the way the company policies and/or directives were sometimes consciously misunderstood by some employees who disregarded the bottom line – the profitability of the company.

Alternatively, you could say, 'You know how it is sometimes with a big company. People lose awareness of the cost of things. There never seemed to be much concern about economy or efficiency. Everyone wanted his or her year-end bonus, but only worried about it just before it was going to be announced. The rest of the year, nobody gave a hoot. I think that's the kind of thing we could be aware of almost every day, don't you agree?'

Another is, 'I didn't like the way some people gave lip-service to "the customer comes first"', but really didn't go out of their way to keep the customer satisfied. I don't think it was a fault of management, just a general malaise that seemed to affect a lot of people.'

'What do you feel is a satisfactory attendance record?'

There are two answers to this question – one if you are in management, one if you are not. As a manager, 'I believe attendance is a matter of management, motivation and psychology. Letting the employees know you expect their best efforts and won't accept half-baked excuses is one thing. The other is to keep your employees motivated by a congenial work environment and the challenge to stretch themselves. Giving people pride in their work and letting them know you respect them as individuals have a lot to do with it, too.'

If you are not in management, the answer is even easier: 'I've never really considered it. I work for a living, I enjoy my job and I'm rarely ill.'

'What is your general impression of your last company?'

Always answer positively. Keep your real feelings to yourself, whatever they might be. There is a strong belief among the management fraternity that people who complain about past employers will cause problems for their new ones. Your answer is, 'Very good' or 'Excellent.' Then smile and wait for the next question.

'What are some of the problems you encounter in doing your job and what do you do about them?'

Note well the old saying, 'A poor workman blames his tools.' Your awareness that careless mistakes cost the company good money means you are always on the lookout for potential problems. Give an example of a problem you recognized and solved.

For example, 'My job is fairly repetitive, so it's easy to overlook problems. Lots of people do. However, I always look for them – it helps keep me alert and motivated, so I do a better job. To give you an example, we make computer memory disks. Each one has to be machined by hand and, once completed, the slightest abrasion will turn one into a reject. I have a steady staff and little turnover and everyone wears cotton gloves to handle the disks. Yet, about six months ago, the reject rate suddenly went through the roof. Is that the kind of problem you mean? Well, the cause was one that could have gone unnoticed for ages. Jill, the section head who inspects all the disks, had lost a lot of weight, her diamond engagement ring was slipping around her finger and it was scratching the disks as she passed them and stacked them to be shipped. Our main client was dissatisfied over it, so my looking for problems and paying attention to detail really paid off.'

The interviewer was trying to get you to reveal weak points, but you avoided the trap.

'What are some of the things you find difficult to do? Why do you feel that way?'

This is a variation on a couple of earlier questions. Remember, anything that goes against the best interests of your employer is difficult to do. If you are pressed for a job function you find difficult, answer in the past tense as, that way, you show that you recognize the difficulty, but you obviously handle it well.

'That's a tough question. There are so many things that are difficult to learn in our business if you want to do the job right. I used to have 40 clients to sell to every month and I was so busy keeping in touch with all of them, I never got a chance to sell to any of them. So, I graded them into three groups. I called on the top 20 per cent with whom I did business every three weeks. The next group were those I sold to occasionally. I called on them once a month, but with a difference – each month, I marked 10 of them to spend time with and really get to know. I still have difficulty reaching all 40 of my clients in a month, but my sales have tripled and are still climbing.'

'Jobs have pluses and minuses. What were some of the minuses on your last job?'

A variation on the question, 'What interests you least about this job?', which was handled earlier. Use the same type of answer. For example, 'Like any salesperson, I enjoy selling, not doing the paperwork. However, as I cannot expect the customer to get the goods and me my commission without following through on this task, I grin and bear it. Besides, if I don't do the paperwork, that holds up other people in the company.'

If you are not in sales, use the salesforce as a scapegoat. 'In accounts receivable, it's my job to get the money in to do the payroll and positive things like that. Half the time, the goods get shipped before I get the paperwork because sales say, "It's a rush order". That's a real minus to me. It was so bad at my last company, we tried a new approach. We had a meeting with sales and explained our problem. The result was that incremental commissions were based on cash in, not on bill date. They saw the connection and things are much better now.'

'What kinds of people do you like to work with?'

This is the easy part of a tricky three-part question. Obviously, you like to work with people who have pride, honesty, integrity and dedication to their work. On to part 2.

'What kinds of people do you find it difficult to work with?'

The second part of the same question. You could say, 'People who don't follow procedures or slackers – the occasional rotten apples who don't really care about the quality of their work. They're long on complaints, but short on solutions.' This brings us to the third part of the question.

'How have you successfully worked with this difficult type of person?'

This is the most difficult part to answer. You might reply, 'I stick to my guns, stay enthusiastic and hope some of it will rub off. I had a big problem with one guy – all he did was complain and always in my area. Eventually, I told him how I felt. I said if I were a millionaire, I'd have all the answers and wouldn't have to work, but, as it was, I wasn't, and had to work for a living. I told him that I really enjoyed his company, but I didn't want to hear it any more. Every time I saw him after that, I presented him with a work problem and asked his advice. In other words I challenged him to come up with positives, not negatives.'

You can go on to say that sometimes you've noticed that such people simply lack enthusiasm and confidence and that energetic and cheerful colleagues can often change that. If the interviewer follows up with an enquiry about what you would do if no amount of good effort on your part solved the problem, respond, 'I would maintain cordial relations, but not go out of my way to seek more than a business-like acquaintance. Life is too short to be demotivated by people who always think their cup is half empty.'

'How did you get your last job?'

The interviewer is looking for initiative. If you can, show it. At the least, though, show determination.

'I was actually turned down for my last job for having too little experience. I asked the manager to give me a trial before she offered it to anyone else. I went in and asked for a list of companies they'd never sold to, picked up the phone and, within that hour, I arranged two appointments. How did I get the job? In a word, determination!'

'How would you evaluate me as an interviewer?'

This question is dangerous – maybe more so than the one asking you to criticize your boss. Whatever you do, of course, don't tell the truth if you think the interviewer is an incompetent. It may be true, but it won't get you a job offer. This is an instance where honesty is not the best policy. It is best to say, 'This is one of the toughest interviews I have ever been through and I don't relish the prospect of going through another. Yet, I do realize what you are trying to achieve.' Then go on to explain that you understand the interviewer wants to know whether or not you can think on your feet, that there is pressure in the job and that he or she is trying to simulate some of that real-life pressure in the interview. You may choose to finish the answer with a question of your own: 'How do you think I fit the profile of the person you need?'

'I'm not sure you're suitable for the job'

Don't worry about the tone of the question – the interviewer's 'I'm not sure' really means, 'I'd like to take you on, so here's a wide-open opportunity to sell me on yourself.' He or she is probing three areas from your personal profile: your confidence, determination and listening profiles. Remain calm and put the ball straight back into the interviewer's court: 'Why do you say that?' You need both the information and time to think up an appropriate reply, but it is important to show that you are not intimidated. Work out a plan of action for this question. Even if the interviewer's point regarding your skills is valid, come back with alternative compatible skills. Counter with other skills that show your competence and learning ability and use them to show you can pick up the new skills quickly. Tie the two together and demonstrate that, with your other attributes, you can bring many pluses to the job. Finish your answer with a reflexive question that encourages a 'yes' answer.

'I admit my programming skills in that language are a little light. However, all languages have similarities and my experience demonstrates that, with competence in four other languages, getting up to speed with this one will take only a short while. Plus, I can bring a depth of other experience to the job.' Then, after you itemize your experience: 'Wouldn't you agree?'

If the reason for the question is not a lack of technical skills, it must be a question about one of your professional behaviours. Perhaps the interviewer will say, 'You haven't convinced me of your determination.' This is an invitation to sell yourself, so tell a story that demonstrates determination.

For example: 'It's interesting you should say that. My present boss is convinced of my determination. About a year ago we were having some problems with union organization on the shopfloor. Management's problem was our 50 per cent Asian virtually monolingual production workforce. Despite the fact that our people had the best working conditions and benefits in the area, they were strongly pro-union. If they were successful, we would be the first unionized division in the company. No one in management spoke Hindi, so I took a crash course – two hours at home every night for five weeks. I got one of the maintenance crew to help me with my grammar and diction. Then a number of other production workers started saying simple things to me in Hindi and helping me with the answers. I opened the first meeting with the workforce to discuss the problems, greeting them in their own language – they really appreciated it. We had demonstrated that we cared enough to try to communicate. Our division never did unionize and my determination to take that extra step paid off and allowed my superiors to negotiate from a position of caring and strength. Wouldn't you agree that my work in that instance shows determination?'

'Wouldn't you feel better off in another firm?'

Relax, things aren't as bad as you might assume. This question is usually asked if you are really doing quite well or if the job involves a certain amount of stress. A lawyer, for example, might well be expected to face this one. The trick is not to be intimidated. Your first step is to qualify the question. Relax, take a breath, sit back, smile and say, 'You surprise me. Why do you say that?' The interviewer must then talk, giving you precious time to collect your wits and come back with a rebuttal.

Then answer 'no' and explain why. All the interviewer wants to see is how much you know about the company and how determined you are to join their ranks. Your earlier research will pay off again. Overcome the objection with an example and show how that will help you contribute to the company. End with a question of your own. In this instance, the question has a twofold purpose: one, to identify a critical area to sell yourself; and, two, to encourage the interviewer to consider an image of you working at the company.

You could reply: 'Not at all. My whole experience has been with small companies. I am good at my job and in time could become a big fish in a little pond, but that is not what I want. This company is a leader in its business. You have a strong reputation for encouraging skills development in your employees. This is the type of environment I want to work in. Now, coming from a small company, I have done a little bit of everything. This means that no matter what you throw at me, I will learn it quickly. For example, what would be the first project I would be involved with?'

End with a question of your own that gets the interviewer focusing on those immediate problems. You can then explain how your background and experience can help.

'What would you say if I told you your presentation this afternoon was pretty bad?'

'If' is the key word here, with the accusation there only for the terminally neurotic. The question is designed to see how you react to criticism and so tests your 'manageability.' No company can afford to employ the thin-skinned applicant today. You will come back and answer the question with a question of your own. An appropriate response would be, 'First of all, I would ask which aspects of my presentation were poor. My next step would be to find out where you felt the problem was. If there was miscommunication, I'd clear it up. If the problem was elsewhere, I would seek your advice and be sure that the problem was not recurrent.' This would show that when it is a manager's duty to criticize performance, you are an employee who will respond in a businesslike and emotionally mature manner.

The illegal question

Of course, one of the most stressful – and negative – questions is the illegal one, a question that delves into your private life or personal background. Such a question will make you uncomfortable if it is blatant and could also make you angry.

Your aim, however, is to overcome your discomfort and avoid getting angry. You want to be offered the job and any self-righteousness or defensive reaction on your part will ensure that you *don't* get it. You may feel angry enough to get up and walk out or say things like, 'These are unfair practices; you'll hear from my lawyer in the morning.' However, the result will be that you won't get the job and, therefore, won't have the leverage you need. Remember, no one is saying you can't refuse the job once it's offered to you.

So, what is an illegal question? The Sex Discrimination Act and the Race Relations Act forbid employers from discriminating against any person on the basis of sex, age, race, national origin or religion.

An interviewer may not ask about your religion, church, synagogue or parish, the religious holidays you observe or your political beliefs or affiliations. He or she may not ask, for instance, 'Does your religion allow you to work on Saturdays?' but may ask something like, 'This job requires work on Saturdays. Is that a problem?' Similarly, the interviewer may enquire if the usual number of hours a week required will be acceptable.

An interviewer may not ask about your ancestry, national origin or parentage. In addition, you cannot be asked about the naturalization status of your parents, spouse or children. The interviewer cannot ask about your birthplace, *but* may ask (and probably will, considering the current immigration laws) whether you are a citizen or resident with the right to work in this country.

An interviewer may not ask about your native language, the language you speak at home or how you acquired the ability to read, write or speak a foreign language. *However,* he or she may ask about the languages in which you are fluent, if knowledge of those languages is pertinent to the job.

An interviewer may not ask about your age, date of birth or the ages of your children. *However,* he or she may ask you if you are over 18 years old.

An interviewer may not ask about maiden names or if you have changed your name, your marital status, number of children or dependents or your spouse's occupation or, if you are a woman, whether you wish to be addressed as Miss, Mrs or Ms. *However,* the interviewer may ask about how you like to be addressed (a common courtesy) and if you have ever worked for the company before under a different name. If you have, you may want to mention that, especially as your prospective manager may check your references and additional background information.

As you consider a question that seems to verge on illegality, you should take into account that the interviewer may be asking it innocently and may be unaware of the laws on the matter. Your best bet is to be polite and straightforward, as you would in any other social situation. You also want to move the conversation on to an examination of your skills and abilities, not your status. Here are some sample illegal questions and some possible responses. Remember, your objective is to get job offers; if you later decide that this company is not for you, you are under no obligation to accept the position.

'What religion do you practise?'

If you do practise, you can say, 'I attend my church/synagogue/mosque regularly, but I make it my practice not to involve my personal beliefs in my work. My work for the company and my career are too important for that.'

If you do not practise a religion, you may want to say something like, 'I have a set of personal beliefs that are important to me, but I do not attend any organized services. And I do not mix those beliefs with my work, if that's what you mean.'

'How old are you?'

Age discrimination is still prevalent, but with older people joining the workforce every day and the increasing need for experienced workers, you will hear this question less and less. Answer the question in terms of your experience. For example, 'I'm in my fifties and have more than 25 years of experience in this field.' Then list your skills as they apply to the job.

'Are you married?'

If you are, the company is concerned with the impact your family duties and future plans will have on your time there. Your answer could be, 'Yes, I am. Of course, I make a separation between my work life and my family life that allows me to give my all to a job. I have no problem with travel or late hours – those things are part of this line of work. I'm sure my references will confirm this for you.'

'Do you plan to have children?'

This isn't any of the interviewer's business, but he or she wants to know whether or not you will leave the company early to raise a family. You can answer 'no' of course. If you answer 'yes' you might add, 'but those plans are for the future and they depend on the success of my career. Certainly, I want to do the best, most complete job for this company I can. I consider that my skills are right for the job and that I can make a long-term contribution. I certainly have no plans to leave the company just as I begin to make meaningful contributions.' However, unless this question is also asked of male applicants, it could be considered as discriminating against women. The skilful interviewer can usually elicit such information without asking a direct question.

If the questions become too pointed, you may want to ask, innocently, 'Could you explain the relevance of that issue to this position? That response, however, can seem confrontational, so you should only use it if you are extremely uncomfortable or are quite certain you can get away with it. Sometimes, the interviewer will drop the line of questioning.

Illegal questions tend to arise not out of brazen insensitivity, but, rather, out of an interest in you. The employer is familiar with your skills and background, feels you can do the job and wants to get to know you as a person. Outright discrimination these days is really quite rare. With illegal questions, your response must be positive – that's the only way you're going to be offered the job and winning that creates a platform for getting other jobs. You don't have to work for a discriminatory company, but you can certainly use the firm to get to something better.

Mock meetings, role plays and in-tray tests

Some employers use even more elaborate versions of the stress interview when selecting staff. Groups of candidates may be put in a room together and asked to stage a mock meeting or give an impromptu presentation. You may even be asked to demonstrate your organization and time management skills by sorting out and acting on an in-tray full of an overwhelming amount of supposedly urgent material, all the while being interrupted by telephone calls.

Collectively, these approaches are referred to as assessment centre techniques. They are frequently run – on an employer's behalf – by a third-party operation that specializes in this corporate manifestation of the Spanish Inquisition. Some companies use this approach when deciding on executives, some for choosing sales and customer service professionals and others for identifying the best candidates for administrative positions. Unfortunately, assessment centre techniques are so common today that anyone in the job market risks facing their myriad tortures. The good news is that I have one or two techniques that can help you face these latter-day dungeons of delight with equanimity.

One of the reasons that assessment centre techniques are growing in popularity is the corporate world's increasing focus on teamwork. Many employers think they can choose the best workers for a team environment by using group interviews. (Forget the fact that assessment centres haven't proved themselves better or worse than other selection methods!) As you may encounter this old–new approach during your job search, I want you to be ready for it.

Racks, beds of nails and iron maidens

Assessment centres use a broad variety of techniques, including:

I mock meetings;

I in-tray tests;

I role playing.

Let me give you some background on each of these techniques and show you how you can prepare yourself to make a great impression in any situation. With these selection techniques, forewarned is fore-armed. With a little bit of time to prepare and an understanding of how these situations work, you can survive anything they might throw at you. Besides, it's only pretend, so there's no need to break out in a cold sweat.

Mock meetings: taking control, taking charge and being a team player

Some employers will want to see you take charge of, or perhaps take over, the leadership of the group, while others want to see your skills at interacting with people and some will want to see both. Your first step in preparing for a mock meeting is to outline the challenges you would face in the average daily routine of the job you've applied for. These challenges are likely to form the basis of the situations you'll be asked to respond to. For example, if your job will involve making sales presentations for expensive items to groups of people, you can expect the mock meeting to include all of the difficult questions, problems and people you would be likely to meet in such a context. There are only two differences. First, the whole range of problems is going to appear in one meeting and, second, it's just pretend. If you are a competent professional and react to the situations you face in a professional manner, you will do just fine.

Your assessors may set up a leaderless group discussion and watch what happens. These groups may include an assortment of applicants, existing employees and selection centre staff, some of them 'planted' there to cause disruption or otherwise throw you off-balance. Just knowing who is who and why they're there can be a big help. This is a test of your assertiveness skills.

Anything you face in one of these situations will mirror the challenges you face in the real work world. If your appraisal of the job is that 'taking control' and 'demonstrating leadership' are likely to be the goals of the mock meeting, *how* you take control and demonstrate leadership will be crucial to your success. You need to set a standard of democratic leadership; you have to become the parent who sets firm limits, but gives support. Be sure to give everyone 'air time' while keeping the group on-target and on-schedule.

Sometimes taking charge can be dangerous, however. If you come across as too tough, bossy or autocratic, forget it! You can't just say, 'OK, this is a test of my decision-making and leadership skills, so move over, and let *me* take over.' You should encourage a more team-oriented approach: 'Let's take a moment to gather our thoughts, then each, in turn, address the issues from our unique perspective.' You must keep the meeting moving if someone tries to dominate the discussion or move it away from the agenda. You can then demonstrate your leadership by thanking everyone for their contributions.

If someone else beats you to it and assumes the leadership role, don't try to show everyone how tough you are by fighting to regain control. Instead, act like the archetypal active team member. Use the time you have while the leader is busy managing the meeting to plan your strategy and develop your contributions to the idea or plan the group is working on. Position yourself as a team player and consensus builder, but show you can take the initiative, too.

From this position, you can be ready to scoop the opposition at the end of the meeting. While the 'leader' is busy making sure that every voice is heard, you can prepare to help the group summarize its common ground and establish possible next steps.

For more information on what the testers will be looking for in terms of teamwork and leadership, see the related questions on pages 168–70.

In-tray: a test of organized action

You're staring at a huge stack of reports, memos and phone messages on your desk. The red light on the phone is flashing to let you know you've got voice mail messages. The computer screen glares at you with a dozen as yet unread e-mail messages. Confronting applicants with a virtual day at the office is yet another technique companies use to screen out the wheat from the chaff. In this example, you're facing an in-tray test and it is being used primarily to examine your time management and organization skills.

The in-tray test confronts the job candidate with overwhelming amounts of information and often conflicting priorities. Then the observers sit back, put their feet up and watch you wither or shine before their eyes. There are many ways to tackle this kind of test, but the main thing is to make sure that you come prepared with a system to prioritize and organize the work.

Alan Lakein, the godfather of time management, introduced me to a wildly effective and widely accepted approach to time management. Take everything out of the in-tray and place each document in one of three piles:

- the A pile is *urgent* and you will act on it 'today' – in other words, during the test;

- the B pile is *important* and needs attention – you'll start on it when and if you get through your A pile; if not, much of it will move into your A pile, as you plan for 'tomorrow' at the end of 'today';

- the C pile is to file or just put in a drawer – it is still important work, but not as urgent as your A and B work, and if someone makes it urgent for you, via a telephone call or an urgent e-mail message, you'll know where to find it.

Working out these priorities is the first step to winning in an in-tray test. Once established, you'll be able to prioritize those pesky interruptions that are always programmed into this particular type of test. When the calls come in, as they will, you must have a system in place that can help you decide how to respond. For example, you need to find out:

- who's calling and what that person does – you want to establish his or her name, department and reporting relationship so that, if your 'boss' of the day calls, you instantly know he or she has the power to move something from your C pile directly to your A pile;

▌ what the person is calling about – you can put him or her on hold while you find the appropriate paperwork, consider the relative importance of the call and decide how to handle it with efficiency and professionalism.

It is important, at the end of the test, to make sure that the assessor understands that you have been using an effective and logical system.

For more information on what assessors are looking for in this kind of test, see the question about scheduling on page 171 and the question on working methods on page 182.

Role playing

You may be asked to handle a sticky staff problem, an employee calling in sick from the golf course, a malfunctioning team, an inventory problem, a broken machine or cold calls to a series of prospective 'clients'. The goal of role playing is invariably to see how you handle the people and situations that are likely to crop up in the day-to-day execution of your duties.

Are you a hard-nosed so-and-so or do you cave in under the slightest pressure? Do you want the world to love and admire you or are you out to settle a score? How do you handle a belligerent customer or salvage a tough sale when it turns sour at the last moment?

What's the best way to handle these situations? Consider the role you are playing – is it to land a job as a customer service representative, sales training specialist, finance director or union lawyer? In handling role-playing tests, you need to be clear about the job you're facing and the challenges it typically generates. You will then understand exactly what the testers are looking for and the role you should choose to play in their scenarios.

In each of these stressful interviewing situations the key is to determine which professional hat you should be wearing and the behaviour the testers will expect from someone wearing that hat.

Interviewers may pull all kinds of tricks on you, but you will come through with flying colours once you realize that they're trying to discover something extremely simple – whether or not you can take the heat. After all, those interviewers are only trying to sort out the good corporate warriors from the walking wounded. If you successfully handle these trick and negatively phrased questions, the interviewer will end up looking at you favourably. Stay calm, give as good as you get and take it all in your stride. Remember that no one can intimidate you without your permission.

15 *Welcome to the real world*

For the school or college leaver or graduate, here are some tough questions specifically tailored to discover your business potential.

Of all the steps a recent school or college leaver or graduate will take up the ladder of success over the years, none is more important or more difficult than getting a foot on the first rung. The interviewing process designed for recent graduates is particularly rigorous because management regards the taking on of entry-level professionals as one of its toughest jobs.

When a company employs experienced people, there is a track record to evaluate. With recent graduates, there is little or nothing. Often, the only solid things an interviewer has to go on are examination results. That's not much on which to base an employment decision – the results don't tell the interviewer whether or not you will fit in or make a reliable employee. Many recruiters liken the gamble of employing recent school and college leavers and graduates to laying down wines for the future: they know that some will develop into full-bodied, reliable vintages, but that others will be disappointments. So, recruiters have to find different ways to predict your potential accurately.

After relying, as best they can, on performance in exams to evaluate your ability, interviewers concentrate on questions that reveal how willing you are to learn and get the job done and how manageable you are likely to be, both on average days and when the going gets rough.

Your goal is to stand out from all the other entry-level candidates as someone altogether different and better. For example, don't be like thousands of others who, in answer to questions about their greatest strength, reply lamely, 'I'm good with people' or 'I like working with others.' As you know by now, such answers do not separate you from the herd. In fact, they brand you as average. To stand out, you must recount a past situation that illustrates exactly how good you are with people or one that demonstrates an ability to be a team player.

Fortunately, the key professional behaviours discussed throughout the book are just as helpful for getting your foot on the ladder as they are for aiding your climb to the top. They will guide you in choosing what aspects of your personality and background you should promote at an interview.

It isn't necessary to have snap answers ready for every question, because you never will. In fact, it is more important for you to pause after a question and collect your thoughts before answering: you must show that you think before you speak. That way, you will demonstrate your analytical abilities, which age feels youth has in short supply.

By the same token, occasionally asking for a question to be repeated is useful to gain time and is quite acceptable, as long as you don't do it with every question. If a question stumps you, as sometimes happens, do not stutter incoherently. It is sometimes best to say simply, 'I don't know' or you might say, 'I'd like to come back to that later' – the odds are even that the interviewer will forget to ask again; if he or she doesn't, at least you've had some time to come up with an answer.

Knowing everything about a certain entry-level position is not necessary, because business feels it can teach you most things. However, as a vice-president of Merrill Lynch once said, 'You must bring to the table the ability to speak clearly.' So, knowing what is behind those questions designed especially for entry-level applicants will give you the time to build informative and understandable answers.

'How did you get your summer jobs?'

All employers look favourably on recent graduates who have any work experience, no matter what it is. 'It is far easier to get a fix on someone who has worked while at school,' says Dan O'Brien, head of employment at Grumman. 'They manage their time better, are more realistic and more mature. Any work experience gives us much more in common.' So, as you make your answer, add that you learnt that business is about making a profit, doing things more efficiently, adhering to procedures and putting in whatever effort it takes to get the job done. In short, treat your summer jobs, no matter how humble, as any other business experience.

With this particular question, the interviewer is looking ideally for something that shows initiative, creativity and flexibility. Here's an example: 'In my town, summer jobs were hard to come by, but I applied to each local restaurant for a position as a waiter, called the manager at each one to arrange an interview and finally landed a job at one of the most prestigious. I was assigned to the afternoon shift, but with my quick work, accurate billing and ability to keep customers happy, they soon moved me to the evening shift. I worked there for three summers and, by the time I left, I was responsible for the training and management of the night-shift waiters, the allotment of tips and the evening's final closing and accounting. All in all, my experience showed me the mechanics of a small business and of business in general.'

'Which of the jobs you have held have you liked least?'

The interviewer is trying to trip you up. It is likely that your work experience contained a certain amount of repetition and drudgery, as all early jobs in the business world do. So, beware of saying that you hated a particular job 'because it was boring'. Avoid the negative and say something along these lines: 'All of my jobs had their good and bad points, but I've always found that if you want to learn, there's plenty to be picked up every day. Each experience was valuable.' Then describe a seemingly boring job, but show how it taught you valuable lessons or helped you hone different aspects of your professional behaviour.

'What are your future vocational plans?'

This is a fancy way of asking, 'Where do you want to be five years from now?' The trap all entry-level professionals make is to say, 'In management' because they think that shows drive and ambition. It has become such a trite answer, though, that it immediately generates a string of questions that most recent graduates can't answer. What is the definition of management? What is a manager's prime responsibility? A manager in what area?

Your safest answer identifies you with the profession you are trying to break into and shows you have your feet on the ground. 'My vocational plans are that I want to get ahead. To do that I must be able to channel my energies and expertise into those areas my industry and employer need. So, in a couple of years I hope to have become a thorough professional with a clear understanding of the company, the industry and where the biggest challenges, and therefore opportunities, lie. By that time, my goals for the future should be sharply defined.' An answer like that will set you far apart from your contemporaries.

'What university did you attend and why did you choose it?'

The university you attended isn't as important as your reasons for choosing it – the question is trying to examine your reasoning processes. Emphasize that it was your choice and that you didn't go there as a result of your parents' desires or because generations of your family have always gone there. Focus on the practical. 'I went to X University in London – it was a choice based on practicality. I wanted a university that would give me a good education and prepare me for the real world. It has a good record for turning out students fully prepared to take on responsibilities in the real world. It is [or isn't] a big university, but/and it has certainly taught me some big lessons about the value of [whatever professional behaviours apply] in the real world of business.'

If the interviewer has a follow-up question about the role your parents played in selection of your college or university, be wary – he or she is plumbing your maturity. It is best to reply that the choice was yours, though you did seek the advice of your parents once you had made your selection and that they supported your decision.

'Are you looking for a permanent or temporary job?'

The interviewer wants reassurance that you are genuinely interested in the position and won't disappear in a few months to pursue postgraduate studies in Paris. Try to go beyond saying simply 'yes'. Explain why you want the job. You might say, 'Of course, I am looking for a permanent job. I intend to make my career in this field and I want the opportunity to learn the business, face new challenges and learn from experienced professionals.' You will also want to qualify the question with one of your own: 'Is this a permanent or a temporary position you are trying to fill?' Don't be scared to ask. The occasional unscrupulous employer will hire someone fresh out of college or university for a short period of time – say, for one particular project – and then let him or her go.

'How did you pay for university?'

Avoid saying, 'Oh, Dad handled all of that', as it probably won't create quite the impression you'd like. Your parents may well have helped you out, but you should explain, if it's appropriate, that you worked part-time and took out loans (as most of us must during university).

'We have tried to hire people from your university before and they never seem to work out. What makes you different?'

Here's a stress question to test your poise and analytical skills. You can shout that, yes, of course you are different and can prove it. So far, though, all you know is that there was a problem, not what caused the problem. Respond this way: 'First, may I ask you exactly what problems you've had with people from this background?' Once you know what the problem is (if one really exists at all – it may just be a ploy to test your poise), then you can illustrate how you are different, but only then. Otherwise, you run the risk of your answer being interrupted with, 'Well, that's what everyone else said before I employed them. You haven't shown me that you are different.'

'I'd be interested to hear about some things you learnt at university that could be used on the job'

While specific job-related courses could form part of your answer, they cannot be all of it. The interviewer wants to hear about 'real-world' skills, so oblige by explaining what the experience of college taught you rather than a specific course. In other words, explain how the experience honed your relevant professional behaviours. 'Within my subject, I tried to pursue those courses that had most practical relevance, such as… However, the greatest lessons I learnt were the importance of…' and then list your professional behaviours.

'Do you like routine tasks/regular hours?'

A trick question. The interviewer knows from bitter experience that most recent graduates hate routine and are hopeless as employees until they come to an acceptance of such facts of life. Explain that, yes, you appreciate the need for routine, that you expect a fair amount of routine assignments before you are entrusted with the more responsible ones and that that is why you are prepared to accept it as necessary. As far as regular hours go you could say, 'No, there's no problem there. A company expects to make a profit, so the doors have to be open for business on a regular basis.'

'What have you done that shows initiative and willingness to work?'

Again, tell a story about how you landed or created a job for yourself or even got involved in some volunteer work. Your answer should show initiative in that you both handled unexpected problems calmly and anticipated others. Your willingness is demonstrated by the ways you overcame obstacles. For example, 'I worked for a summer in a small warehouse. I found out that a large shipment was due in a couple of weeks and I knew that room had to be made. The inventory system was outdated and the rear of the warehouse was disorganized, so I came in on a Saturday, figured out how much room I needed, cleaned up the mess at the rear and catalogued it all on the new inventory forms. When the shipment arrived, the truck just backed in. There was even room to spare.'

Often after an effort above and beyond the call of duty, a manager might congratulate you and, if it had happened to you in this instance, you might conclude your answer with the verbal endorsement, 'The divisional manager happened along just when I was finishing the job and said he wished he had more people who took such pride in their work.'

'Can you take instructions without feeling upset or hurt?'

This is a manageability question. If you take offence easily or bristle when your mistakes are pointed out, you won't last long with any company. Competition is fierce at entry level, so take this as another chance to set yourself apart. 'Yes, I can take instruction – and, more important, I can take constructive criticism without feeling hurt. Even with the best intent, I will still make mistakes and at times someone will have to put me back on the right track. I know that if I ever expect to rise in the company, I must first prove myself to be manageable.'

'Have you ever had difficulties getting along with others?'

This is a combination question, probing for willingness *and* manageability. Are you a team player or are you going to disrupt the department and make the interviewer's life miserable? This is a closed question that requires only a yes/no answer, so give one and shut up.

'What type of position are you interested in?'

This again is one of those questions that tempts you to mention management. Don't. Say you are interested in what you will be offered, which is an entry-level job. 'I am interested in an entry-level position that will enable me to learn this business inside and out and will give me the opportunity to grow when I prove myself, either on a professional or a managerial ladder.'

'What qualifications do you have that will make you successful in this field?'

There is more to answering this question than reeling off your academic qualifications. In addition, you will want to stress relevant work experience and illustrate your strong points as they match the key professional behaviours that apply to the position you seek. It's a simple, wide-open question that says, 'Hey, we're looking for an excuse to employ you. Give us some help.'

'Why do you think you would like this type of work?'

This is a deceptively simple question because there is no pat answer. It is usually asked to see if you really understand what the specific job and profession entails on a day-to-day basis. So, to answer it requires you to have researched the company and job functions as carefully as possible. Preparation for this should include a call to another company in the field and a request to speak to someone doing the job you hope to get. Ask what the job is like and what that person does day to day. How does the job fit into the department? What contribution does it make to the overall efforts of the company? Why does he or she like that type of work? Armed with that information, you will show that you understand what you are getting into; most recent graduates do not.

'What's your idea of how industry works?'

The interviewer does not want a long dissertation, just the reassurance that you don't think it works along the same lines as a registered charity. Your understanding should be something like this: 'The role of any company is to make as much money as possible, as quickly and efficiently as possible and in a manner that will encourage repeat business from the existing client base and new business as a result of word of mouth and reputation.' Finish with the observation that it is every employee's role to play as a team member in order to achieve these goals.

'Why do you think this industry will sustain your interest over the long haul?' *or* 'Why do you think you will shine in this profession?'

Your answer should speak both to your pragmatism and to your motivation. An answer along the following lines will work in both instances: 'At this point in my career, I am looking at the industry because I believe it offers stability and professional growth potential over the years [explain why]. Also, I'll be using skills [itemize strong skill sets that are relevant to the job] that are areas of personal strength, from which I derive great personal satisfaction.'

'What do you know about our company?'

This can be a simple conversation gambit, helping the interviewer know where to start in explaining the company activities, or it can be a more loaded question. In the tight job race we have today, the offer always goes to the person who is most knowledgeable and enthusiastic about the company. It makes sense when you think about it, because that knowledge and enthusiasm are endorsements of both the work and the place that the interviewer is a part of for the majority of his or her waking hours.

The enthusiasm for your profession and the job is a matter of your attitude. Knowing something about the company is as simple as a little internet research and personal networking. For the internet research aspect, browse the company website, and enter the company name and/or their products and services into a couple of search engines, and absorb as much as time allows. Print out as much as you can and use it as bedtime reading the night before the interview.

For the networking aspect, talk to acquaintances who have knowledge of the company. Without a doubt, membership in the local branch of a professional association is the best bet for learning about any company in your town.

You can't answer this question unless you have enough interest to research the company thoroughly. If you don't have that interest, you should expect someone who has made the effort to get the job.

'What do you think determines progress in a good company?'

Your answer will include all the positive professional behaviours you have been illustrating throughout the interview. Include allusions to the listening profile, determination, ability to take the rough with the smooth, adherence to systems and procedures and the good fortune to have a manager who wants you to grow.

'Do you think your exam results should be considered by first employers?'

If your results were good, the answer is obviously 'yes'. If they weren't, your answer needs a little more thought. 'Of course, an employer should take everything into consideration and, along with results, will be an evaluation of willingness and manageability, an understanding of how business works and actual work experience. Combined, such experience and professional skills can be more valuable than results alone.'

Many virtuous candidates are called for entry-level interviews, but only those who prepare themselves to answer the tough questions will be chosen. Interviews for recent school and college leavers and graduates are partly sales presentations. The more you interview, the better you get, so don't leave preparing for them until the last minute. Start now and hone your skills to get a head start on your peers. Finally, here's what a professor from a top-notch business school once told me: 'You are taking a new product to market. Accordingly, you've got to analyse what it can do, who is likely to be interested and how you are going to sell it to them.' Take some time to get to know yourself and your particular values as they will be perceived in the world of business.

16 *The graceful exit*

Is parting such sweet sorrow? The end of an interview will more likely mean relief, but here are some dos and don'ts to bear in mind as your meeting comes to a close.

To paraphrase Shakespeare, all the employment world's a stage, and all the people on it merely players making their entrances and exits. Curtains rise and fall and your powerful performance must be capped with a professional and memorable exit. To ensure you leave the right impression, this chapter will review the dos and don'ts of leaving an interview.

A signal that the interview is drawing to a close comes when you are asked if you have any questions. Ask questions and, by doing so, highlight your strengths and show your enthusiasm. Your goal at the interview is to generate a job offer. Make sure your exit is as graceful as your entrance.

Dos

Ask appropriate job-related questions

When the opportunity comes to ask any final questions, review your notes. Bring up any relevant strengths that haven't been addressed.

Show decisiveness

If you are offered the job, react with enthusiasm. Then sleep on it. If it's possible to do so without making a formal acceptance, lock the job up now and put yourself in control; you can always change your mind later. However, before you make any commitment with regard to pay, see Chapter 19, 'Negotiating the offer'.

When you are interviewed by more than one person, be sure you have the correct spellings of their names

'I enjoyed meeting your colleagues, Ms Smith. Could you give me the correct spellings of their names, please?' This question will give you the names you forgot in the heat of battle and will demonstrate your consideration.

Review the job's requirements with the interviewer

Match them point by point with your skills and attributes.

Find out if this is the only interview

If so, you must ask for the job in a positive and enthusiastic manner. Find out the time frame for a decision and finish with, 'I am very enthusiastic about the job and the contributions I can make. If your decision will be made by the fifteenth, what must I do in the meantime to ensure I get the job?'

Ask for the next interview

When there are subsequent interviews, ask for the next interview in the same honest and forthright manner. 'Is now a good time to schedule our next meeting?' If you do not ask, you do not get.

Keep yourself in contention

A good leading question to ask is, 'Until I hear from you again, what particular aspects of the job and this interview should I be considering?'

Always depart in the same polite and assured manner in which you entered

Look the interviewer in the eye, put on a smile (there's no need to grin), give a firm handshake and say, 'This has been an exciting meeting for me. This is a job I can do and I feel I can contribute to your goals, because the atmosphere here seems conducive to doing my very best work. When will we speak again?'

Don'ts

Don't discuss salary, holidays or benefits

It is not that the questions are invalid, just that the timing is wrong. Bringing such topics up before you have been offered the job is asking what the company can do for you – instead, you should be saying what you can do for the company. These topics are part of the negotiation (handled in Chapter 19, 'Negotiating the offer') and, without an offer, you have nothing to negotiate.

Don't press for an early decision

Of course you should ask, 'When will I know your decision?' but don't press it. Also, don't try to use the 'there are other opportunities I have to consider too' gambit as leverage when no such offers exist – that annoys the interviewer, makes you look foolish and may even force you to negotiate from a position of weakness. Timing is everything; the issue of how to handle other opportunities as leverage is explored in detail later.

Don't show discouragement

Sometimes you can be offered a job on the spot. Usually, though, you won't, so don't show discouragement if you are not offered the job at the interview, because discouragement shows a lack of self-esteem and determination. Avoiding making a bad impression is merely laying the foundations for leaving a good one, and the right image to leave is one of enthusiasm, guts and openness – just the traits you have been projecting throughout the interview.

Don't ask for an evaluation of your interview performance

To do so forces the issue and puts the interviewer in an awkward position. You *can*, though, say that you want the job and ask what you have to do to get it.

Part IV

Finishing Touches

Statistics show that the last person to interview usually gets the job. Here are some steps you can take that will keep your impression strong.

The successful completion of every interview is a big stride towards getting job offers, yet it is not the end of your job hunt.

A company rarely takes on the first competent person they see. A hiring manager will sometimes interview as many as 15 people for a particular job, but the strain and pace of conducting interviews naturally dim the memory of each applicant. Unless you are the last person to be interviewed, the impression you make will fade with each subsequent interview the interviewer undertakes. If you are not remembered, you will not be offered the job. You must develop a strategy to keep your name and skills constantly in the forefront of the interviewer's mind. These finishing touches often make all the difference.

Some of the suggestions here may not seem earth-shattering, just simple, sensible demonstrations of your manners, enthusiasm and determination, but remember that today all employers are looking for people with that extra little something. You can avoid the negative or merely indifferent impression and be certain of creating a positive one by following these guidelines.

17   *Out of sight, out of mind?*

Don't let the interviewer forget you! The follow-up is simple and here are the steps that guarantee the continuation of your candidacy.

The first thing you do on leaving the interview is breathe a sigh of relief. The second is to make sure that 'out of sight, out of mind' will not apply to you. You do this by starting a follow-up procedure immediately after the interview.

Sitting in your car, on the bus, train or plane, do a written recap of the interview while it is still fresh in your mind. Answer the following questions:

■   Who did you meet? (Write down their names and titles.)

■   What does the job entail?

■   What are the first projects, the biggest challenges?

■   Why can you do the job?

■   What aspects of the interview went well? Why?

■   What aspects of the interview went poorly? Why?

■   What is the agreed-on next step?

■   What was said during the last few minutes of the interview?

■ What stage has the employment process reached? When will a decision be made?

Probably the most difficult – and most important – thing to do is analyse what aspects of the interview went poorly. A person is not offered a job based solely on strength. On the contrary, many people get new jobs based on their relative lack of negatives as compared with the other applicants. So, it is mandatory that you look for and recognize any negatives from your performance. That is the only way you will have an opportunity to package and overcome those negatives in your follow-up procedure and during subsequent interviews.

After your analysis of the interview, your next step is to send the follow-up e-mail or letter to the interviewer. Sending a follow-up letter shows that you are organized and enthusiastic and motivated by the opportunity. In a tightly run job race, when there is nothing to choose between the ability and suitability of two candidates, the job offer always goes to the candidate who is most enthusiastic about the opportunity. It's common sense when you think about it from the employer's viewpoint: the enthusiastic person is going to put more effort into the job; additionally, your enthusiasm is flattering to the hiring manager.

Write a follow-up letter to be sent as an e-mail or as a traditional letter, it should make four points clear to the interviewer:

■ you understand the job and can do it;

■ you paid attention to what was being said;

■ you are excited about the job, and want it;

■ you have the experience to contribute to those first major projects.

Use the right words and phrases in your letter

Here are some you might want to include:

■ 'On reflection' or 'Having thought about our meeting…';

■ recognize – 'I recognize the importance of…';

■ listen – 'Listening to the points you made…';

I enthusiasm – talk about your enthusiasm as it is very effective, especially when your letter will arrive while other applicants are nervously sweating their way through the interview;

I impressed – let the interviewer know you were impressed with the people/ product/service/facility/market/position, but do not overdo it;

I challenge – show that you feel you would be challenged to do your best work in this environment;

I confidence – there is a job to be done and a challenge to be met, so let the interviewer know you are confident of doing both well;

I interest – if you want the job (or next interview), say so as, at this stage, the company is buying and you are selling – ask for the job in a positive and enthusiastic manner;

I appreciation – as a courtesy and mark of professional manners, you must express appreciation for the time the interviewer took out of his or her busy schedule.

Mention the names of the people you met at the interview

Do this whenever it is possible and appropriate to do so. Draw attention to one of the topics that was of general interest to the interviewers.

Address the follow-up letter to the main interviewer

Address the follow-up e-mail/letter to the main interviewer. You can send separate e-mails/letters to others in the selection cycle. Each makes a positive impression and shows extra effort and attention to detail.

Don't write too much

Keep it short – less than one page – and don't make any wild claims that might not withstand close scrutiny.

Send the letter within 24 hours of the interview

If the decision is going to be made in the next couple of days, e-mail the letter or hand deliver it. The follow-up letter will help to set you apart from other applicants and will return your image to the mind of the interviewer just when it would normally be starting to dim.

Perhaps call the interviewer

If a hiring decision is to be made imminently, follow up with an e-mail then a telephone call within 24/48 hours as time constraints dictate; your follow-up is dictated by the time constraints of the employer. 'Mr Massie? Martin Yate. We met for an interview on Wednesday afternoon. I know you are making a decision by close of business tomorrow and I wanted to catch up with you personally to say:

Thanks for your time;
I can do the job and this is why;
I am excited about the job and this is why;
I will make a good employee and this is why.'

If you are in an extended interview cycle, you will need to pace yourself a little differently. If you do not hear anything after five days (which is quite normal), put in a telephone call to the interviewer; I have always thought it a good idea to make sure that the interviewer is reminded of your candidacy right before the weekend begins. Cover the same points as addressed in the last item, asking either for the job or the next interview in the cycle, whichever is appropriate.

Sometimes interviews can stretch into weeks and occasionally months, so a couple of considerations here. You can't e-mail and call every week, but you can touch base every couple of weeks. Google has a nice feature that allows you to track news on any topic you choose. Taking advantage of this allows you to keep up to speed on your profession and factors affecting it, and this knowledge gathering can be put to additional good use.

E-mail a quick note with a link: 'Mr Massie, I just came across this article about the impact of X on productivity in our profession and thought you might like to see it. By the way, I am still determined to be your next [title]. Regards, Martin Yate.'

Even better, print it out and, with a neatly hand-written note, send it by post (instead of or in addition to e-mail). You think I'm crazy? Think again; everyone gets a ton of e-mail every day but regular mail has diminished to a similar degree, so by sending useful information through a less trammelled medium will help you stand out.

Now while you will follow up enthusiastically with all your interviews, you should recognize a difficult fact of life: the longer an interview cycle drags out, the less likelihood of it resulting in an offer. So while you will follow up conscientiously with all your interviews, you will not place your professional future on the wings of a prayer. Instead you will continue to work your plan, making new contacts and generating new interviews on a consistent basis.

This is simply the sensible approach. Just as every job is not right for you, you will not be right for every job, so occasionally you may be told you are no longer in the running. In most instances this will be a signal to shrug your shoulders and move on, but once in a while it will happen with a job that you really want. The next chapter will show you practical ways to snatch victory from the jaws of defeat.

18 Snatching victory from the jaws of defeat

Rejection? Impossible! Then again, you won't be right for every job. Here are some techniques that help you to create opportunity even in the face of rejection.

During the interviewing process, there are bound to be interviewers who erroneously come to the conclusion that you are not the right person for the job they need to fill. When that happens, you will be turned down. Such an absurd travesty of justice can occur in different ways:

∎ at the interview;

∎ in a letter of rejection;

∎ during your follow-up telephone call.

I have stressed the wisdom of having at least a few interviews in process at the same time – being rejected when you have no others in the pipeline can be devastating to your ego. But it needn't be, so long as you are emotionally and intellectually prepared to take advantage of the opportunity being offered to you.

You will get turned down. No one can be right for every job. The right person for a job doesn't always get it, however – the best-prepared and most determined often does. While you may be responsible in part for the initial rejection, you still have the power to correct the situation and get the job in the end. What you do with the claimed victory is a different matter – you will then be in a seller's market with choice and control of your situation.

To turn around a rejection often requires only willpower and determination. Almost every job you desire is obtainable once you understand the process from the interviewer's side of the desk. Your initial – and temporary – rejection is attributable to one of these reasons:

▮ the interviewer does not feel you can do the job;

▮ the interviewer feels you lack a successful profile;

▮ the interviewer did not feel your personality would contribute to the smooth functioning of the department – perhaps you didn't portray yourself as either a team player or as someone willing to take the extra step.

With belief in yourself, you can still succeed. Repeat to yourself constantly through the interview cycle, 'I will get this job because no one else can give as much to this company as I can!' Do that and implement the following plan immediately when you hear of rejection, whether in person, via a letter or over the telephone.

Step 1

Let's suppose you get the rejection when the interview finishes. Thank the interviewer for his or her time and consideration. Then ask politely, 'To help my future job search, why wasn't I chosen for the position?' Assure the interviewer that you would truly appreciate an honest, objective analysis. Listen to the reply and do not interrupt regardless of the comments. Use your time constructively and take notes furiously. When the interviewer finishes speaking, show you understood the comments. (Remember, understanding and agreeing are different animals.)

'Thank you, Mr Smith – now I can understand the way you feel. Because I am not a professional interviewer, I'm afraid my interview nerves got in the way. I'm very interested in working for your company [use an enthusiastic tone] and am determined to get the job. Let me meet you once again. This time, when I'm not so nervous, I am confident you will see I really do have the skills you require' [then provide an example of a skill you have in the questionable area]. 'You name the time and the place and I will be there. What's best for you, Mr Smith?'

End with a question, of course. An enthusiastic request like that is very difficult to refuse and will usually get you another interview. An interview, of course, at which you must shine.

Step 2

Check your notes and accept the interviewer's concerns. Their validity is irrelevant; the important point is that the negative points represent the problem areas in the interviewer's perception of you. List the negative perceptions and, using the techniques and exercises discussed throughout the book, develop different ways to overcome or compensate for every negative perception.

Step 3

Reread Part III of this book.

Step 4

Practise aloud the statements and responses you will use at the interview. If you can practise with someone who plays the part of the interviewer, so much the better. That will create a real interview atmosphere and be helpful to your success. Lacking a role-play partner, you can create that live answer by putting the anticipated objections and questions on a tape and responding to them.

Step 5

Study all available information on the company.

Step 6

Congratulate yourself continually for getting another interview after initial rejection. This is proof of your self-worth, ability and tenacity. You have nothing to lose and everything to gain, having already risen phoenix-like from the ashes of temporary defeat.

Step 7

During the interview, ask for the job in a positive and enthusiastic manner. Your drive and staying power will impress the interviewer. All you must do to win the job is overcome the perceived negatives and you have been given the time to prepare. Go for it.

Step 8

Even when all has failed at the subsequent interview, do not leave without a final request for the job. Play your trump card: 'Mr Smith, I respect the fact that you allowed me the opportunity to prove myself here today. I am convinced I am the best person for the job. I want you to give me a trial and I will prove on the job that I am the best decision you have made this year. Will you give us both the opportunity?'

A reader once wrote to me as I was revising this book. The letter read, in part, 'I read the chapter entitled 'Snatching victory from the jaws of defeat', and did everything you said to salvage what appeared to be a losing interview. My efforts did make a very good impression on the interviewer, but, as it was finally explained to me, I really did not have equal qualifications for the job and finally came in a close second. I really want to work for this growing company and they say they have another position coming up in six months. What should I do?'

I know of someone in the airline business who wanted a job working on Concorde. He had been recently laid off and had high hopes for a successful interview. As it happened, he came in second for the Concorde position. He was told that the firm would speak to him again in the near future. So he waited – for eight months. Finally, he realized that waiting for the job could only leave him unemployed. The moral of the story is that you must be brutally objective when you come out second-best and, whatever the interviewer says, you must sometimes assume that you are getting a polite brush-off.

With that in mind, let's see what can be done on the positive side. First of all, send a thank you note to the interviewer, acknowledging your understanding of the state of affairs and reaffirming your desire to work for the company. Conclude with a polite request that he or she bear you in mind for the future.

Then, keep an eye out for any news item about the company in the press. Whenever you see something, cut it out and post it to the interviewer with a very brief note that says something like, 'I came across this in *The Financial Times* and thought you might find it interesting. I am still determined to be your next account manager, so please keep me in mind when the next opening occurs.'

You can also call the interviewer once every couple of months, just to check in. Remember, of course, to keep the phone call brief and polite – you simply want to keep your name at the top of the interviewer's mind.

Maybe something will come of it. Ultimately, however, your only choice is to move on. There is no gain to be had from waiting on an interviewer's word. Go out and keep looking because chances are that you will come up with an even better job. Then, if you still want to work for the company that gave you the brush-off, you will have some leverage.

Most people fail in their endeavours by quitting just before the dawn of success. Follow these directions and you can win the job. You have proven yourself to be a fighter and that is universally admired. The interviewer will want you to succeed because you are made of stuff that is rarely seen today. You are a person with guts, drive and endurance – the hallmarks of a winner. Being turned down for a job is an opportunity to exercise and build on your strengths and, by persisting, you may well add to your growing number of job offers, now and in the future.

19 Negotiating the offer

They want you! Before you sign on the dotted line, however, you should be well schooled in the essentials of good salary and benefits negotiations. After all, you're never going to have this much leverage again unless you start over from square one.

The crucial period after you have received a formal offer and before you accept it is probably the one point in your relationship with an employer at which you can say with any accuracy that you have the whip hand. The advantage, for now, is yours. They want you but don't have you and their wanting something they don't have gives you a negotiating edge. An employer is also more inclined to respect and honour a person who has a clear understanding of his or her worth in the marketplace – they want a savvy and businesslike person.

You don't have to accept or reject the first offer, whatever it is. In most instances you can improve the initial offer in a number of ways, but you have to know something about the existing market conditions for those employed in your area of endeavour. If you are female, bear in mind that simply settling for a few points above your current rate of pay is bad advice for anyone and downright crazy for you.

Statistics tell us that men out-earn women in nearly every field. (For what it's worth, my research could not turn up a single industry in which this was not the case.) Even if a woman's responsibilities, background, and accomplishments are exactly the same as those of her male colleague, she is statistically unlikely to take home a payslip equal to his. According to statistics, male engineers make 14.3 per cent more than their female counterparts. Male mathematicians make 16.3 per cent more. Male advertising and public relations professionals make 28 per cent more. Male lawyers and judges make 28 per cent more. And male editors and reporters make a whopping 43 per cent more than women performing the same or comparable work. My belief is that much of the gap can be attributed to a simple lack of knowledge of professional negotiating skills, and that women in the workplace are picking these skills up fast.

Man or woman, there is no guarantee that you are being paid what you are worth at the moment. The simple facts are these: if you don't get it while they want you and don't have you, you sure can't count on getting it once they do have you. Remember, too, that if you start at a reduced figure, every subsequent pay rise will come from a proportionately lower base, so the real amount of money lost over an entire career span could actually be substantial.

To get what you have coming at the negotiating table, you must take the time to understand what you have achieved, what you have to offer and what you are worth to the employer. You should be able to get a better handle on that final item by doing good research, but remember that regional influences can affect pay levels, as can current business conditions.

Everything in this book has been written with the aim of maximizing your professional worth and salary negotiation is certainly no exception. Please bear in mind that there are no shortcuts. The ideas presented in this chapter will be helpful to you if they represent the culmination of your successful campaign to set yourself apart from the competition, but you cannot negotiate a terrific salary package if an employer is not convinced that you are in the top tier of applicants.

Follow this three-step procedure when planning your salary discussions with employers.

Step 1

Before getting into negotiations with any employer, work out your minimum cash requirements for any job – you must know what it is going to take to keep a roof over your head and bread on the table. It's necessary to know this figure, but you need never discuss it with anyone – knowing it is the foundation of getting both what you need and what you are worth.

Step 2

Get a grip on what your skills are worth in the current market. There are several ways to do that. Consider the resources and methods outlined below:

▪ you can find salary surveys at online employment sites;

▪ you may be able to find out the salary range for the level above you and the level beneath you at the company in question;

▪ ask headhunters – they know better than anyone what the market will bear and you should, as a matter of career prudence, establish an ongoing relationship with a reputable headhunter because you never know when his or her services will come in handy;

▪ many professional journals publish annual salary surveys that you can consult and look in recent newspapers and compare salaries offered to people with your skills.

Step 3

This is the fun part. Come up with the figure that would make you smile, drop dead and go to heaven on the spot (but try to keep it somewhere within the bounds of reality – multimillion-pound offers with stock options and other benefits being in relatively short supply for most of us).

You now have three figures: a minimum, a realistic middle of the road desired salary and a dream salary.

Your minimum is, you will recall, what you need to cover personal consumption – never discuss it with anyone. Put it aside and what do you have left? A salary range, just like the one every employer has for every interview you attend. Yours extends from your midpoint to your dream salary. Yes, that range represents the 'top half' of what you want or, more accurately, could conceivably accept, but there's a reason for that. In the event, you will find that it is far easier to negotiate down than it is to negotiate up and you must find a starting point that gives you every possible advantage.

Negotiate while you can

Although questions of salary are usually brought up after you are under serious consideration, you must be careful to avoid painting yourself into a corner when you fill out the initial company application form that contains a request for required salary. Usually you can get away with 'open' as a response; sometimes the form will instruct you not to write 'open', in which case you can write 'negotiable' or 'competitive'.

So much for basic considerations. Let's move on to the money questions that are likely to be flying around the room.

The salary/job negotiations begin in earnest in two ways. The interviewer can bring up the topic with statements like the following:

■ 'How do you think you would like working here?'

■ 'People with your background always fit in well with us.'

■ 'You could make a real contribution here.'

■ 'Well, you certainly seem to have what it takes.'

Alternatively, if it is clearly appropriate to do so, you can bring on the negotiating stage. In that case, you can make mirror images of the above, which make the interviewer face the fact that you certainly are able to do the job and that the time has therefore come to talk frankly:

■ 'How do you think I would fit in with the group?'

■ 'I feel my background and experience would definitely complement the work group, don't you?'

■ 'I think I could make a real contribution here. What do you think?'

■ 'I know I have what it takes to do this job. What questions are lingering in your mind?'

Now then. What do you do when the question of money is brought up before you have enough details about the job to negotiate from a position of knowledge and strength? Postpone money talk until you have the facts at hand. Do that by asking something like, 'I still have one or two questions about my responsibilities and it will be easier for me to talk about money when I have cleared them up. Could I first ask you a few questions about…?'

Then proceed to clarify duties and responsibilities, being careful to weigh the relative importance of the position and the individual duties to the success of the department you may join.

The employer is duty-bound to get your services as reasonably as possible, while you have an equal responsibility to do the best you can for yourself. Your goal is not to settle for less than will enable you to be happy in the job – unhappiness at work can taint all the other areas of your life. As noted earlier, it is far easier to negotiate down than it is to negotiate up. The value of the offer you accept depends on your performance throughout the interviewing process and, especially, the finesse you display in the final negotiations. The rest of this chapter is going to address the many questions that might be asked or that you might ask to bring matters to a successful conclusion.

'What is an adequate reward for your efforts?'

A glaring manageability question and money probe all in one. The interviewer probably already has a typist on staff who expects a Nobel Prize each time he or she gets out a faultless letter. Your answer should be honest and cover all angles. 'My primary satisfaction and reward comes from a job well done and completed on time. The occasional good word from my boss is always welcome. Last but not least, I think everyone looks forward to a salary review.'

'What is your salary history?' *or* 'How did your salary progress in your last job?'

The interviewer is looking for a couple of things here. First, for the frequency, percentage and monetary value of your pay rises, which, in turn, tell him or her about your performance and the relative value of the offer that is about to be made. What you want to avoid is tying the potential offer to your salary history – the offer you negotiate should be based solely on the value of the job in hand. Again, this is even more important if you are a woman.

Your answer needs to be specifically vague. Perhaps, 'My salary history has followed a steady upwards path and I have never failed to receive merit increases. I would be glad to give you the specific numbers if needed, but I shall have to sit down and give it some thought with a pencil and paper.' The odds are that the interviewer will not ask you to do that; if he or she does, nod in agreement and say that you'll get right to it when you get home. Don't begin the task until you are requested a second time, which is unlikely.

If for any reason you find yourself with your back against the wall with this one, be sure to include in the specifics of your answer that 'one of the reasons I am leaving my current job is that pay rises were standard for all levels of employees, so, despite my superior contributions, I got the same percentage rise as the poor employee. I want to work in an environment where I will be recognized and rewarded for my contributions.' Then end with a question: 'Is this the sort of company where I can expect that?'

'What were you earning at your last job?'

A similar but different question. It could also be phrased, 'What are you earning now?' or 'What is your current salary?'

While I have said that your current earnings should bear no relation to your starting salary on the new job, it can be difficult to make that statement clear to the interviewer without appearing objectionable. Although the question asks you to be specific, you needn't get too specific. Instead, you should try to draw attention to the fact that the two jobs are different. A short answer might be, 'I am earning £X, although I'm not sure how that will help you in your evaluation of my worth for this job, because the two jobs are somewhat different.'

It is important to understand the areas of allowable fudge. For instance, if you are considerably underpaid, you may want to include the monetary value of such perks as medical and other health plans, pay in lieu of holidays, profit-sharing and pension plans, bonuses, stock options and other incentives. For many people, these can add between 20 and 35 per cent to their basic salary, so you might honestly be able to mention a higher figure than you at first thought possible. Also, if you are due for a pay rise imminently, you are justified in adding it in.

It isn't common for current or previous salaries to be verified by employers, although certain industries, because of legal requirements, check more than others do. Before your 'current salary' figure disappears through the roof, however, it is safest to remain within credible bounds. After all, once you have been given the job and are starting work at the company, you will have to hand over your P45 and your present salary could be extrapolated from that.

'Have you ever been refused a salary increase?'

This implies that you asked. An example of your justifiable request might parallel the following true story. An accountant for a tyre distributorship made changes to an accounting system that saved thousands of pounds a year, plus 30 staff hours a week. Six months after the methods were obviously working smoothly, he requested a salary review, was refused, but was told he would receive a year-end bonus. He did: £75. If you can tell a story like that, by all means tell how you were turned down for a pay rise. If not, it is best to play it safe and explain that your work and salary history showed a steady and marked continual improvement over the years.

'How much do you need to earn to support your family?'

As we have seen, your best advice is to find some way to sidestep this by discussing your midpoint desired salary.

This question is sometimes asked of people who will be working in a sales job, where remuneration is based on a draw against forthcoming commissions. If this scenario describes your income patterns, be sure you have a firm handle on your basic needs before you accept the position.

For salaried positions, this question is of little relevance. It implies the employer will try to get you at a subsistence salary, which is not why you are there. In this instance, give a range from your desired high-end salary down to your desired midpoint salary.

'How much will it take to get you?' 'How much are you looking for?' 'What are your salary expectations?' 'What are your salary requirements?'

You are being asked to name a figure here. Give the wrong answer and you can find you're eliminated. It is always tempting to ask for the moon, knowing you can come down later, but there are better approaches. It is wise to confirm your understanding of the job and its importance before you start throwing numbers around, because you will have to live with the consequences. You need to ensure the best possible offer without pricing yourself out of the market, so it's time to dance with one of the following responses.

'Well, let's see if I understand the responsibilities fully...' You then proceed to itemize exactly what you will be doing on a daily basis and the parameters of your responsibilities and authority. Once that is done you will seek agreement: 'Is this the job as you see it or have I missed anything?' Remember to describe the job in its most flattering and challenging light, paying special attention to the way you see it fitting into the overall picture and contributing to the success of the department, work group and company. You can then finish your response with a question of your own: 'What figure did you have in mind for someone with my track record?' or 'What range has been authorized for this position?' Your answer will include, in part, something along the lines of,'I believe my skills and experience will warrant a starting salary between _____ and _____.'

You also could ask, 'What would be the salary range for someone with my experience and skills?' or 'I naturally want to make as much as my background and skills will allow. If I am right for the job, and I think my credentials demonstrate that I am, I am sure you will make me a fair offer. What figure do you have in mind?'

Another good response is, 'I would expect a salary appropriate to my experience and ability to do the job successfully. What range do you have in mind?'

Such questions will get the interviewer to reveal the salary range and concentrate his or her attention on the challenges of the job and your ability to accept and work with those challenges.

When you are given a range, you can adjust your money requirements appropriately, latching on to the upper part of the range. For example, if the range is £30,000–£35,000 a year, you can come back with a range of £34,000–£37,000.

Consequently, your response will include: 'That certainly means we have something to talk about. While your range is £30,000–£35,000, I am looking for a minimum of £34,000 with an ideal of £37,000. Tell me, what flexibility is there at the top of your salary range?' You need to know this to put yourself in the strongest negotiating position and this is the perfect time and opportunity to gain the information and the advantage.

All this fencing is aimed at getting the interviewer to show his or her hand first. Ask for too much and it's 'Oh dear, I'm afraid you're overqualified', to which you can reply, 'So, overpay me.' (Actually, that works when you can carry it off with an ingratiating smile.) If your request is too low, you are likely to be ruled out as lacking the appropriate experience.

When you have tried to get the interviewer to name a range and failed, you must come up with a specific figure. At this point, the key is to understand that all jobs have salary ranges attached to them.

Consequently, the last thing you will ever do is come back with a specific figure – that traps you. Instead, you will mention your own range, which will not be from your minimum to your maximum, but, rather, from your midpoint to your maximum. Remember, as before, you can always negotiate down, but rarely negotiate up.

'What kind of salary are you worth?'

This is a 'How much do you want?' question with a slight twist. It is asking you to name a desired figure, but the twist is that it also asks you to justify that figure. It requires that you demonstrate careful analysis of your worth, industry norms and job requirements. You are recommended to try for a higher figure rather than a lower one. 'Having compared my background and experience with industry norms and salary surveys, I feel my general worth is in the region of £X to £Y. My general background and credentials fit your needs and my first-hand knowledge of the specific challenges and projects I would face in this job are an exact match, so I feel worthy of justifying an offer towards the top of this range. Don't you agree?'

After your response to a salary question, you can expect to hear, 'That's too much' or 'Oh, that is more than we were hoping to pay' or 'That would be stretching the budget to the breaking point.' When this happens, accept it as no more than a negotiating gambit and come back with your own calm rebuttal: 'What did you have in mind?'

'What do you hope to be earning two to five years from now?'

A difficult question. The interviewer is probing your desired career and earning path and is trying to see if you have your sights set high enough – or too high. Perhaps a jocular tone doesn't hurt here: 'I'd like to be earning just about as much as my boss and I can work out!' Then, throw the ball back with your own question: 'How much is it possible to make here?'

If you give a specific figure, the interviewer is going to want justification. If you come up with a salary range, you are advised also to have a justified career path to go along with it.

You could also say, 'In two years, I will have finished my exams, so with that plus my additional experience, industry norms say I should be earning between £X and £Y. I would hope to be earning at least within that range, but hopefully, with a proven track record of contributions, I would be making above the norm.' The trick is to use industry statistics as the backbone of your argument, express confidence in doing better than the norm and, whenever possible, stay away from specific job titles unless pressed.

'Do you think people in your occupation should be paid more?'

This one can be used prior to serious salary negotiation to probe your awareness of how your job really contributes to the bottom line. Otherwise, it can occur in the middle of salary negotiations to throw you off-balance. The safe and correct answer is to straddle the fence. 'Most jobs have salary ranges that reflect the job's relative importance and contribution to a company. Those salary ranges reflect the norm for the great majority of people within that profession. That does not mean, however, that the extraordinary people in such a group are not recognized for their extra performance and skills. There are always exceptions to the rule.'

Good offers, poor offers

After a period of bantering back and forth like this, the interviewer names a figure, hopefully meant as a legitimate offer. If you aren't sure, qualify it: 'Let me see if I understand you correctly: Are you formally offering me the position at £X a year?'

The formal offer can fall into one of two categories.

It sounds fair and equitable

In that case, you still want to negotiate for a little more – employers almost expect it of you, so don't disappoint them. Mention a salary range again, the low end of which comes at about the level of their offer and the high end somewhat above it. You can say, 'Well, it certainly seems that we are close. I was hoping for something more in the range of £X to £Y. How much room do we have for negotiation here?'

No one will withdraw an offer because you say you feel you are worth more. After all, the interviewer thinks you are the best person for the job and has extended a formal offer – the last thing he or she needs now is to start from square one again. The employer has a vested interest in bringing the negotiation to a satisfactory conclusion. In a worst case scenario, the interviewer can stick to the original offer.

It isn't quite what you expected

Even if the offer isn't what you thought it would be, you still have options other than accepting or rejecting it as it stands. However, your strategy for now is to run the money topic as far as you can in a calm and businesslike way. Then, once you have gone that far, you can back off and examine the other potential benefits of the job. That way you will leave yourself with an opening, if you need it, to hit the money topic once more at the close of negotiations.

If you feel the salary could do with a boost, say so: 'I like the job and I know I have what it takes to be successful in it. I would also be prepared to give you a start date of 1 March, to show my sincerity, but, quite honestly, I couldn't justify it with your initial salary offer. I hope that we have some room for negotiation here.'

Alternatively, you can say, 'I could start on 1 March and I do feel I could make a contribution here and become an integral part of the team. The only thing standing in the way is my inability to make ends meet based on your initial offer. I am sincerely interested in the opportunity and flattered by your interest in me. If we could just solve this money problem, I'm sure we could come to terms. What do you think can be done about it?'

The interviewer will probably come back with a question asking how much you want: 'What is the minimum you would be prepared to work for?' Respond with your range again – with your minimum really your midpoint – and the interviewer may well then come back with a higher offer and ask for your concurrence. This is the time to be non-committal but encouraged and move on to the benefits included with the position: 'Well, yes, that is a little better. Perhaps we should talk about the benefits.'

Alternatively, the interviewer may come back with another question: 'That's beyond our salary range for this job title. How far can you reduce your salary needs to fit our range?'

That question shows good faith and a desire to close the deal, but don't give in too easily – the interviewer is never going to want you as much as he or she does now. Your first response might be: 'I appreciate that, but if it is the job title and its accompanying range that is causing the problem, couldn't we upgrade the title, thereby putting me near the bottom of the next range?' Try it – it often works. If it doesn't, it is probably time to move to other negotiable aspects of the job offer, but not before one last try. You can take that final stab by asking, 'Is that the best you can do?' With this question, you must look the interviewer directly in the eye, ask the question and maintain eye contact. It works surprisingly well. You should also remember to try it as a closing gambit at the very end of negotiations when you have received everything you can hope for. You may get a pleasant surprise.

Negotiating your future salary

At this point, you have probably ridden present salary as hard as you reasonably can (for a while, anyway), so the time has come to shift the conversation to future remuneration.

'Even though the offer isn't quite what I'd hoped for to start the job, I am still interested. Can we talk about the future for a while?' Then you move the conversation to an on-the-job focus. Here are a few arrangements corporate headhunters frequently negotiate for their recruits.

A single lump sum signing bonus

Known as a 'golden hello', it is nice to have, though it is money that is here today and gone tomorrow. Don't make the mistake of adding it on to the basic salary figure. If you get a £2,500 signing bonus, that money won't be included when it comes to your year-end review – your pay rise will be based on your actual salary – so the bonus is a little less meaningful than it appears.

A performance review with pay rise attached

You can frequently negotiate a minimum percentage increase here, if you have confidence in your abilities.

Promotion

You might be able to negotiate a review after a certain period of time.

▪ **An end-of-year bonus.** When you hear talk about an end-of-year bonus, don't rely on 'what it's going to be this year' or 'what it was last year', because the actual bonus will never bear any resemblance to either figure. Base the realism of any bonus expectations on a five-year performance history.

▌ **Things other than cash.** Also in the realm of real disposable income are things like a company car, petrol, maintenance, and insurance. They represent hard cash you would not have to spend. It's not unusual to hear of employers paying car or insurance allowances, picking up servicing bills for your personal vehicle, or paying petrol up to a certain amount each month. But if you don't ask, you can never expect an employer to offer. What have you got to lose? Remember to get any of those unusual goodies in writing – even respectable managers in respected companies can suffer amnesia.

Influencing and evaluating the offer

No two negotiations are going to be alike, so there is no absolute model you can follow. Nevertheless, when you have addressed present and future remuneration, this might be the time to get some more information about the company and the job itself.

Even if you haven't agreed on money, you are probably beginning to get a feeling as to whether or not you can put the deal together – you know the employer wants to. Many of the following questions will be appropriate here; some might even be appropriate at other times during the interview cycle.

Full knowledge of all the relevant facts is critical to your successful final negotiation of money and benefits. Your prudent selection of questions from this list will help you negotiate the best offers and choose the right job for you. (At this point, asking some pertinent questions from the following list also serves as a decompression device of sorts for both parties.)

The questions come in these categories:

▌ nuts-and-bolts job clarification;

▌ job and department growth;

▌ corporate culture;

▌ company growth and direction.

The following section is also worth reading between first and second interviews.

Nuts and bolts

First, if you have career aspirations, you want to land a job in an outfit that believes in promoting from within. To find out, ask a few of these questions: 'How long has the job been open?' 'Why is it open?' 'Who held the job last?' 'What is he/she doing now?' 'Promoted, fired, quit?' 'How long was he/she in that job?' 'How many people have held this job in the last three years?' 'Where are they now?' 'How often and how many people have been promoted from this position and to where?'

You could also ask, 'What is the timetable for filling the position?' The longer the job has been open and the tighter the time frame for filling it, the better your leverage. That can also be determined by asking, 'When do you need me to start? Why on that date particularly?'

Here are some more good questions:

■ 'What are the first projects to be addressed?' or 'What are the major problems to be tackled and conquered?'

■ 'What do you consider the five most important day-to-day responsibilities of this job? Why?'

■ 'What personality traits do you consider critical to success in this job?'

■ 'How do you see me complementing the existing group?'

■ 'Will I be working with a team or on my own? What will be my responsibilities as a team member? What will be my leadership responsibilities?'

■ 'How much overtime is involved?'

■ 'How much travel is involved?' and 'How much overnight travel?' With overnight travel you need to find out the number of days per week and month and, more importantly, whether or not you will be paid for weekend days or given time off in lieu. I have known companies that expect you to get home from a long weekend trip at 1 o'clock in the morning and be at work at 8.30 am on Monday – all without extra pay or time off.

■ 'How frequent are performance and salary reviews? What are they based on – standard pay rises for all or are they weighted towards merit and performance?'

■ 'How does the performance appraisal and reward system work? Exactly how are outstanding employees recognized, judged and rewarded?'

■ 'What is the complete financial package for someone at my level?'

Job and department growth

Gauging the potential for professional growth in a job is very important for some; for others, it comes slightly lower down the list. Even if you aren't striving to head up the company in the next few years, you will still want to know what the promotional and growth expectations are so that you don't end up with a company expecting you to scale the heights. Here are some questions you will find useful for finding these things out:

■ 'To what extent are the functions of the department recognized as important and worthy of review by upper management?' If upper management takes an interest in the doings of your work group, rest assured you are in a visible position for recognition and reward.

■ 'Where and how does my department fit into the company pecking order?'

■ 'What does the department hope to achieve in the next two to three years? How will that help the company? How will it be recognized by the company?'

■ 'What do you see as the strengths of the department? What do you see as weaknesses that you are looking to turn into strengths?'

■ 'What role would you hope I would play in these goals?'

■ 'What informal/formal benchmarks will you use to measure my effectiveness and contributions?'

■ 'Based on my effectiveness, how long would you anticipate me holding this position? When my position and responsibilities change, what are the possible titles and responsibilities I might grow into?'

■ 'What is the official corporate policy on internal promotion? How many people in this department have been promoted from their original positions since joining the company?'

▮ 'How do you determine when a person is ready for promotion?'

▮ 'What training and professional development assistance is available to help me grow professionally?'

▮ 'Does the company encourage outside professional development training? Does the company sponsor all or part of any costs?'

▮ 'What are my potential career paths within the company?'

▮ 'To what jobs have people with my title risen in the company?'

▮ 'Who in the company was in this position the shortest length of time? Why? Who has remained in this position the longest? Why?'

Corporate culture

All companies have their own way of doing things – that's corporate culture. Not every corporate culture is for you. To find out more, try asking the following questions:

▮ 'What is the company's mission? What are the company's goals?'

▮ 'What approach does this company take to its marketplace?'

▮ 'What is unique about the way this company operates?'

▮ 'What is the best thing you know about this company? What is the worst thing you know about this company?'

▮ 'How does the reporting structure work? What are the accepted channels of communication and how do they work?'

▮ 'What kinds of checks and balances, reports or other work-measurement tools are used in the department and company?'

▮ 'What do you and the company consider important in my fitting into the corporate culture – the way of doing things round here?'

▮ 'Will I be encouraged or discouraged from learning about the company beyond my own department?'

Company growth and direction

For those concerned about career growth, a healthy company is mandatory; for those concerned about stability of employment, the same applies. See how things are by asking the following questions:

- 'What expansion is planned for this department, division or organization?'

- 'What markets does the company anticipate developing?'

- 'Does the company have plans for mergers or acquisitions?'

- 'Currently, what new endeavours is the company actively pursuing?'

- 'How do market trends affect company growth and progress? What is being done about them?'

- 'What production and employee redundancies and cutbacks have you experienced in the last three years?'

- 'What production and employee redundancies and cutbacks do you anticipate? How are they likely to affect this department, division or organization?'

- 'When was the last corporate reorganization? How did it affect this department? When will the next corporate reorganization occur? How will it affect this department?'

- 'Is this department a profit centre? How does that affect pay?'

The package

Take-home pay is, naturally, the most important part of your package. (You'll probably feel that the only thing wrong with your pay is that it gets taxed before you get to take it home!) That means you must carefully negotiate any possible benefits accruing to the job that have a monetary value, but are tax deductible and/or add to your physical and mental happiness. The list is almost endless, but below you will find those most commonly available. Although many of these benefits are available to all employees at some companies, you should know that, as a rule of thumb, the higher up the ladder you climb, the more benefits you can expect. Because the corporate world and its concepts of creating a motivated and committed workforce are constantly in flux, you should never assume that a particular benefit will not be available to you.

The basic rule is to ask – if you don't ask, there is no way you will get. A few years ago, it would have been unthinkable for anyone but an executive to expect something as glamorous as a leisure club membership in a benefits package. Today, however, more companies have a membership as a standard benefit; an increasing number are even building their own health club facilities. What's this benefit worth in your area? Call a club and find out.

Benefits to your package may include some of the following:

I   investment opportunities

I   insurance plans

I   car allowance

I   car insurance or an allowance

I   car servicing and petrol or an allowance

I   car

I   time off in lieu – as recompense for unpaid overtime/business travel time

I   country club or health club membership

I   accidental death insurance

I   deferred compensation

I   dental insurance – note deductibles and the percentage that is employer-paid

I   employment contract and/or termination contract

I   expense account

I   financial planning help and tax assistance

I   life assurance

I   medical insurance – note deductibles and percentage that is employer-paid

I   pension plans

- personal days off

- profit sharing

- short- or long-term disability compensation plans

- shares

- more holidays.

Evaluating the offer

Once the offer has been negotiated to the best of your ability, you need to evaluate it – which doesn't have to be done on the spot. Some of your requests and questions will take time to be answered and, very often, the final parts of negotiation – 'Yes, Mr Jones, we can give you the extra £2,000 and six weeks of holiday you requested' – will take place over the telephone. Regardless of where the final negotiations are completed, never accept or reject the offer on the spot.

Be positive, say how excited you are about the prospect and that you would like a little time (overnight, a day, two days) to think it over, discuss it with your spouse, whatever. Not only is this delay standard practice, but it will also give you the opportunity to influence other offers, as discussed in the next chapter.

Use the time you gain to speak to your mentors or advisers. However, a word of caution: when asking advice from those close to you, be sure you know exactly where that advice is coming from – you need clear-headed objectivity at this time.

Once the advice is in, and not before, weigh it up along with your own observations – no one knows your needs and aspirations better than you do. While there are many ways of doing that, a simple line down the middle of a sheet of paper, with the reasons to take the job written on one side and the reasons to turn it down on the other, is about as straightforward and objective as you can get.

You will weigh salary, future earnings and career prospects, benefits, journey time, lifestyle, and stability of the company, along with all those intangibles that are summed up in that technical term 'gut feelings'. Make sure you answer these next questions for yourself:

- Do you like the work?

■ Can you be trained in a reasonable period of time, thus having a realistic chance of success on the job?

■ Are the title and responsibilities likely to provide you with a challenge?

■ Is the opportunity for growth in the job compatible with your needs and desires?

■ Are the company's location, stability and reputation in line with your needs?

■ Is the atmosphere/culture of the company conducive to your enjoying working at the company?

■ Can you get along with your new manager and immediate work group?

■ Is the money offer and total compensation package the best you can get?

Notice that money is but one aspect of the evaluation process. There are many other factors to take into account as well. Even a high-paying job can be less advantageous than you think. For instance, you should be careful not to be foxed by the gross figure. It really is important that you get a firm handle on that actual, spendable, after-tax money – the money that pays the rent or mortgage and puts food on the table, and all those other necessities. Always look at an offer in the light of how much spendable money a week it will put in your pocket.

Evaluating the new boss

When all that is done, you must make a final, but immensely important, decision – whether or not you will be happy with your future manager. Remember, you are going to spend the majority of your waking hours at work and the new job can only be as good as your relationship with your new boss. If you felt uncomfortable with the person after an interview or two, you need to evaluate carefully the kind of discomfort and unhappiness it could generate over the coming months and years.

You'll want to know about the manager's personal style. Is he or she confrontational, authoritarian, democratic, hands-off? How would reprimands or differing viewpoints be handled? Does he or she share information on a need to know basis, the old military-management style of keep 'em in the dark? When a group member makes a significant contribution, who gets the credit as far as senior management is concerned – the person, manager or group? You can find out some of that information from the manager; other aspects you'll need to review when you meet team members or the people from HR.

Accepting new jobs, resigning from others

Once your decision has been made, you should accept the job verbally. Spell out exactly what you are accepting: 'Mr Smith, I'd like to accept the position of engineer at a starting salary of £X. I will be able to start work on 1 March. I understand my package will include life, health, and dental insurance and a company car.' Then, you finish with: 'I will be glad to start on the above date pending a written offer received in time to give my present employer adequate notice of my departure. I hope that's acceptable to you.'

Until you have the offer in writing, you have nothing. A verbal offer can be withdrawn – it happens all the time. That's not because the employer suddenly doesn't like you, but because of reasons that affect, but bear no real relationship to, your candidacy. I have known of countless careers that have stalled through reneged verbal offers – they lead to unemployment, bitterness and even lawsuits. So, avoid the headaches and play it by the numbers.

Once you have the offer in writing, notify your current employer in the same fashion. Resigning is difficult for almost everyone, so you can write a pleasant letter, walk into your boss's office, hand it to him or her, then discuss things calmly and pleasantly once he or she has read it.

You will also want to notify any other companies who have been in negotiation with you that you are no longer on the market, but that you were most impressed with meeting them and would like to keep communications open for the future. (See the next chapter for details on how to handle – and encourage – multiple job offers.)

20 Multiple interviews, multiple offers

Relying on one interview at a time can only lead to anxiety, so you must create and foster an ever-growing network of interviews and, consequently, job offers.

False optimism and laziness lead many job hunters to be content with only one interview in process at any given time. That severely reduces the odds of landing the best job in town within your chosen time frame. Complacency guarantees that you will continue to operate in a buyer's market.

The recommended approach is to generate as many interviews as possible in a two- to three-week period. Interviewing skills are learnt and consequently improve with practice. With the improved skills comes a greater confidence and those natural interview nerves disperse. Your confidence shows through to potential employers and you are perceived in a positive light. Also, because other companies are interested in you, everyone will move more quickly to secure your services. That is especially important if you are unfortunate enough to be unemployed. Being out of work is when you need money the most and is the time when the salary you can command on the open market is substantially reduced. The interview activity you generate will help offset this.

By generating multiple interviews, you bring the time of the first job offer closer and closer. That one job offer can be quickly multiplied into a number of others. With a single job offer, your unemployed status has, to all intents and purposes, passed.

Immediately, you can call every company with whom you've met and explain the situation. 'Mr Johnson, I'm calling because, while still under consideration by your company, I have received a job offer from one of your competitors. I would hate to make a decision without the chance of speaking to you again. I was very impressed by my meeting with you. Can we get together in the next couple of days?' End, of course, with a question that carries the conversation forward.

If you were in the running at all, your call will usually generate another interview – Mr Johnson does not want to miss out on a suddenly prized commodity. Remember, it is human nature to want the very things one is about to lose. So, you see, your simple offer can be multiplied almost by the number of interviews you have in process at the time.

A single job offer can also be used to generate interviews with new firms. It is as simple as making your usual telephone networking presentation, but you end it differently. You would be very interested in meeting them because of your knowledge of the company/product/service, but also because you have just received a job offer – would it be possible to get together in the next couple of days?

Relying on one interview at a time can only lead to prolonged anxiety, disappointment and, possibly, unemployment. That reliance is due to the combination of false optimism, laziness and fear of rejection. These are traits that cannot be tolerated, except by confirmed defeatists, for defeat is the inevitable result of these traits. As Heraclitus said, 'Character is destiny.' Headhunters say, 'The job offer that cannot fail will.'

Self-esteem, on the other hand, is vital to your success and happiness is found with it. Also, with it you will begin to awake each day with a vitality previously unknown. Vigour will increase, your enthusiasm will rise and desire to achieve will burn within. The more you do today, the better you will feel tomorrow.

Even when you follow this plan to the letter, not every interview will result in an offer. However, with many irons in the fire, an occasional firm 'no' should not affect your morale. It won't be the first or last time you face rejection. Be persistent and, above all, close your mind to all negative and discouraging influences. The success you experience from implementing this plan will increase your store of willpower and determination, affect the successful outcome of your job hunt and enrich your whole life. Start today.

The key to your success is preparation. Remember, it is necessary to plan and organize in order to succeed. Failing is easy – it requires no effort. It is the achievement of success that requires effort, which means effort today, not tomorrow, for tomorrow never comes. So, start building that well-stocked briefcase today.

21 *Conclusion: the glittering prizes*

All victories have their foundation in careful preparation and, having read this book, you're ready to win.

Your attitude is positive and active – dream jobs don't come to those who sit and wait – and you realize that success depends on getting out and generating interviews for yourself. At those interviews, you will maintain the interviewer's interest and attention by carrying your half of the conversation. What you ask will show your interest, demonstrate your analytical abilities and carry the conversation forward. If in doubt about the meaning of a question, you will ask one of your own to clarify it.

The corporate body recognizes that its most valuable resource is those employees who understand and contribute towards its goals. These people have something in common: they all recognize their differing jobs as a series of challenges and problems, each to be anticipated, met and solved. It's that attitude that lands jobs and enhances careers.

People with such an attitude advance their careers faster than others because they possess a critical awareness of universally admired business practices and value systems. They then advance their careers by projecting the personality traits that most closely complement those practices and values.

As I said at the beginning of this book, your job search can be seen as a ritualized mating dance. The name of that dance is 'attitude'. Now that you know the steps, you are ready to whirl away with the glittering prizes. There is no more to say except go to your next interview and knock 'em dead.

Appendix: psychometric tests

Psychometric tests are multiple choice or short answer tests that are claimed to measure intelligence and ability. They are designed by occupational psychologists and are a commonplace feature of many interviews.

How to perform to the best of your ability on tests

Our experience over many years of preparing candidates for both selection tests and public examinations leads us to suggest that if you want to perform to the best of your ability on tests you should:

■ make sure that you know what you have to do before you start – if you do not understand ask the test administrator;

■ read the instructions carefully before the test starts in order to make sure that you understand them – skim reading through them can cause you to overlook important details and make silly mistakes;

■ assume that the instructions (and the worked examples) are not the same as they were the last time you took the test – they may well have been changed, so read them as carefully as you can;

■ highlight or underline the 'command words' in the instructions, ie those words that tell you what you have to do;

■ work as quickly and accurately as you can once the test begins – every unanswered question is a scoring opportunity missed;

■ check frequently to make sure that the question you are answering matches the space you are filling in on the answer grid;

■ avoid spending too much time on questions you find difficult – leave them and go back to them later if you have time;

■ enter your best reasoned choice if you are uncertain about an answer (but avoid simply guessing);

■ go back and check all your answers if you have any spare time after you have answered all the questions;

■ keep working as hard as you can throughout the test – the more correct answers you get the higher your score will be;

■ concentrate your mind on the test itself and nothing else – you cannot afford to allow yourself to be distracted;

■ be positive in your attitude – previous failures in tests and examinations should not be allowed to have a detrimental effect on your performance on this occasion; don't allow yourself to be 'beaten before you begin'!

Sample psychometric test questions

Kogan Page publishes a wide range of books on this subject area, and what follows is a selection of questions drawn from those books. The questions vary in their level of difficulty, with the more basic questions first. For a full list of titles available please see page 301.

Number problems

1. Two out of every 8 cyclists are questioned in a spot-check. Out of 408 cyclists, how many are questioned?

A	B	C	D	E
102	100	88	80	40

Answer =

2. If I pay £4.40 for lunch and £2.75 for tea, how much in total have I spent?

A	B	C	D	E
£6.95	£7.05	£7.15	£7.25	£7.35

Answer =

3. A worker's shift begins at 05.30 and lasts for 9 hours. What time does it end?

A	B	C	D	E
15.30	15.00	14.30	14.00	13.30

Answer =

4. How much would it cost to buy 3 bicycle lights at £3.50 each?

A	B	C	D	E
£9.50	£11.50	£12.00	£11.00	£10.50

Answer =

5. If I pay 23p for a bus ticket, £2.35 for a train ticket and £10.40 for a taxi fare, how much have I spent in total?

A	B	C	D	E
£2.98	£5.75	£9.98	£10.63	£12.98

Answer =

6. If my bus journey takes 35 minutes and my train journey takes 55 minutes, how long is my journey in total?

A	B	C	D	E
1½ hours	1¼ hours	70 minutes	¾ hour	85 minutes

Answer =

7. I leave my house at 06.00 and return at 14.15. How many hours have I been out of my house?

A	B	C	D	E
20½	18¾	8¼	6	2¼

Answer =

8. If 5 cars fill up their tanks with 120 litres of diesel each, how many litres of diesel are used in total?

A	B	C	D	E
6,000	600	500	460	240

Answer =

9. A car park holds 550 cars when it is full. How many cars does it hold when it is half full?   .

A	B	C	D	E
1,100	250	55	275	350

Answer =

10. In a car park of 660 cars, 20 per cent are yellow cars. How many yellow cars are in the car park?

A	B	C	D	E
680	230	330	132	33

Answer =

11. Yousuf sets off on the annual London to Cambridge bike ride. He cycles at a steady pace of 9 miles an hour and crosses the finishing line 6 hours later. What is the distance of the London to Cambridge ride?

Answer =

12. Jo walks along the South Downs Way at a rate of 4.5 miles per hour. After walking for 3½ hours, she still has 6 miles left to walk. What is the total distance she intends to walk?

Answer =

13. A singer is on stage with a bass guitarist. Part of the dance routine requires them to move to opposite ends of the stage for one section of the song. Standing together, they start to move away from each other. The singer shimmies across the stage at the speed of 1 ft every 10 seconds, while the bassist shuffles at the speed of 1 ft every 20 seconds. After 2 minutes, they both reach the edges of the stage. How wide is the stage?

Answer =

14. If a rowing boat travels at an average speed of 1/1000 mile every second, how far will the boat travel in 2 hours?

Answer =

15. A farmer leaves a bale of hay every morning at a location on Dartmoor for the wild ponies, while another farmer leaves a bucket of oats at another location in the evening. One pony trots along a track to the location of the oats at a rate of 12 mph and remains at that location for the night. In the morning, he walks to the hay at a rate of 6 mph along the same track. His round trip journey takes exactly 2 hours and he always starts the journey at the location of the hay or oats. What is the distance between the location of the hay and the location of the oats?

Answer =

16. On a particular stretch of railway line, a speed restriction of 50% of the maximum speed of 100 mph is imposed on parts of the track. What is the minimum time a traveller must allow to complete a journey of 375 miles?

Answer =

17. A hosepipe discharges water at a rate of 4 gallons per minute. How long, in hours, does it take to fill a paddling pool with a 300-gallon capacity?

Answer =

18. Mike drives from his flat to the seaside in 1½ hours. On the way home he is in a hurry to watch the start of the Crystal Palace match and drives one and a half times as fast along the same route. How much time does he spend driving?

Answer =

19. Two cars, 100 miles apart, set off driving towards each other. One is travelling at 70 mph and the other is travelling at 80 mph. After how long will the two cars meet?

Answer =

20. A small car with an engine size of 848 cc and a family car with an engine size of 3 litres set off on a journey of 480 miles. The family car completes the journey in 8 hours. The small car travels at an average speed of 5/6 of the speed of the family car. How much later after the family car will the small car arrive at the destination?

Answer =

21. The perimeter of Jenny's local park measures 5.5 miles and it takes Jenny 3 hours to run four times around the park. What is her average speed?

Answer =

22. Jake rides his new tricycle for half an hour in the park and covers ¾ mile. What is his average speed in miles per hour?

Answer =

23. Bob drives a cab in London. He picks up a passenger at Gatwick Airport on a Friday afternoon and drives 26 miles to a Central London location, a journey of 2 hours and 15 minutes. Then he drives an additional 4 miles to Waterloo station, which takes another 45 minutes. What is Bob's average speed for the Friday afternoon journeys?

Answer =

24. An egg timer contains 18,000 grains of sand. The sand passes at a consistent rate between the top and the bottom cylinders. After 2 minutes and 24 seconds, 14,100 grains of sand have passed through the middle. At what rate per second does the sand pass through the timer per minute?

Answer =

25. In the Ironman Triathlon, athletes are expected to swim for 2.4 miles, bike for 112 miles and run a full marathon distance of 26.2 miles. Rayne enters the competition and is given the following split times for each leg of the competition:

Swim: 48 minutes Bike: 4 hours 59 minutes Run: 6 hours 43 minutes

To the nearest mph, what is Rayne's average speed for the triathlon?

Answer =

Recommended further reading

Intermediate: *How to Pass Numerical Reasoning Tests* (2006), Heidi Smith
Advanced: *How to Pass Advanced Numeracy Tests* (2008), Mike Bryon

Missing words

1. The section of dual _____ was closed due to _____.

A	B	C	D
carrigeway	carriageway	carrigeway	carriageway
alterations	allterations	allterations	alterations

   E   None of these

Answer   =

2. The road _____ was _____ by a stray dog.

A	B	C	D
acident	accident	accident	acident
coursed	caused	coursed	caused

   E   None of these

Answer   = .

3. The _____ happened late on _____ night.

A	B	C	D
atack	atack	attack	attack
Saterday	Saturday	Saterday	Saturday

   E   None of these

Answer   =

4. His _____ new car was a complete _____-off.

A	B	C	D
beautiful	beutiful	beatiful	beautiful
write	right	write	right

   E   None of these

Answer   =

5. The girl could not _____ her insurance _____.

A	B	C	D
prodduce	produce	produce	prodduce
certificate	certifecate	certifficate	certifficate

   E   None of these

Answer   =

6. It is _____ to keep doing the _____ in order to improve.

A	B	C	D
importent	importent	important	important
exercises	exercices	exercices	exercises

E   None of these   Answer   =

7. Our new _____ is a very _____ worker.

A	B	C	D
colleague	coleague	collegue	colleague
competent	competant	competent	competant

E   None of these   Answer   =

8. The _____ _____ were excellent to use.

A	B	C	D
new	knew	new	knew
diaries	diaries	dairies	dairies

E   None of these   Answer   =

9. The _____ policies were said by many to be _____.

A	B	C	D
goverment	government	government	goverment
complicated	complecated	complicated	complecated

E   None of these   Answer   =

10. The old _____ who lived alone were very _____.

A	B	C	D
poeple	people	people	poeple
lonely	loneley	lonely	lonly

E   None of these   Answer   =

11. We drove there _____ car. Can you remember whether or not we paid _____ cheque or _____ cash?

    A. in my   by   in
    B. by my   in   by

> Answer =

12. How many adjectives are in the sentence:

The beautiful young woman was wearing a blue and green dress.

> Answer =

13. Which of the following sentences contain an error?

    A. The design was one of the most unique.
    B. The design was the most unique
    C. The design was unique.
    D. None

> Answer =

14. It rained _____ much and for _____ long time.

    A. such   so
    B. so   such
    C. a   a

> Answer =

15. The man was wearing a _____ coat.

    A. long and red
    B. red and long
    C. long, red
    D. long red

> Answer =

16. Peter is a good friend _____ lives in Italy, a country _____ I have never visited.

    A. and   what
    B. that   whom
    C. who   which

    Answer =

17. Which is a plural reflective pronoun?

    A. myself
    B. my
    C. ours
    D. mine
    E. yourself
    F. themselves

    Answer =

18. _____ rugby team scored three kick goals.

    According to the timetable the train runs _____ day twice _____ hour.

    A. every   each   each
    B. each   every   every

    Answer =

19. With little money but _____ time you can visit a _____ museums.

    A. little   little
    B. few   much
    C. much   few

    Answer =

20. Tom is lazy and never has _____ work while Joe always has
    _____ work to do.

    A. some   any
    B. any   some

    > Answer =

21. _____ a new cinema opened in town but when I went _____ was
    closed.

    A. It   there
    B. there   there's
    C. their   their
    D. there's   it

    > Answer =

Recommended further reading

Intermediate: *The Ultimate Psychometric Test Book* (2006), Mike Bryon
Advanced: *The Graduate Psychometric Test Workbook* (2005), Mike Bryon;
How to Pass Advanced Verbal Reasoning Tests (2008), Mike Bryon

Identify the *correct* sentences:

1.
A There are redundancies when the managing director arrived.
B There will be redundancies after the managing director arrived.
C After the new managing director arrived, there were redundancies.
D After the new managing director arrived, there will be many redun-
   dancies.
E None of these.

Answer

2.

A   As soon as the sales figures are available, the directors knew they had achieved their targets.

B   As soon as the sales figures were available, the directors knew they had achieved their targets.

C   As soon as the sales figures are available, the directors knew they have achieved their targets.

D   None of these.

Answer

3.

A   Although the business plan look promising the bank manager suspected that the proposal is unlikely to succeed.

B   Although the business plan looks promising the bank manager suspects the proposal was unlikely to succeed.

C   Although the business plan looked promising the bank manager suspected that the proposal was unlikely to succeed.

D   None of these.

Answer

4.

A   If you were to contact the client you might find that they would buy.

B   If you are to contact the client you might find that they would buy.

C   If you were to contact the client you will find that they will buy.

D   None of these.

Answer

5.
A   While the photocopier is broken you will have to go across the road to the copy shop.
B   While the photocopier was broken you will have to go across the road to the copy shop.
C   When the photocopier is broken you went across the road to the copy shop.
D   None of these.

Answer

6.
A   My new colleague is the one who has the red car.
B   My new colleague was the one whom had the red car.
C   My new colleague will be the one who had the red car.
D   None of these.

Answer

7.
A   The family will eating their meal in the restaurant.
B   The family was eating its meal in the restaurant.
C   The family were eating their meal in the restaurant.
D   None of these.

Answer

8.
A   Neither you nor I is able to make sense of this.
B   Neither you nor I are able to make sense of this.
C   Neither you nor I won't be able to make sense of this.
D   None of these.

Answer

9.

A Bill, as well as the rest of his colleagues, is going to the annual office dinner.

B Bill, as well as the rest of his colleagues, are going to the annual office dinner.

C Neither of these.

Answer

10.

A You girls over there what do you think you are doing.

B You girl over there what do you think you are doing.

C Neither of these.

Answer

Data interpretation

Table A.1 The market demand and supply of potatoes

Price of potatoes (pence per kg)	Total market demand (tonnes)	Total market supply (tonnes)
4	700	100
8	500	200
12	350	350
16	200	530
20	100	700

1. How many potatoes will be demanded if the price per kg were 16p?

A	B	C	D
200	350	500	100

Answer =

2. If the price per kg of potatoes were 4p, how many tonnes would be supplied by the market?

A	B	C	D
700	350	100	200

Answer =

3. If the price of potatoes were to rise from 8p to 12p per kg, what effect would this have on the demand?

A	B	C	D
Increase by 350 tonnes	Decrease by 350 tonnes	Increase by 150 tonnes	Decrease by 150 tonnes

Answer =

4. What is the equilibrium price in this market?

A	B	C	D
4p	8p	12p	16p

Answer =

5. If the price of potatoes were set at 8p per kg by the government, what would be the effect on the market?

A   Shortage of 300 tonnes
B   Surplus of 300 tonnes
C   Shortage of 500 tonnes
D   Surplus of 200 tonnes

Answer =

6. How much more surplus would be created if the price rose from 16p to 20p per kg of potatoes?

A	B	C	D
700 tonnes	530 tonnes	350 tonnes	270 tonnes

Answer =

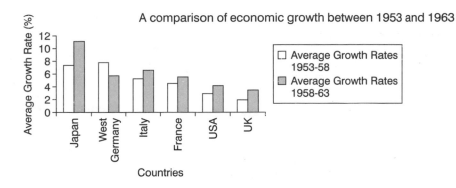

7. What is the average growth rate for the UK between 1953 and 1958?

A	B	C	D
1%	2%	3%	4%

Answer =

8. Which country had the highest average growth rate between 1958 and 1963?

A	B	C	D
Japan	West Germany	Italy	France

Answer =

9. In which country is the average growth rate for 1953–58 greater than the one for 1958–63?

A	B	C	D
UK	USA	France	West Germany

Answer =

10. Which country experiences the largest rise in average growth rate?

A	B	C	D
France	Italy	West Germany	Japan

Answer =

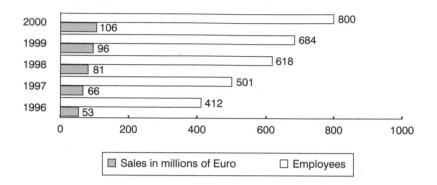

11. By approximately what percentage did total staff numbers change from year 1996 to 2000?

A
387

B
94%

C
90%

Answer =

12. By what percentage did the total profit change from year 1996 to 2000?

A
100%

B
53 million EUR

C
50%

Answer =

13. If the number of employees in the year 2001 has increased by 25% over 2000, what was the total number of new recruits in 2001 compared with 2000?

A
200

B
1000

C
1200

Answer =

14. Between 1996 and 2000, which year showed the smallest and largest staff profit numbers?

A   B   C
1996   1999   1999
& 2000   & 1996   & 1998

Answer =

15. If 1 euro = £0.65, then the profit in 1999 was approximately

A   B   C
£6,240,000   £62.4 million   € 624,000,000

Answer =

16. If there are 300 additional recruits in 2001 and the average growth of sales and staff remain constant, how much greater would the total sales volume in EUR for 2001 be?

A   B   C
£39.75 million   EUR 3,975,000   EUR 39,750,000

Answer =

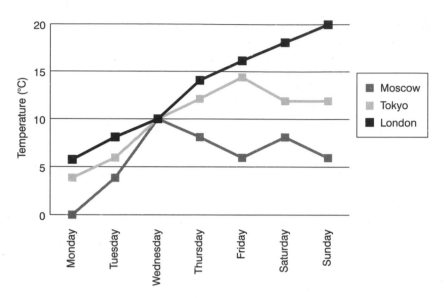

17. On which day did the three capitals have the same temperature?

A
Monday

B
Wednesday

C
Friday

Answer =

18. Which day showed the largest increase in temperature in Moscow?

A
Wednesday

B
Saturday

C
Monday

Answer =

19. In which capital was the trend of temperature consistent throughout the week?

A
London

B
Moscow

C
Tokyo

Answer =

20. What was the average temperature for the week in Moscow?

A	B	C
8°	5.5°	6°

Answer =

21. What was the average temperature for the week in Tokyo?

A	B	C
7°	8°	10°

Answer =

22. What was approximately the percentage increase in temperature between Monday and Sunday in London?

A	B	C
237	33%	245

Answer =

23. What was the ratio of temperature in London on Sunday to the temperature in Moscow on Tuesday?

A	B	C
5:1	1:5	4/20

Answer =

Answers

Number problems

1. A
2. C
3. C
4. E
5. E
6. A
7. C
8. B
9. D
10. D
11. 54 miles
12. 21¾ miles
13. 18 feet
14. 7.2 miles
15. 8 miles
16. 7½ hours
17. 1 hour 15 minutes
18. 2 hours and 30 minutes
19. 40 minutes
20. 1 hour 36 minutes
21. 7 ⅓ mph
22. 1 ½ mph
23. 10 mph
24. 6000 grains per minute
25. 2 mph

Missing words

1. D

2. B

3. D

4. A

5. E

6. D

7. A

8. A

9. C

10. C

11. Answer: A
    Explanation: We say 'in my car' or, for example, 'in the bus' or 'by bus' and 'by car' and 'by cheque' but 'in cash'.

12. Answer: 4 – beautiful, young, blue, green
    Explanation: Adjectives add detail so beautiful and young add detail to what is known about the woman and blue and green add detail to what is known about the dress.

13. Answer: A and B
    Explanation: Both sentences misuse the meaning of the word 'unique' which means one of a kind, unlike anything else.

14. Answer: B
    Explanation: 'so' and 'such' serve to add emphasis; 'so' is used with adjectives and 'such' with nouns.

15. Answer: D
    Explanation: Adjectives such as 'long' and 'red' are normally put in the order of size then colour. We would only use 'and' if a list was formed, for example a long red and white coat.

16. Answer: C
    Explanation: 'who' introduces the clause that provides the extra information about where Peter lives. 'Which' and 'what' refer to objects, 'who' and 'whom' to people. We use 'which' rather than 'what' because we are referring to something already mentioned.

17. Answer: F – themselves
    Explanation: 'myself', 'my' and 'ours' are possessive pronouns. The rest are reflective but only 'themselves' is plural.

18. Answer: B
    Explanation: 'each' and 'every' are often interchangeable but in these instances we are referring to the teams in the particular games, not every rugby team. Also, when we describe how often something occurs we use 'every'.

19. Answer: C
    Explanation: 'much' and 'little' are used with unspecified quantities; 'much' is correct because the 'but' implies a tension with 'little'. 'Few' is used for plural subjects.

20. Answer: B
    Explanation: 'some' is used to make a positive point while 'any' is used in a negative situation.

21. Answer: D
    Explanation: When we introduce something for the first time we refer to it as 'there's'; for subsequent references 'it' is used. 'There's' is an abbreviation for 'there is'. 'Their' is used when the subject is a person, 'there' for a place.

Correct sentences

1. C

2. B

3. C

4. A

5. A

6. A

7. B Note that family is a collective noun and should therefore take a singular verb.

8. B

9. A

10. C

Data interpretation

1. A (can clearly be seen from the table)

2. C (can clearly be seen from the table)

3. D (500 (demand at 8p) – 350 (demand at 12p) = 150 tonnes; decrease rather than increase because as price rises, demand decreases)

4. C (the price where the quantity demanded equals the quantity supplied; the price where there is no shortage or surplus)

5. A (500 (demand at 8p) – 200 (supply at 8p) = 300; shortage for the price is below the equilibrium price of 12p)

6. D (surplus created at 16p = 530 – 200 = 330 tonnes. Surplus created at 20p = 700 – 100 = 600 tonnes. Therefore, surplus will increase by 270 tonnes)

7. B (as is clearly illustrated from the UK's first bar in the graph)

8. A (as the graph clearly shows that Japan has the highest second bar (approximately 11%))

9. D (West Germany is the only country to experience this drop in average growth rate; 8% for 1953–58, whereas 6% for 1958–63)

10. D (as the graph clearly shows; approximately 7% for 1953–58, whereas approximately 11% for 1958–63 (4% increase))

11. B

12. A

13. A

14. B

15. B

16. C

17. B

18. A

19. A

20. C

21. C

22. B

23. A

Further reading from Kogan Page

Titles in the testing series

Career, Aptitude and Selection Tests, rev edn, Jim Barrett, 2006
How to Master Personality Questionnaires, 2nd edn, Mark Parkinson, 2000
How to Master Psychometric Tests, 4th edn, Mark Parkinson, 2008
How to Pass Advanced Aptitude Tests, rev edn, Jim Barrett, 2008
How to Pass Advanced Numeracy Tests, rev edn, Mike Bryon, 2008
How to Pass Advanced Verbal Reasoning Tests, Mike Bryon, 2008
How to Pass the Civil Service Qualifying Tests, 3rd edn, Mike Bryon, 2007
How to Pass Graduate Psychometric Tests, 3rd edn, Mike Bryon, 2007
How to Pass the New Police Selection System, rev 2nd edn, Harry Tolley, Billy Hodge and Catherine Tolley, 2007
How to Pass Numeracy Tests, 3rd edn, Harry Tolley and Ken Thomas, 2006
How to Pass Numerical Reasoning Tests, rev edn, Heidi Smith, 2006
How to Pass Professional Level Psychometric Tests, 2nd edn, Sam Al-Jajjoka, 2004
How to Pass Selection Tests, 3rd edn, Mike Bryon and Sanjay Modha, 2005
How to Pass Technical Selection Tests, 2nd edn, Mike Bryon and Sanjay Modha, 2005
How to Pass Verbal Reasoning Tests, 3rd edn, Harry Tolley and Ken Thomas, 2006
How to Succeed at an Assessment Centre, 2nd edn, Harry Tolley and Bob Wood, 2005

IQ and Psychometric Tests, 2nd edn, Philip Carter, 2007
Succeed at IQ Tests, Ken Russell and Philip Carter, 2008
Test And Assess Your IQ, Ken Russell and Philip Carter, 2008
Test Your Own Aptitude, 3rd edn, Jim Barrett and Geoff Williams, 2003
The Advanced Numeracy Test Workbook, Mike Bryon, 2003
The Aptitude Test Workbook, rev edn, Jim Barrett, 2008
The Times Book of IQ Tests – Book Five, Ken Russell and Philip Carter, 2005
The Times Book of IQ Tests – Book Four, Ken Russell and Philip Carter, 2004
The Times Book of IQ Tests – Book Three, Ken Russell and Philip Carter, 2003
The Times Book of IQ Tests – Book Two, Ken Russell and Philip Carter, 2002
The Times Book of IQ Tests – Book One, Ken Russell and Philip Carter, 2001

Also available on CD ROM in association with The Times

Published by Kogan Page Interactive, *The Times* Testing Series is an exciting new range of interactive CD ROMs that will provide invaluable practice tests for both job applicants and for those seeking a brain-stretching challenge. Each CD ROM features:

▌ over 1000 unique interactive questions;

▌ instant scoring with feedback and analysis;

▌ hours of practice with randomly generated tests;

▌ questions devised by top UK MENSA puzzles editors and test experts;

▌ against-the-clock, real test conditions.

current titles available:
Psychometric Tests, 2002
Test Your IQ, 2002
Test Your Aptitude Volume 1, 2002

Interview and career guidance

A–Z of Careers and Jobs, 13th edn, Susan Hodgson, 2008
Changing Your Career, Sally Longson, 2003
Choosing Your Career, 2nd edn, Sally Longson, 2004
Graduate Job-Hunting Guide, Mark Parkinson, 2001

How You Can Get That Job!, 3rd edn, Rebecca Corfield, 2002
Odd Jobs, 2nd edn, Simon Kent, 2002
Online Job-Hunting: Great Answers to Tough Interview Questions, Martin John Yate and Terra Dourlain, 2002
Preparing Your Own CV, 3rd edn, Rebecca Corfield, 2003
Readymade CVs, 3rd edn, Lynn Williams, 2004
Readymade Job Search Letters, 3rd edn, Lynn Williams, 2004
Successful Interview Skills, 4th edn, Rebecca Corfield, 2006
The Ultimate CV Book, Martin Yate, 2002
The Ultimate Job Search Letters Book, Martin Yate, 2003
Your Job Search Made Easy, 3rd edn, Mark Parkinson, 2002

Please visit the website at the address below for more details.

The above titles are available from all good bookshops. For further information, please contact the publisher at the following address:

Kogan Page Limited
120 Pentonville Road
London N1 9JN
Tel: 020 7278 0433
Fax: 020 7837 6348
www.koganpage.com

Index to the questions